QUEER INDIGENOUS CINEMAS

Latinx Pop Culture

SERIES EDITORS

Frederick Luis Aldama and Arturo J. Aldama

QUEER INDIGENOUS CINEMAS

Sovereign Genders from Seven Directions

Gabriel S. Estrada

THE UNIVERSITY OF
ARIZONA PRESS
TUCSON

The University of Arizona Press
www.uapress.arizona.edu

We respectfully acknowledge the University of Arizona is on the land and territories of Indigenous peoples. Today, Arizona is home to twenty-two federally recognized tribes, with Tucson being home to the O'odham and the Yaqui. The university strives to build sustainable relationships with sovereign Native Nations and Indigenous communities through education offerings, partnerships, and community service.

ISBN-13: 978-0-8165-5640-3 (paperback)
ISBN-13: 978-0-8165-5641-0 (ebook)

Cover design by Leigh McDonald
Typeset by Leigh McDonald in 10.5/13.5 Warnock Pro with Futura Std

Library of Congress Cataloging-in-Publication Data
Names: Estrada, Gabriel S., 1970– author
Title: Queer Indigenous cinemas : sovereign genders from seven directions / Gabriel S. Estrada.
Other titles: Latinx pop culture
Description: [Tucson] : University of Arizona Press, 2026. | Series: Latinx pop culture | Includes bibliographical references and index.
Identifiers: LCCN 2025029997 (print) | LCCN 2025029998 (ebook) | ISBN 9780816556403 paperback | ISBN 9780816556410 ebook
Subjects: LCSH: Indigenous peoples in motion pictures | Sexual minorities in motion pictures | Indigenous films—History and criticism | Indian sexual minorities | Sexual minorities—Identity
Classification: LCC PN1995.9.I49 E88 2026 (print) | LCC PN1995.9.I49 (ebook)
LC record available at https://lccn.loc.gov/2025029997
LC ebook record available at https://lccn.loc.gov/2025029998

Printed in the United States of America
♾ This paper meets the requirements of ANSI/NISO Z39.48-1992 (Permanence of Paper).

CONTENTS

ILLUSTRATIONS

ACKNOWLEDGMENTS

To the four black, red, yellow, and white colors of humanity, and all the mixes in between.

To my Estrada/Villalobos family, and to my nanas/tatas/abuelxs/grandparents, their waterways flowing from La Sierra Madre Occidental to the hue at / the Pacific Ocean (and noting Indigenous Peoples of those rivers): Grandma Sarah, Río Papigochi (Rarámuri, Ndé); Grandma Lupe, Río Valle de Topia (Acaxee, Ódami); Tata Santiago, Arroyo Huiscolco–Río Juchipila (Caxcan); Grandpa Joe, Río Jomulco–Río Grande de Jerez (Guachichil/Wixárika, Zacateco). And to the waters of my diverse ancestral migrant and settler colonial ancestors from Turtle Island and beyond: Lago Texcoco (Mexica/Hñähñu); The Gambia River (Mandinka, Fula, Wolof) and Odò Ògùn (Yorùbá); Zubitegi Erreka–Ego Ibaia–Deba Ibaia (Euskaldunak) and Baztan Ibaia–Bidasoa Ibaia (Euskaldunak); Caldera de Taburiente–Barranco de Las Angustias (Guanche/Amazigh).

To all Indigenous LGBTQI2+ circles and friends, but especially, Gay American Indians, City of Angels Two-Spirit Society, Indigenous Pride Los Angeles, Bay Area American Indian Two-Spirits, Montana Two Spirit Society, Two Spirit & Native LGBTQ+ Center for Equity, and Red Circle Project/AIDS Project Los Angeles.

QUEER INDIGENOUS CINEMAS

INTRODUCTION TO THE SPACE, TIME, AND GENDERS OF *QUEER INDIGENOUS CINEMAS*

¡Cuali tonal/Buenos días/Good day![1] Identifying with my Rarámuri matrilineage, Caxcan patrilineage, and racially mixed Xicanx ancestry of Mexico, I greet you where you are, knowing that this book's readership may both span the globe and someday rise above it.[2] Such a wide audience would be fitting, as *Queer Indigenous Cinemas: Sovereign Genders from Seven Directions* makes broad relationships across Indigenous cinemas, genders, and spaces.[3] This book features not only contemporary film images of Indigenous peoples from the North and Central American areas of Abiayala (land of plenitude and maturity/the Americas), but also from across the Polynesian moana (ocean/Pacific Ocean), and the Yorùbá Yemayá ayaba omi o (queen of water) who spans the Atlantic okun (ocean) and Taíno Caribbean.[4] I begin with this description of cultural regions because space is a main feature of this book's analysis, especially the following seven Indigenous directions: east, south, west, north, down, up, and center. Also in focus are the many Indigenous genders and sexualities that may or may not overlap with contemporary constructions of lesbian, gay, bisexual, transgender, queer, intersex, and two-spirit (LGBTQI2+) identities. A third book emphasis is on Indigenous LGBTQI2+ cinema and streaming videos. This introduction takes time to define these main book concepts. Its first section considers Indigenous understandings of space and seven directions. Next come definitions of LGBTQI2+ terms, followed by LGBTQI2+ Indigenous film histories that spiral out from Hollywood. Summaries of the book's seven chapters finish this introduction.

Reorienting Indigenous LGBTQI2+ Cinemas to Seven Directions

Queer Indigenous Cinemas structures LGBTQI2+ Indigenous movements through regions of Abiayala, moana, and okun media spaces. This book features seven chapters for seven Indigenous directions, building upon previous articles on directional analysis on LGBTQI2+ Mexica, Anishinaabe, Zapotec, and Mixtec images.[5] *Queer Indigenous Cinemas* expands from four cardinal directions in part I to include central directions of below, above, and center in part II. Each of the directional chapters considers various genders from different Indigenous peoples as represented in film. This book's seven-directions spatial approach has its own Indigenous intellectual genealogy of sovereignty from several sources. Visual artist Jolene Rickard (Tuscarora Nation) makes spatial connections between Indigenous spirituality, political sovereignty, and images in her landmark 1994 article "Sovereignty: A Line in the Sand."[6] Rickard notes how George Longfish's (Six Nations of the Grand River) *America 500* mixed-media collage portraits teach that "everything is relational," in "Indigenous thought . . . [and] space" and that "locating . . . the center of the universe as being within the individual" is a key spatial aesthetic that integrates Indigenous sovereignty, mapping, and science.[7] Rickard's sovereign concept of the personal being the relative middle of the universe is shared widely in the directional spaces of many Indigenous peoples.

For some Indigenous scholars, four cardinal directions around the personal center is the spatial framing. For example, Roger Kuhn (Poarch Creek Indians) gives the common name "medicine wheel" for this four-directions system. His work on two-spirit "somacultural liberation," a "somatic, intellectual, emotional, and existential modality," connects with the medicine wheel's integrated practices of healing the body, mind, heart, and spirit, correlating respectively with the four directions.[8] Gay Chicano Francisco X. Alarcón's English/Spanish/Nahuatl 1992 *Snake Poems: An Aztec Invocation* included a "Four Directions/Cuatro Direcciones/Nauhcampa" poem, which has stanzas for the "west/oeste/cihuatlampa," "north/norte/mictlampa," "east/oriente/tlapcopa," and "south/sur/huitzlampa," perhaps modeled on the 1400s Codex Borgia (Yohualli Ehecatl) Mexica four directions.[9] Joseph Pierce includes the "seven directions" of his Cherokee Nation of Oklahoma within the larger project of queer Indigenous "worlding" in which "love" is "not simply relationality, but a specific type of engaging in relations . . . a way of naming the speculative process by which our embodied relations take shape across beings, across those limitations of the body that we call desire."[10] Lawrence Gross (Anishinaabe White Earth Nation) explains that the seventh direction is the center arrived after moving through the directions of "east, south, west, north, down, and up."[11] Feminist Niimiipuu/Tejana Inés Hernández-Ávila (Confederated Tribes of the Colville Reservation) also shares medicine directions, but from a Mexica and Chicana perspective: "East. West. North. South. A balanced cross. Each of us is at the center of this cross—each of us . . . emanates from this center towards the four directions, but also towards the EarthMother and the SkyWorld. Four directions. Seven points."[12]

Queer Indigenous Cinemas features a seven-directions method of film analysis that helps to critique the European-language and settler-colonial mappings of earth. All seven chapters in this queer film book take a partial Indigenous-language approach, linking seven directions across seven distinct Indigenous nations and languages. To deepen sovereign cultural, spatial, and gender understandings, *Queer Indigenous Cinemas* expands upon Renee Pualani Louis's *Kanaka Hawai'i Cartography* insights that Indigenous mappings of space/time are uniquely embedded in Indigenous language and dynamic localized practices.[13] This book also benefits from the Diné language philosophy, four directions, and "hane' (story/narrative/wisdom)" insights within Renae Watchman's (Navajo Nation) 2024 land and transgender film analysis in *Restoring Relations Through Stories: From Dinétah to Denendeh*.[14] Figure 1 maps the Diné (Navajo) in the east, Caxcan (Chichimeca) in the south, Kānaka Maoli (Native Hawaiian) in the west, and Nêhiyawak (Cree) in the

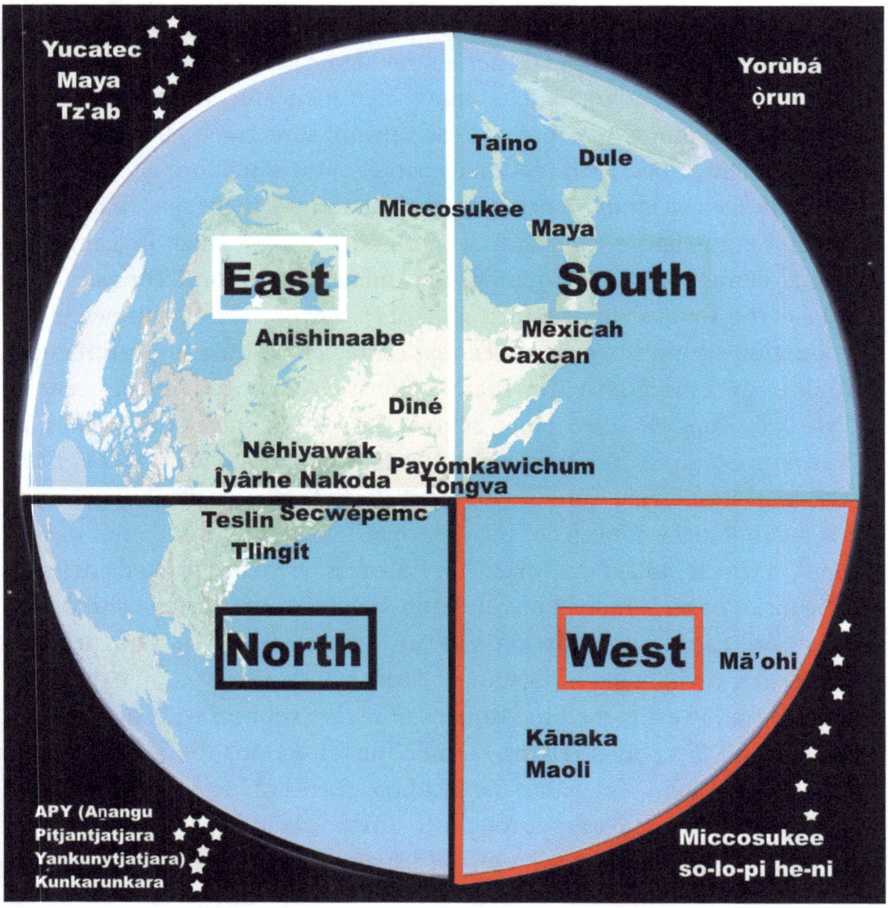

Figure 1 Medicine wheel on map (Google Earth, © 2025) of Turtle Island and Hawai'i.

north, featured respectively in chapters 1, 2, 3, and 4. Figure 1's Indigenous names help decenter English-language settler-colonial mappings, as does the medicine wheel's position over the northwest quadrant of a global map.

Figure 1's eastern orientation follows the east-facing map of Diné territory on the Great Seal of the Navajo Nation, and Diné traditions of beginning the day with prayers facing east and proceeding from the east in a clockwise motion. In the map, colors and directions displace the Western cartographies that commonly label these areas as the United States of America in the east, Mexico in the south, Polynesia in the west, and Canada in the north, with the Tongva area of Hollywood, Los Angeles, as the map's implied center. The four white, blue, red, and black colors have cultural and spatial significance, with Diné, Wixárika, Kānaka Maoli, and Îyarhe Nakoda (Stoney) respectively inspiring the east/white, south/blue, red/west, and black/north directional colors. Figure 1 shows the Anishinaabe in the east; the Mexica in the south; the Mā'ohi (Tahitians) in the west; the Teslin Tlingit, Nêhiyawak (Plains Cree), and Tk'emlúpsemc or Tk'emlúps te Secwépemc in the north; and the Payómkawichum (Luiseño) of the center. In the night sky are constellations from the A̲nangu, Pitjantjatjara, and Yankunytjatjara; Yucatec Maya; Yorùbá; and Miccosukee Seminole to represent the upward direction. All these people appear in their respective directional chapter shown in figure 1.

While Tongva lands lie below the center and the night sky shines above the center in the figure 1 map, the seventh direction is inside, an unmapped personal center. Nepanta Tovaangar/en medio del mundo Tongva/in the middle of the Tongva world, and in sight of Hollywood, I locate myself in this introduction within the nepanta/centro/center of my own seven-directions spatiality.[15] As Luiseño/Tongva Theresa Stewart-Ambo explains, referencing the work of Tongva/Acjachemen scholar Charles Sepulveda, at best, I am a "kuuyam . . . guest" on Tongva land, rather than simply a "visitor" or an "invader."[16] If, following Euro-Australian Patrick Wolfe, settler/Indigenous is the absolute binary concept of the day, then I offer the formulation of "settler/ed" in which Indigenous mixed-race peoples have complicated attributes and histories of both Indigenous and non-Indigenous ancestors, and potential for both further assimilation and "un-settler/ed-ing" movement of reclaiming and revitalizing Indigenous culture.[17] Like a tocat/araña/spider on a web's center, I've attached the threads of my perception wide in this book with all seven directions relative to me. This directionality is a movement of unsettler/ed-ing, of resisting the insidious forms of cis-heteropatriarchal settler-colonial mapping first brought to Turtle Island in the early 1500s by some of my Euskaldunak (Basque) and Españoles (Spanish) forbearers who later settled the temperate eastern flanks of the Sierra Madre Occidental, where most of my Indigenous ancestors originated. In one oral tradition of my Chicana matrilineage, the Rarámuri peoples of Chihuahua, Mexico, the American continent was created on the back of a great turtle, Gawí, the inspiration for the turtle shell pattern on this book's front cover. This account is one of many Turtle Island oral traditions that represent the Americas as a living entity bound by four cardinal directions, whose shell of twenty-eight panels can also serve as a twenty-eight-day lunar calendar for menstruation.[18]

While I still reside on this great turtle continent, I am like my Chicana/o parents, born not only outside my ancestral Sierra Madre Occidental of Northern Mexico and in the settler-colonial empire of the United States of America, but also across a rapidly militarizing border in the Trump presidency of the mid-2020s. Despite my family's migration to the USA occurring more than a century ago, I am still subject to increased border scrutiny that targets darker and more Indigenous people, though undocumented Indigenous peoples in the USA are impacted to a greater extent, reflecting Tria Blu Wakpa's observation that "Many people incarcerated at the U.S.-Mexico border are Indigenous, their incarceration continuing a long-enacted strategy of targeting underrepresented communities to maintain the stability of the settler state."[19] While my mom's mom and father's father identified with their specific Indigenous origins, my Chicana/o parents were differently detribalized by the border, more generally identifying with mestizaje, being racially mixed with mostly Mexican Indigenous and Spanish/Basque peoples. However, within the larger Xicanx communities in which I've lived in Sacramento, Tucson, Long Beach, and Berkeley, ongoing ancestral identification with detribalized Apache, Yoeme, Navajo, Hopi, and other U.S. Southwest Indigenous peoples is common, as are the more southern identifications with Zapotec, Mexica, Purépecha, Maya, and Wixárika of Mexico. To reflect both my grandparents and parents, I self-identify with the Indigenous *x* to begin and end "Xicanx." The first *X* borrowed from the Mexica Nahuatl language signals a return to indigeneity. The final gender-neutral *x* expresses my own genderqueer identity in place of a feminine *-a* or masculine *-o* ending in Spanish.[20] Because the intertribal Xicanx is too often Mexica-centric, I am retaining the Caxcan identity as a reminder of Chichimeca difference with nationalized or intertribal Mexica/n indigeneity.

I chose four broad directional regions in figure 1 to reflect some of the diverse Indigenous LGBTQI2+ communities and films that I have encountered over the past twenty years of living in the greater Los Angeles region. I first went to the Native American Red Circle Project/AIDS Project Los Angeles for services as an HIV-positive person in 2009. In the Red Circle Project, I attended the "gay" rather than the "transgender" subgroups once the main group divided in two, even though I consider both these identities as important parts of the larger two-spirit community and to my own gendered path. I eventually worked with the group's founder Elton Naswood (Navajo Nation) to do community screenings and discussions of the 2010 Fred Martinez (Navajo Nation) queer hate crime murder film *Two Spirits* (2009). As part of the City of Angels Two-Spirit Society (CATSS) in the 2010s, I partnered in some of those screenings to fulfill the CATSS vision "to provide support to the City of Angels American Indian/ Alaska Native/1st Nation/Indigenous Two-Spirit community and engender awareness of our traditional sacred role to the community of greater Los Angeles."[21] The CATSS vision, which purposefully includes "American Indian/Alaska Native/1st Nation/Indigenous," also guides the geographically broad formation of this book beyond settler-colonial borders. CATSS collaborations grew a new partnership with Indigenous Pride Los Angeles, helping to replace Columbus Day city celebrations in 2018 with an annual Indigenous LGBTQI2+ event. A reflection of many Indigenous peoples in the greater LA area, the online 2020 third annual Indigenous Pride LA celebration streamed a Tongva welcome, an Afro-Indigenous Zoom panel, two-spirit Mexica dancers, and Kānaka Maoli hula. *Queer Indigenous Cinemas* features this global Indigenous community diversity that is only slowly integrating Hollywood representations.

International Indigenous film production is a reality in Hollywood, and this book acknowledges that many Indigenous peoples are drawn locally to one of the larger cinema production centers in the world. I was able to witness this Indigenous diversity firsthand as background cast in the Disney+ short film "The Roof" (2023), which starred Academy Award–winning actor Wes Studi (Cherokee Nation of Oklahoma). Filmed just north of Hollywood in Tataviam territory, "The Roof" brought together many Indigenous LGBTQI2+ talents. The streaming short was written by the two-spirit W. A. W. Parker (Northern Cheyenne Tribe), directed by Kānaka Maoli Alexander Boccieri, and cast by Salvadoran Nahua Candido Cornejo. On set, Buffalo Barbie (Navajo Nation) and John Sneezy (San Carlos Apache Tribe) helped the lead actor Phoenix Wilson (M'Chigeeng First Nation) learn the Jingle Dress Dance for the film. Landa Lakes (Miko Thomas, Chickasaw Nation) and the Tongvetam/Ajachmem/Rarámuri L. Frank Manriquez filled the two-spirit elder roles in a climactic two-spirit powwow scene. I've learned from these two-spirit community members as much as I have from the Indigenous intellectuals I cite in this book. As a transborder Caxcan/Xicanx author interested in land-based directionality, I've had to be open to learning what is outside of my personal gender, national, and cultural experience from local community and more grounded Indigenous scholars from across the globe.

Not only is *Queer Indigenous Cinemas: Sovereign Genders from Seven Directions* the first book wholly focused on LGBTQI2+ Indigenous film, but it is also the first monograph to emphasize queer Indigenous Hispanophone Mexican, Caribbean, and Central American media, plus some LGBTQ2+ Indigenous-language media from both the Global North and Global South. As this media analysis looks north and south, it necessarily expands upon the largely Global North Anglophone approaches of *Queer Indigenous Studies* and *Sovereign Erotics,* two of the more impactful anthologies in the respective fields of global queer Indigenous gender theory and literature.[22] A concerted neoliberal politics of settler neocolonialism from the Global North has helped to mute the voices and images of contemporary Indigenous peoples of the Global South, even as it fuels Indigenous migrations to the United States and the greater Los Angeles region, where Indigenous Latinx peoples form the majority of the Indigenous population.[23] This erasure in queer Indigenous film representation is also ironic given that over 80 percent of the Indigenous population of the Americas live south of the U.S. border.[24] Settler-colonial Hispanophone language repression of LGBTQI2+ Indigenous directors is also at work in this crisis of queer Indigenous representation in the film record of the Global South parts of Abiayala. This book's LGBTQI2+ approach reconnects the queer Indigenous Global South and North in a way that rarely appears in print, with the "International Queer Indigenous" special issue of the *Yellow Medicine Review* being one notable exception, though in the field of literature.[25]

International Indigenous media rights that transcend Global North and South demarcations are modeled in the Indigenous rights literature. The 2007 United Nations Declaration on the Rights of Indigenous Peoples (UNDRIP) documented resistance to the ongoing state suppression of sovereign Indigenous media direction, production, and distribution. Written within an Indigenous African, Asian, Pan-American, Oceanian, and European context, UNDRIP article 16 advocates for increased Indigenous media access, stating, "Indigenous peoples have the right to establish their own media in their own languages. . . . States shall take effective measures to ensure that State-owned media duly reflect indigenous cultural diversity . . . [and] encourage privately owned media to adequately reflect indigenous cultural diversity."[26] While these are excellent principles of Indigenous media sovereignty, UNDRIP's media rights are difficult to enforce internationally and among transborder Indigenous diasporas. Written broadly, UNDRIP also struggles to account for Indigenous gender, culture, language, politics, and protocol nuances. For example, UNDRIP does not mention sexual orientation and Indigenous gender variants within its list of rights.

Queer Indigenous Cinemas necessarily expands upon filling the LGBTQI2+ absences within UNDRIP while practically drawing from its general global advocacy for Indigenous media. This book features healing gender relations in relationship with sovereign land and directionality. Following Andrew J. Jolivétte's queer urban Native American writings, this text centers "contemporary modes of Two-Spirit subjectivity as a reclamation of traditional, non-Western mechanisms for healing, self-love, and decolonization."[27] It also draws from Joanne Barker's (Delaware Tribe of Maryland) feminist concern for the "ethics and responsibilities of gendered and sexed land-based . . . cultural protocols and practices"[28] as well as Daisy Ocampo's Caxcan affirmation that "spiritual sovereignty based on sacred geographies is a critical process for Indigenous people's restoration, healing, and futurities."[29] Combining sovereign insights from Jolivétte, Barker, and Ocampo leads to an understanding that land grounds and heals Indigenous bodies and genders, even while often living in urban or transnational spaces, as Tonawanda Band of Seneca feminist Mishuana Goeman might remind.[30]

Recent Evolutions of Sovereign Gender Terms

The ending of the 1980s and beginning of the 1990s was the time in which both the "queer" and "two-spirit" gender/sexual identity umbrella terms were first popularized through disparate social movements. In 1990 members of the AIDS Coalition to Unleash Power (ACT UP) redefined their umbrella gender/sexuality identity by reclaiming the derogatory term "queer," which meant odd or strange, and forming an LGBTQ Queer Nation movement through their New York City activism.[31] Following Judith Butler, *Queer Indigenous Cinemas* takes the "queer" signifier to mean "nonnormative," in terms of sexualities that deviate from "the cultural assumption that only different-sex desire and eroticism are normal, natural, and beneficial to society," along with queer gender expression and trans identities that do not adhere to the Western cisgender expectation that gender should conform to the binary sex choice assigned at birth.[32] Author Joshua Whitehead (Peguis First Nation) popularized the combination of the words "Indigenous" and "queer" in the identity "Indigiqueer," a term that has gained use among younger generations since the 2010s. Indigiqueer is a fusion of nonnormative Indigenous sexualities, genders, and the identities within the larger context of setter-colonial cis-heteropatriarchy.[33]

The "two-spirit" term migrated out from the central prairies/plains to eventually reach the East and West Coasts of Turtle Island. Originating from late 1980s LGBTQI2+ Indigenous conversations, "two-spirit" was also a name heard by Myra Laramee (Fisher River Cree Nation) from the "Creator or Great

Mystery."[34] She confirmed this vision at the 1990 Third Native American/First Nations Gay and Lesbian Conference in Winnipeg, where "two-spirit" was adopted as an Indigenous umbrella gender and sexual identity. "Two-spirit" was formed as a reclamation of Indigenous gender variants that were traditionally honored and respected. It was also created to replace the colonial-era Jesuit and early anthropological term "berdache," which was deemed culturally inappropriate with its French and Arabic origins in words for catamite or a boy sexual servant.[35] For some LGBTQI2+ Indigenous people, the "two" in "two-spirit" describes having both a masculine and feminine spirit. For others, "two-spirit" means to transcend the limited gender binaries of femininity/masculinity. Never intended for non-Indigenous Euro-American adoption, two-spirit identity is but a shorthand way of speaking about queer gender and sexuality within complex relationships of Indigenous nation, language, kinship, and history. In Canada and the USA, "two-spirit" gained prominence through regional two-spirit societies and health activisms in the 1990s–2020s, though many prefer other identity terms.[36]

Diverse LGBTQI2+ identifications continue to evolve and increasingly include transgender identities.[37] Saylesh Wesley (Stó:lō Nation) offers an important approach to these multiple identities. She is clear about her own "two-spirit, transgender, and queer identity as a Stó:lō 'sts'iyóye smestíyexw slhá:li (twin-spirited woman),'" the last term being one her Stó:lō maternal grandmother created and gifted to her. She also honors the ever-evolving nature of gender/sexual identifications for others.[38] Transgender voices like Wesley's are important to reflect gender diversity for those who disidentify with their sex attributed at birth. Transgender Métis/Nishnaabe scholar Kai Pyle (Sault Tribe of Chippewa Indians) confirms that two-spirit discussions need to include transgender people so that "the reclamation of Two-Spirit places of belonging in Indigenous communities" is not left "incomplete."[39] While *Queer Indigenous Cinemas* considers Indigenous butch, femme, intersex, two-spirit, and Indigenous mixed genders in film history, it especially responds to Pyle's community call to improve the underrepresentation of transgender Indigenous peoples, who have a double invisibility of being Indigenous and trans in a settler-colonial and cis-heteropatriarchal popular culture. This transgender inclusion is more important than ever as Trump-appointed U.S. American courts move to increasingly deny transgender rights. Complicating the transgender identity, this book's film analysis is "trans*Indigenous," an original term foregrounding nonbinary gender systems as well as seven Indigenous directions. Trans*Indigenous prefaces "Indigenous" with "trans" plus the Boolean-search-inspired asterisk to denote "not only identities such as transgender, transsexual, trans man, and trans woman . . .

but also . . . genderqueer, neutrios, intersex, agender, two-spirit, cross-dresser, and genderfluid."[40] In this spatial trans*Indigenous analysis, the asterisk center is surrounded by six lines that represent the six directions, east, south, west, north, above, and below, making "trans*Indigenous" a signifier operating across Indigenous genders and spaces.

A Brief Indigenous LGBTQI2+ Film History

This book fills gaps in the LGBTQI2+ Indigenous film history literature. One of these gaps pertains to Lisa Tatonetti's 2014 call for a full queer Indigenous cinema book, which has remained unfulfilled for over a decade.[41] To date, only articles, book chapters, and shorter book sections of analysis on LGBTQI2+ Indigenous films have made publication. For example, the milestone *Reservation Reelism: Redfacing, Visual Sovereignty, and Representations of Native Americans in Film* (2010) by Michelle Raheja integrated threads of queer theory into her film history of "visual sovereignty," the aesthetics of Indigenous-made film, and its political and cultural service back to its Indigenous communities and nations of origin.[42] While this partial integration of two-spirit films marks an important evolution in the Native American and Indigenous film literature, the greater historical erasures of LGBTQI2+ Indigenous peoples remain mostly unarticulated to film analysis. *Reservation Reelism* and other works do not attempt to explain the sustained impact of LGBTQI2+ censorship across Indigenous cinema history. To fill the gap in the Anglophone North American two-spirit film history literature, I wrote "Ojibwe Lesbian Visual AIDS: On the Red Road with Carol laFavor, *Her Giveaway* (1988) and Native LGBTQ2 Film History," and "Trans Indigenous Visual Sovereignty: From *Little Big Man* (1970) to *Drunktown's Finest* (2013)."[43] I merge lesbian and transgender analyses from both articles in this introduction and expand from previous works to cover broader Indigenous areas of Canada, Africa, Latin America, and Oceania. While male homoerotic and transfeminine characters predominate in the classic and new Hollywood discussion herein, the extended examples of women's cross-dressing predominate in Tongva silent and classic Hollywood analysis in chapter 6.

Native American Hollywood film analysis anthologies of the 1980s, 1990s, and 2000s mostly established the prevalence of "Indian" stereotypes in cinema history with little integrated analysis of LGBTQI2+ images.[44] Similar to the early 1990s and 2000s writings by Māori director Barry Barclay for an Indigenous "Fourth Cinema," 2010s Indigenous film analysis increasingly emphasized "visual sovereignty" and self-representation in the Indigenous United States, Aotearoa/New Zealand, and Mexico,[45] but often without giving historical context to Indigenous LGBTQI2+ film. Visual sovereignty and

Fourth Cinema analyses provide strong models for this book that also integrates queer film histories. The silent, classic, and contemporary Hollywood eras film history approach taken by *The Celluloid Closet* documentary, directed by Rob Epstein and Jeffrey Friedman and based upon Vito Russo's 1981 *The Celluloid Closet*, is also a film history model for this literature review and introduction to LGBTQI2+ Indigenous Hollywood history. It follows Russo's basic understanding of the limitations of the silent era's humorous LGBTQI2+ images of the late 1890s–1930s, the classic era's severe LGBTQI2+ censorship from 1934 to 1969,[46] and the new Hollywood era's 1970s–1980s confusing mix of tepid support for burgeoning LGBTQI2+ images and continued suppression of contemporary LGBTQ2+ representations.

Raheja reveals that the Native American actors, directors, and producers created relatively sympathetic and visually sovereign images in early 1900s silent Hollywood;[47] however, it was not a time in which LGBTQI2+ Indigenous gender and erotic sovereignty were clearly depicted in film. There was instead more cinematic openness for gender and sexuality variants in which Indigenous queer and transgender images were considered humorous or marked racial difference. Angela Aleiss's brief mention of the comical cross-dressing in *The Squaw's Mistaken Love* (1911) establishes an early queer silent-era baseline film when a cross-dressed Euro-American woman is humorously mistaken for a biological man by a Native American woman interested in courtship.[48] However, in silent Hollywood of the late 1890s through the early 1930s, Native American characters often blurred human and animal, gender, and erotic boundaries as embodiments of supposedly wild Indigenous lands to be tamed within the cis-heterosexist white settler-colonial imagination. Laura Horak's analysis of the queer aspects of silent film Native American cross-dressing in *The Red Girl and the Child* (1910) and *The Snowbird* (1916) highlights the irony, repressed homoeroticism, and racialization of these early cross-dressing images.[49]

In the 2010s, shorter LGBTQI2+ Indigenous analyses included coded homoeroticism among warrior archetypes in classic Hollywood. Raheja argues that seeking to understand Indigenous visual sovereignty masked by a white-dominated silent and classic Hollywood is something akin to the project that queer scholars have in teasing out queer resistance from a history of cis-heteronormative Hollywood images. In her reading of Native American classic Hollywood, Raheja articulates both queer and racist censorship set out within the 1930 Motion Picture Production Code, or Hays Code, which dominated film images from 1934 to 1968. Championed by the Catholic church, the Hays Code prohibited both racial "miscegenation" of Native American and white U.S. American subjects as well as "sexual perversion," the code's euphemism for what are now known as LGBTQI2+ representations.[50] While homoerotic and mixed-race couplings were often treated in a humorous or melodramatic way in silent film, they were reviled as perverse images during classic Hollywood Hays Code censorship. The Motion Picture Production Code would allow open representations of miscegenation and LGBTQ narratives so long as the films' offending characters were brutally punished for their supposed racial, sexual, or gender transgressions by the end of the film. As explained in chapter 6, *The Outsider* (1961) presented a coded suicide by its Akimel O'odham World War II veteran Ira Hayes, who expressed intense homosocial, physically intimate, and sexual banter with his war buddy and bedmate. Raheja's findings on the male-male homosocial bonding inherent in many Westerns such as *Sitting Bull* (1950) provided a useful insight into rereading classic Indigenous film with a queer lens, and she later picked up the dropped thread of gay sexuality by showing how the murder in the contemporary Lakota drama *Imprint* (2007) is coded homophobia.[51]

After the more erotically and racially permissive 1968 Motion Picture Code replaced the Hays Code, *Little Big Man* (1970) included the first openly transgender Native American representation in Hollywood, featuring a feminine male-bodied Northern Cheyenne two-spirit, Little Horse (Robert Little Star), who both marries a man and openly proposes marriage to the straight cisgender male protagonist Little Big Man (Dustin Hoffman). This character is massacred along with other Northern Cheyenne, thus keeping the two-spirit openness safely in a disappearing past having fulfilled her comedic role, a trope critiqued by trans hemaneh Adria Jawort (Northern Cheyenne Tribe), Margo Kasdan, and Susan Tavernetti in the trans film documentary *Disclosure* (2020).[52] Although the porn-inspired 1970 independent film *Song of the Loon* did supply gay settler fantasies of naked homoerotic Native Americans, such graphic gay sex was not at all the norm in Native American Hollywood film. Fearing transphobic and homophobic box office impacts, Native American Hollywood film directors and actors faced de facto censorship into the 1970s and beyond. Directed by Euro-American Richard Morse and adapted as a screenplay by N. Scott Momaday (Kiowa Tribe of Oklahoma) from Momaday's eponymous 1968 novel, the film *House Made of Dawn* (1972) features a stoic Vietnam veteran protagonist and subtle homophobia. After threatening and caressing the Pueblo film lead Abel (Larry Littlebird, Laguna/Santo Domingo Pueblo) in an oddly intimate way, the albino witch (Skeeter Vaughan) meets a nasty death when Abel stabs him to death. This ending follows classic modes of coded queer deaths even when the censorship had already officially ended. Euro-American Nancy Walker's *Can't Stop the Music* (1980) also follows a general pattern of coded contemporary LGBTQI2+ erasure. In this new Hollywood musical that traces the rise of Pete Rose's disco band phenomenon Village People, Rose's 1990s public self-identifications as gay, non-enrolled Lakota, and Puerto Rican remain masked by a straight Afro-Caribbean persona.[53] *Little Big Man, Song of the Loon, House Made of Dawn,* and *Can't Stop the Music* show that open gay and transfemme Native American representations were either limited to the Native Americans of the late 1800s or heavily suppressed in the contemporary Hollywood film settings in 1968–80 new Hollywood.

It isn't until the global rise of LGBTQI2+ Indigenous independent videos of the 1980s–2020s that there is a larger restoration of the self-representation of LGBTQI2+ Indigenous images from the colonial, cis-heteropatriarchal, and genocidal tropes reflected across silent, classic, and new Hollywood film. Fueled by cheaper video recording equipment, LGBTQI2+ Indigenous activism, and AIDS funds,[54] this period saw an expansion of queer Indigenous media in which Indigenous visual, erotic, and spiritual sovereignty combined. Morgensen documents the increase in early LGBTQI2+ Indigenous media in a context of AIDS documentaries in the 1980s, 1990s, and 2000s that resist a biopolitics of queer settler colonialism. He traces an increase in Indigenous multimedia "health sovereignty" that begins to include queer gender, sexual, two-spirit, HIV+, addict, and Indigenous identities.[55] Morgensen also places HIV campaigns and early Native gay/lesbian documentaries *Her Giveaway: A Spiritual Journey with AIDS* (1988), *Honored by the Moon* (1990), *Two Spirit People* (1991), and *It Gets Better* (2005) as decolonial moments within two-spirit communities and multimedia AIDS education. The lesbian AIDS-diagnosed Ojibwe representation by Carol laFavor in *Her Giveaway* is an especially important example of a new fusion of gender, visual, and spiritual sovereignty going into the 1990s, with Lisa Tatonetti affirming that laFavor was "an important voice not only in queer Native literature but also in the rise of HIV/AIDS education and activism."[56]

In the wake of Queer Nation, AIDS activism, and a slate of aggressively queer films, Euro-American lesbian B. Ruby Rich coined the term "New Queer Cinema" in 1991 and emphasized how the defiant New Queer Cinema defied social constructs of "positive images" desired within both homonormative and heteronormative perspectives.[57] Rich lauded how New Queer Cinema questioned the oppositional category binaries such as heterosexual/homosexual and highlighted queer spectatorship.[58] This queer sensibility carried through subsequent queer film and film analysis of the 2000s and 2010s, with transgender representation also becoming more prevalent in the 2010s and 2020s. However, despite the 1990s New Queer Cinema's critiques of classist and heterosexist intersections, settler Euro-American New Queer Cinema directors struggled to portray antiracism and honor the sovereign nature of Indigenous genders. For example, the New Queer Cinema film *My Own Private Idaho* relies upon tropes of appropriation, as its major coming-out scene is accompanied by Native American reminiscent drumming, as if to equate wild queerness with wild indigeneity. *My Own Private Idaho* displays New Queer Cinema's ongoing settler-colonial fantasy that appropriating "Indian" freedom in nature equates to white queer sexual freedom, a trope replicated in the earlier gay films like *Parting Glances* (1986) that features fantasy redface performances from its gay white protagonists.[59]

The limited representation of two-spirit characters continued into non-Indigenous films of the 2000s like *Big Eden* (2013). B. Ruby Rich's *New Queer Cinema: The Director's Cut* (2013) only tangentially references *Big Eden*'s queer Montana Indigenous character, further indicating how impactful queer film analysis is often unable to account for settler colonialism.[60] P. Jane Hafen also writes a short review of *Big Eden* (2000) with the historical context of the film "as part of a second generation of gay cinema . . . more romantic comedy than coming-out drama or confronting AIDS and its consequences,"[61] without noting the gaps in Indigenous representation. In contrast, Tatonetti faults *Big Eden,* directed by the non-Indigenous Thomas Bezucha, for its tokenized gay Indigenous character.[62] A focus on the quick-witted two-spirit character Seymour Polotkin (Adam Evens, Tla'amin First Nation) in Sherman Alexie's (Spokane Tribe of Indians) *The Business of Fancydancing* (2002) is found in works by Joanna Hearne, Amy Corbin, Dean Rader, Quentin Youngberg, Theo Van Alst, Gabriel Estrada, and Lee Schweninger, and marks a breakthrough in both two-spirit film and two-spirit film analysis.[63] Films like *Fancy Dance* (2023), in which the Blackfeet and Niimiipuu actor Lily Gladstone stars as a lesbian from the Seneca-Cayuga reservation, also mark visibility for queer women who are less often featured in film. The seven chapters in *Queer Indigenous Cinemas* emphasize LGBTI2+ Indigenous media featuring Indigenous directors, writers, and actors that mark a key upsurge in visual, erotic, and theological sovereignty in the 2000s–2020s, after a century of Hollywood suppression. As will be seen in later chapters, these mostly post-millennial films' analyses within Indigenous, gender, and film studies also mark key evolutions in the scholarly record.

In a binational U.S./Mexico context, Linda Fregoso offered an important chapter titled "Nepantla in Gendered Subjectivity," with queer HIV/AIDS insights into the Latinx San Francisco and Indigenous Oaxacan Day of Dead ceremonies as depicted in the film documentary *La ofrenda* (1989) by Lourdes Portillo and Susana Muñoz. Via the feminist Mexican luminary Sor Juana de la Cruz, Fregoso translates her Nahuatl "nepantla" title word as "spaces in between" and applies it to gender instability and in-betweenness.[64] With a related Indigenous Oaxacan focus, Gustavo Subero highlights the cinematic "muxeninity" of the Zapotec third-gender muxe in the documentary *Muxes: Auténticas intrépidas buscadoras de peligro* (2005).[65] Paul Julian Smith also wrote a short analysis of the muxe film *Carmín tropical* (2014) that confronts violence against the third-gender muxes in Oaxaca.[66] Estrada's spatial analysis of queer Mexica, transgender Mixtec, and Zapotec muxe representations complements these writings on LGBTQI2+ Indigenous Oaxaca.[67]

However, with a notable exception, most queer Mexican film analysis is concerned with hegemonic queer Mestizo and Hispanic images. When Rich fills in the broad Latin American queer cinema sweep of last century that increasingly opens up to LGBTQI2+ images, she does so with little emphasis on Indigenous queer images, only briefly mentioning the generalized "Indigenous religion" background in Leduc's *Friday Kahlo* (1983) film.[68] Queer Latinx media books are similarly problematic. Gustavo Subero's *Queer Masculinities in Contemporary Latin American Film* (2014),[69] Sergio de la Mora's *Cinemachismo: Masculinities and Sexualities in Mexican Film* (2006), and Daniel Enrique Pérez's *Rethinking Chicana/o and Latina/o Popular Culture* (2009) are Mestizo or Hispanic centered and do not center sovereign Indigenous queer images. De la Mora explains, "Mexican cinema of the 1990s is overwhelmingly middle-class, urban, and white; the Indigenous population figure mostly as local color and secondary players."[70] María de la Cruz Castro Ricalde affirms a similar twenty-first-century Mexican queer film preference for "the social environments that privilege a middle or upper-middle class, that is neither Indigenous nor politically active."[71] Joseph Pierce notes that even the heterosexual "Indian" (Mixtec) miscarriage narrative centered in the Academy Award–winning 2018 film *Roma* directed by Mestizo Mexican Alfonso Cuarón still essentially serves the upper-class "colonial" imaginary in which Indigenous people have no real past and future outside of colonial servitude.[72]

Recent documentaries of Indigenous peoples of South America have focused on anti-LGBTQI2+ violence grounded in colonial Catholicism. The 2022 short film "Two Spirit" by the non-Indigenous director Monica Taboada-Tapia highlights the dire poverty and outcast standing of a Wayuu transgender woman who face various kinds of violence from her community in Colombia.[73] Directed by the non-Indigenous Álvaro Delgado-Aparicio, *Retablo* (2017) also recounts Indigenous violence against their own LGBTQI2+ population, but this time it is a bisexual Quechua married family man who eventually dies by suicide when his homoerotic practices are discovered by his Catholic Peruvian Andes community. In a review of *Retablo*, Micaela Giesecke-Chero reports the colonial conservative source of this violence, writing, "Catholics and other Christians operate in alliance with conservative political parties to reduce efforts to improve the social and political conditions of the LGBTQI+ population in Peru."[74] Two-spirit Quechua actor Sergio Papa Ruark is set to positively queer this homophobic Peruvian cinematic streak in a longer version of the short film "The Inka of Malvas," the plot of which follows "Sergio, a queer Quechua, return[ing] home to continue the legacy of the Inka of Malvas."[75] The relative lack of LGBTQI2+ Indigenous cinema analysis also indexes the low Indigenous film distribution across Latin America. These deficits in both Indigenous film analysis and film distribution throughout Latin America occur despite reports of local Indigenous renaissances in local media production that are especially strong in Indigenous-language use.[76]

LGBTQI2+ Indigenous film analysis in Canada also finds fragmented scholarly discussions in broader queer film analysis. Thomas Waugh's *The Romance of Transgression in Canada: Queering Sexualities, Nations, Cinemas* (2006) queers a century of Canadian film by documenting the Canadian government's uneven purging of "homosexuals" from the movies during the post–World War II Canadian Cold War.[77] He includes mostly paragraph-long media portraits of key Indigenous filmmakers including actor Even Adams (Tla'amin First Nation), Dene director Clint Alberta, Métis filmmaker Marjorie Beaucage, director/actor Theo Jean Cuthand (Little Pine First Nation), Cree/Métis director Adam Garnet Jones, Sayisi Dene director Zachery Longboy, director Gail Maurice of the Cree/Métis community of Beauval, and artist Kent Monkman (Fisher River Cree Nation). Unable to confirm a combined political, erotic, and visual sovereignty, Thomas Waugh concludes, "I don't come away from this research with a strong sense of coherent two-spirit or aboriginal queer corpus" of cinema.[78]

In clear contrast to Waugh's diminishment of visual sovereignty, Tatonetti calls for cinema to reflect the community power of national two-spirit spaces, criticizing the lesbian-themed *Johnny Greyeyes* (2000) by non-Indigenous director Jorge Manzano for portraying queerness as only existing openly off the Indigenous reserve.[79] The film *Fire Song* (2015) by two-spirit Cree/Métis director Adam Garnet Jones found minor critiques for its uneven depictions of First Nation women's suicide and two-spirit resilience. Beenash Jafri observes, "*Fire Song* problematically positions queer futurity alongside the antifuturity of young Native women: whereas Shane and David negotiate their existence amid colonial conditions, Destiny and Tara are unable to survive."[80] This seconds Estrada's sense that the film's planned escape from a queerphobic reserve is problematic given the unresolved rape and suicide of the two-spirit protagonist's jilted girlfriend.[81] The film's final family support for the two-spirit couple is a key healing moment in the often tense film.

In a more positive light, Tatonetti celebrates the "non-cis masculinity" of Plains Cree/Scots filmmaker Theo Jean Cuthand's many films, including their transition as a trans man depicted in the 2012 film *Boi O Boi*.[82] June Scudeler's Métis application of the Cree "kinship" word "wâhkôhtowin" to explain

Cuthand's inclusion of "friends in the film" "2 Spirit Introductory Special $19.95" is a good example of using an Indigenous-language approach to analyzing Indigenous queer film.[83] Like Tatonetti, Sophie Mayer aims to "queer/indigenize" postmillennial film analysis, lauding the manner in which Dene director Clint Alberta's *Deep Inside Clint Star* (2009) puts forth complicated Indigenous issues of documentary genres, urban community, sexual abuse, homoerotic desire, and First Nation identity.[84] While Kerstin Knopf highlights the gay, urban, Indigenous "Other" antagonist within director Shelley Niro's (Mohawks of the Bay of Quinte First Nation) 1998 detective parody *Honey Moccasin*, Elizabeth Weatherford includes AIDS and gay activism as a positive context for the creation of *Honey Moccasin* in an insightful interview with the film's Kanien'kehà:ka director, Shelley Niro.[85] Drawing evidence from director Duane Gastant' Aucoin's (Teslin Tlingit First Nation) films "Kichx Anagaat Yatx'i: Children of the Rainbow" (2003) and "My Own Private Lower Post" (2008), Kristin Dowell notes how Aucoin manifests his "desire to honor two-spirit individuals and reclaim the traditional roles of two-spirit people."[86] Part of what is so powerful about "My Own Private Lower Post" is that it is one of the few two-spirit films to this day to depict intergenerational Indigenous alcoholism as stemming from the Christian heteropatriarchal Indian residential school programs of Canada, unlike two-spirit films like those of Sherman Alexie's (Spokane Tribe of Indians) *The Business of Fancydancing* (2010), Adam Garnet Jones's Cree/Métis *Fire Song* (2015), and Dene Clint Alberta's *Deep Inside Clint Star*.[87]

Across the moana, film analyses trace problematic and successful Māori and Kānaka Maoli queer gender/sexuality representations. For example, Martin J. Blythe and Janet Wilson note the colonial cinematic "homosexual" desire for the Māori "Other,"[88] echoing Daniel McMullin's fa'afafine Sāmoan critiques on the queer film fetishization of the Māori male in *Twilight of the Gods* (1996).[89] Fortunately, more affirmative images became available by the 2000s. According to the Māori television venue NZ On Screen, "Takatāpui was the world's first Indigenous gay, lesbian and transgender series," a major breakthrough in media representation in 2005.[90] The gay Māori coming-out film *Kawa* (2010) also emerged, thanks to the famed queer Māori fiction and screenwriting of Whiti Ihimaera of the Te Whānau-a-Kai, Te Aitanga-a-Māhaki, Rongowhakaata, Ngāti Porou, and Tūhoe iwis. Leo Koziol of the Ngāti Rakaipaaka and Ngāti Kahungunu iwis praises the "groundbreaking New Zealand web series-turned-feature film *Rurangi*" directed by white settler New Zealander Max Currie and featuring a Māori transmasculine protagonist Caz Davis, played by Te Whakatōhea and Te Aitanga-A-Māhaki actor Elz Carrad. Kozol also lauds the "stunning" 2018 digital interactive work *FafswagVogue* by the Samoan and Māori Tanu Gago as a "queer Pacific community . . . interactive documentary . . . [on] the LGBTQ vogue dance scene in . . . Auckland, New Zealand."[91]

While an early review by Kānaka Maoli Ty Tengan takes a positive spin on how the Hawaiian film *Ke Kulana He Mahu* (2001) represents the mixed-gender māhū as part of Kānaka Maoli ohana, history, and community, Kānaka Maoli scholar Stephanie Nohelani Teves provided a mixed review of the *Ke Kulana He Mahu,* voicing concerns over the repression of sovereignty in parts of the film by the local Asian directors Kathryn Xian and Brent Anbe.[92] Kānaka Maoli Lisa Hall's brief mention of *Ke Kulana He Mahu* is also complicated, noting how the film reflects a politics of gay marriage rights more than it does Hawaiian sovereignty.[93] In contrast, Kānaka Maoli Kehaulani Watson gave the biographical film *Kumu Hina* (2014) a glowing review for its depiction of the māhū Kumu Hina, writing, Hina "is a community leader and champion. She is stunning and glorious. . . . Hina transformed the role of māhū in Hawai'i."[94] However, Mary Zaborskis and Elizabeth Reich note the tension between *Kumu Hina* Euro-American directors Wilson and Kramer's situating of Kumu Hina within gender identity politics and Kumu Hina's contrasting focus on supporting Kānaka Maoli sovereignty as a māhū.[95]

Queer African and Afrofuturistic cinematic visions are also worth noting. Acknowledging Ken Derry's popularization of the "Afrofuturism" term as "speculative fiction that treats African-American themes and . . . appropriates images of technology and a prosthetically enhanced future," *Queer Times, Black Futures* author Kara Keeling favors Ytasha Womack's *Afrofuturism* redefinition of the term as "an intersection of imagination, technology, the future, and liberation" that includes film.[96] Commenting the "Queer Afrofuturism and New Spatialities in Diego Paulino's *Negrum3*," Ariela Parisia argues for a Brazilian queer of color film critique in which "Afrofuturism . . . breaks down the perceived opposition between 'white science' and 'black magic' . . . in the context of the African religions of *Candomblé* and *Yoruba*."[97] As "a non-African and non-Black scholar," Lindsey Green-Simms finds that "queer African cinema can also register dreams for different possible presents and futures, presents and futures that are often even in conversation with more traditional and fluid understandings of gender and sexuality."[98] Of course, the blockbuster *Black Panther: Wakanda Forever*'s inclusion of queer Dora Milaje women warriors has sparked academic interest.[99] This will be seen in this book's chapter 5, summarized later in this introduction.

Expressing solidarity with Black Americans, Sandy O'Sullivan (Wiradjuri) and colleagues note that while queer Indigenous characters often lack complexity on the film screen, "across so-called Australia, there is a richness of inclusion of queerness across Indigenous-developed and written projects, on streaming television shows including *Black Comedy* (2014–2020), *All My Friends Are Racist* (2021), *Redfern Now* (2012–2015), and *Heartbreak High* (2022–2024)." O'Sullivan and colleagues conclude, "As with *Reservation Dogs*, these shows have Indigenous writers and directors, as well as actors, and this makes a difference," noting the queer representation by Paulina Alexis (Alexis Nakota Sioux First Nation) on the *Reservation Dogs* series by Sterlin Harjo (Seminole Nation of Oklahoma) and Te Whānau-ā-Apanui director Taika Waititi.[100] This inclusion of Indigenous writers and directors in streaming media makes a contrast from the iconic *Adventures of Priscilla, Queen of the Desert* (1994) film, which featured a short glimpse of Australian Indigenous drag, an art that Jojo Zahoe (John Ridgeway, Biripi and Worimi) expanded upon in *RuPaul's Drag Race Down Under* (season 1, 2021).[101] The increasing queer Indigenous representations on television and other media platforms are important to note, as streaming and online media comprise wider audiences, especially through the COVID-19 pandemic of the early 2020s, which restricted public access to theaters. However, while streaming content is increasingly impactful, the history of cinema remains important given its much greater global influence prior to the 2020s.

Summaries of Chapters 1–7

Part I of this book features four directions, east, south, west, and north, and considers the various Indigenous media connections to sovereign directionality, gender, and media in each of these areas as shown in the figure 1 map. Chapter 1, "East: Restoring Hózhǫ́ in Diné Transgender, Nádleehí, and Genderqueer Film," considers the Diné direction of the east and its association of beginnings and thinking at dawn. The film analysis of Nazbah Tom's (Navajo Nation) 2012 digital story "Mountain of Stories" completes a full directional circle that begins with a Diné chant to Tsisnaajiní (Mount Blanca), mountain of the east, as Tom prepares to mail a letter to their mom to openly identify for the first time as queer. The Diné eastern direction teachings on thinking can also explain aspects of the animated short video "Two-Spirit—Injunuity." In that video, the Diné genderqueer Nazbah Tom is one of seven two-spirit people sharing two-spirit history and contemporary experiences to help youth through the process of thinking about their gender identities. The chapter moves to the Red Circle Project/AIDS Project LA HIV/AIDS prevention medicine wheel curriculum co-developed by nádleehí Diné health workers Mattee Jim (Navajo Nation) and Elton Naswood. Using their Medicine Wheel model, and beginning in the east with emotions surrounding identity, the film analysis considers the emotional identities of the gay HIV-positive Ojibwe Damian Grey in the 1996 "I Am" film by nádleehí

Diné director Carrie House (Navajo Nation). Finally, through analyzing the eastward-facing kinaaldá coming-of-age run in *Drunktown's Finest* (2014) by transgender Diné director Sydney Freeland, this chapter expands upon Renae Watchman's establishment of how scenes express erotic, theological, and visual sovereignty by restoring hózhǫ́ (beauty) to the film's protagonists and audiences. While this chapter emphasized the eastern direction teaching, it also introduces the developmental teachings of the south, west, and north, observing Diné protocols to complete the full circle.

In chapter 2, "South: Trans*forming Caxcan Xochipilli on YouTube," the video "Juchipila Zacatecas y el Xuchitl" (2019), directed by Juchipilense filmmaker Alondra Sánchez, explains the link of the Caxcan Flower Dance to the directional winds that bring rain, including those from the south. Daisy Ocampo's Caxcan scholarship helps explain a spatial sovereign reading of the Xochipilli stone sculpture that currently sits upon a fountain and facing from the south, the direction of the Caxcan Creation Mountain, as depicted in Sánchez's video. While the Xochipilli deity is now a queer Mexica icon in pop visual culture, being read as a double of the Mexica pleasure god of the southern direction, Macuilxóchitl, this reading considers the Caxcan Xochipilli with emphasis on sacred plants that are sometimes intersex in nature. In the "Danza de Los Viejos de la Chinana" and "Las fiestas de Moyahua" (2019) videos, a monkey-masked cross-dressed "wife" dancer marks the Catholic conversion of the Caxcans. Her monkey-masked dance that references Central Mexican Nahua representations of Xochipilli and Macuilxóchitl and their southern direction affiliation has both Chichimeca and Nahua gender-subversive nuances.

In chapter 3, "West: Filming Kumu Hina, Aloha ʻĀina, and Māhū in Hawaiʻi," the famed Kumu Hina establishes a Kānaka Maoli sense of the western feminine direction also linked with the red road of Kānaloa that represents sunset and the transition of the kūpuna (ancestors). Kumu Hina also relates a healing practice that begins with sunrise on the eastern horizon and concludes in the west with a culmination of healing at sunset. Thus, ancestral healing linked with the west is the theme of this chapter. The animated "Kapaemahu" (2020) features four Tahitian māhū healers who are commemorated on the western shores Waikīkī for their healing powers centuries ago. Keeping connection to the west of the ancestors, the film *Kumu Hina* especially deals with the maintenance of ancestral traditions such as chanting/mele in this māhū-centered film. "Kapaemahu" animates a historic moment when the four Tahitian māhū healers leave their mana in four stones set on the western shores of Waikīkī. The western direction of healing and letting go also resonates with healing HIV stigma and LGBTQI-phobic colonial trauma in *Ke Kulana He Mahu: Remembering a Sense of*

Place (2001) by Brent Anbe and Kathryn Xian. This film also features the cultural healing of Kumu Hina and the HIV-positive Kānaka Maoli drag performer Cocoa Chandelier.

Chapter 4 reconnects with the sequential stages of life teachings of the east (infants), south (youths), west (adults), and north (elders) began in chapter 1, but with a special emphasis on the northern direction of elders in two-spirit film. This chapter, "North: Healing Kamloops with Two-Spirit and Nêhiyawak Jingle Dress Video," focuses on the healing from the Indian residential school gendercide of two-spirit peoples, with an emphasis on the finding of 215 graves at Kamloops Indian Residential School reported in 2021. Drawing upon Nêhiyawak (Plains Cree) teachings that link elders with the northern direction, this chapter begins to trace the cinematic links of two-spirit Indian residential schools and two-spirit Jingle Dress Dance healings in film. It begins with Sharon Desjarlais's "First Stories—Two Spirited" (2007) short film about the trials and triumphs of a male-bodied Îyârhe Nakodabi (Stoney Nakoda) Jingle Dress dancer who relies on the strong support of elders to dance after being banned from the powwow at Kamloops for wearing women's regalia. Moving across cultures, the chapter considers the absence of these supportive elders within Shelley Niro's two-spirit Jingle Dress Dance film *Honey Moccasin* (1998), as well as the Tsitsistas (Northern Cheyenne) grandfather's heartfelt sponsorship of his grandson's first two-spirit Jingle Dress Dance in screenwriter W.A.W. Parker's (Northern Cheyenne Tribe) "The Roof" (2023). The chapter ends with the Teslin Tlingit two-spirit director Duane Gastant' Aucoin's prayer for the Kamloops lost babies and children. In "My Own Private Lower Post," Aucoin also narrates his mother's escape and healing from the 1900s Indian residential school trauma she experienced upstate from Kamloops in British Columbia.

Having made a full circle of east, south, west, and north in part I, the analysis then considers the three remaining directions in part II, "Seeing Trans*Indigenous Time/Space: Down, Up, and Center." Chapter 5, "Down: Unsettling Hollywood Eras with Tongva Two-Spirit Video" reestablishes Tongva/Gabrielino land connections after a century of cinematic transphobic tropes of Tongva disappearance from the landscape. This chapter first considers Native California women's cross-dressing as a sign of impending genocide and land dispossession in both the silent feature *Ramona* (1928) by Chickasaw director Edwin Carewe and the classic film *Island of the Blue Dolphins* (1964) by Euro-American director James Clark. These silver and golden Hollywood movies differ from the contemporary recovery of two-spirit Tongva images and land connections in the independent videos "L. Frank Manriquez Oral History" (2011) by queer Nordic director Paul Christiaan Klieger and "Indigenous Pride LA Welcome Address: L. Frank Manriquez"

(2020) made by L. Frank themself, and *City of Ghosts* episode 4, "Tovaangar," Netflix animation starring L. Frank as a crow. Reclaiming a connection to Tongva lands across time, the decolonial and gender-inclusive Tongvetam/Ajachmem/Rarámuri L. Frank Manriquez breaks with Hollywood's settler cis-heteropatriarchal spatiality. With a focus on earth, the analysis looks at establishing landscape shots in light of Tongva two-spirit insights.

The upward direction of chapter 6, "Up: Queering Wakandan, Afro-Indigenous, and Bla(c)k Futurisms" begins with examples of Blak sky connections from the A̲nangu singer Zaachariaha Fielding of the Australian Western Desert. This Blak Indigenous futurity contrasts with Afro-Indigenous absence or assimilationist visions within white settler sci-fi found in Stanley Kubrick's *2001: A Space Odessey*; James Cameron's *Avatar* and *Avatar: The Way of Water*; and the Wachowskis and Tom Tykwer's *Cloud Atlas* (2012). While Black sci-fi productions *The Wiz* and *Black Panther* make racial inroads, they do not queer Afrofuturistic and Indigenous futuristic representations as do the FX series *Pose* and the independent film "Chaac + Yum." Briefly featuring a Yorùbá sky connection, *Pose* is partly directed by the trans Black and Kānaka Maoli Janet Mock and features the LGBTQI2+ Latinx and Afro-Indigenous ballroom culture of New York City. Playing Angel, the Afro-Taíno Indya Moore invokes the orishas during *Pose*'s season 1 ballroom competition finale, which prompts analysis on the orí-orun or head-heaven connection in Yorùbá practices of the Caribbean. These orí-orun futuristic connections are also present in the brief lesbian representations in the sci-fi film *Black Panther* and its sequel *Black Panther: Wakanda Forever*. This analysis notes the vertical hierarchy between queerly advanced aboveground African Wakandans and the cis-heteropatriarchal Maya, mutated to live in the ocean depths. This vertical hierarchy contrasts with the outright two-spirit Maya sky/earth erotics of the "Chaac + Yum" film short, written by Snowflake Arizmendi and Xav SF, which queers the rift between past and future Maya.

Chapter 7, "Center: Nepanta Raven Film Reflections" returns to the personal seventh direction voice that I briefly initiated in this introduction. As the coda to this book, it is my personal response to the Crow/Raven rhetorics in the Diné film of the east, Caxcan creation YouTube narratives in the south, the absenting of crows from Mauna a Wākea representations and images in the west, and the Teslin Tlingit Raven clan stories filmed in the north. It concludes with reflections on the crow animations of L. Frank Manriquez that ground the center of this book in Tongva territory and the African enslavement crows of *The Wiz*'s sky-bound Oz, as contrasted with the Afrofuturism of Ryan Coogler's *Sinners*. In this last trans*Indigenous element of my analysis, I am nepanta (in the center) of the book's formation and tell stories to give personal HIV-positive, land-based, and Caxcan/Xicanx context to my film analysis. This chapter recounts my own experience with ravens throughout Washington, California, Arizona, Hawaiʻi, and Mexico, including meetings with and traditions of ravens and crows from Palouse, Nisenan, Miwok, Tohono O'odham, Rarámuri, Chichimeca, Caxcan, and Tongva lands. The rhetorical point here, shared by Lawence Gross, is that the Indigenous stories as told, written, or filmed are meant to elicit relationships to related stories and memories from an Indigenous audience. My Raven reflections are a reminder that my book audience will read from the perspectives of their own seventh direction, inside, to forge new meanings of this book's cinematic contents.

Citing Chadwick Allen's "trans-Indigenous . . . comparisons," Tatonetti cautions about the possibilities that such "comparisons run the risk of flattening out . . . differences."[102] My organization of seven directions is not meant to imply that all Indigenous peoples have the same directionality. They don't. Even the Diné and Anishinaabe, who share some directional elements, have differing origins from below and above, respectively, that change their protocols. Where nations meet waters or approach the polar regions, the four directions often have less use. Differences are so extreme with the Kānaka Maoli that I insert that my interest in their western directionality is a trans-Indigenous Turtle Island concept applied to their media rather than organically coming from the media itself. My four directions retrace migration patterns to Tovaangar/LA and are not a reflection of deeper connections across distant cultures.

I

Orienting Gender to Four Directions

East, South, West, and North

1

EAST

Restoring Hózhǫ́ in Diné Transgender, Nádleehí, and Genderqueer Film

In the 2023 anthology *Nihikéyah: Navajo Homeland*, editor Lloyd L. Lee (Navajo Nation) demonstrates a Diné four-directions organization of scholarly and cultural thought by grouping two thematically linked articles within four book parts: Ha'a'aah/East, 'E'e'aah/West, Shádi'ááh/South, and Náhookǫs/North.[1] With a similar editorial anthology organization in *Indigenous Motherhood in the Academy*, Robin Zape-tah-hol-ah Starr Minthorn (Kiowa Tribe of Oklahoma), Christine A. Nelson (Navajo Nation), and Heather J. Shotton (Navajo Nation) write how they "found that contributors' stories were aligning with planning, processing, living, and reflecting," and so named the four anthology parts after these qualities that represent the Diné four directions teachings to the east, south, west, and north. They conclude, "Chris likened this process to Diné philosophy (Sa'ah Naaghai Bik'eh Hozhoo), so we used this loosely to help us organize each contributor's narrative."[2] With an emphasis on ha'a'aah teachings of the eastern direction, this analysis also applies sovereign Diné (Navajo Nation) directional knowledge—in this case, to interpret four media that feature Diné third and fourth genders and LGBTQI2+ images. Rather than offering a linear film history modeled in this book's introduction, this chapter is instead organized thematically upon three related Diné eastern direction teachings: thinking, praying, and balancing emotions.

The first of the four films to find an east direction analysis is "Mountain of Stories" (2012) directed by Nazbah Tom (Navajo Nation). This analysis points out Tom's initial thinking process and prayers as they plan to reveal their then-lesbian identity to their mother. The genderqueer Tom also gives a history of the thinking about two-spirit peoples prior to the intrusion of Christianity into Diné territories in the animated short "Two Spirit—Injunuity" (2013) by Hopi director Adrian Baker. Trans Diné director Sydney Freeland (Navajo Nation) offers this chapter's only feature-length fictional film, *Drunktown's Finest* (2014). While Freeland weaves together the stories of three Diné youth protagonists living in Gallup, this chapter will focus on one character's decision to fulfill her nádleehí (third-gender) family blessing ceremonial roles oriented to the east on the Navajo Nation rather than travel as a transgender woman sex worker in New York City. This film chapter culminates with a reading of "I Am" (1997) directed by the nádleehí Carrie House (Navajo Nation), which features 1990s interviews, activisms, and performances from various San Francisco Bay Area two-spirit/Indigenous LGBTQI2+ peoples. Reflecting an eastern direction perspective on balancing emotions, this concluding section explains how House artfully documents the emotional trauma and recovery of Damien Grey along his Ojibwe journey of becoming HIV-positive during the height of the 1990s AIDS pandemic of San Francisco.

"Mountain of Stories" (2012)

The white title words "Mountain of Stories" enlarge to fill the full length of a black screen in the first twenty-four seconds of this digital storytelling video composed of photographs, a background chant, and Tom's narration. From this beginning, the diegetic song "Honor Your Drum" by Jay Begaye (Navajo Nation) from the album *Honoring Our Ways* (1995) plays, dominating all sound in the first moments of the four-minute short. In this Diné language chant, Begaye first invokes the mountain Tsisnaajiní, also known as Mount Blanca, the mountain of the east. And then in clockwise fashion, he chants the names of the other three directional mountains of the south, west, and north: Tsoodził, Dook'o'oosłííd, and Dibé Nitsaa. Infusing Diné language and philosophy into her film analysis, Renae Watchman (Navajo Nation) explains the spatiality of these four sacred mountains linked to cardinal directions, writing, "Navajo origin stories tell of four sacred mountains, originally created by the Diyin Dine'é to demarcate traditional territory. . . . The eastern mountain is Tsisnaajiní (Mount Blanca). . . . The southern mountain is Tsoodził (Mount Taylor). . . . The west is Dook'o'oosłííd (San Francisco Peaks). . . . The mountain to the north is Dibé Ntsaa (Mount Hesperus)."[3] Since Tsisnaajiní is the mountain of the east for the Diné, this chant immediately establishes the underlying directional intentions of the digital storytelling media made of moving photographs and narrated by Nazbah Tom. The four names of the chant cycle again and again throughout the video. Through the consistent east, south, west, and north order of the respective mountain names Tsisnaajiní, Tsoodził, Dook'o'oosłííd and Dibé Nitsaa, Tom clearly demarcates a protocol of east first and Tsisnaajiní first by including this chant that accompanies the narrative to a harmonious end.

Expanding on Diné spatiality, Vincent Werito (Navajo Nation) succinctly explains these "T'áá shá bik'ehgo na'nitin, or the Sun Wise Path Teachings," writing, "the Diné philosophy is associated with and orientated to the four cardinal directions, starting with the east direction; the four seasons, starting with spring; and the four parts of the day, beginning with early dawn and moving around in a clockwise direction with the path of the sun."[4] More importantly for this first close film reading, Werito shares that the eastern direction is also part of an "orientation" for living that begins in the east with "nitsáhákees" that represents a period of prayer, thinking, and "a conceptualization of the mind and the realization of self for positive outcomes." To this t'áá shá bik'ehgo na'nitin, Lloyd L. Lee adds the "four stages of life (birth, adolescence, adulthood, and old age)," and the "four sacred minerals (white shell, turquoise, abalone, and back jet)" as a part of those teachings.[5] Thus, when Tom begins their video with a sung invocation of Tsisnaajiní, they are honoring this cycle of directions that begins in the east with its associations of sunrise, birth, white, white shell, spring, and thinking that guide this video analysis.

A photo image of the northern Mount Hesperus emerges from the blackness after the white title introduction in a moment that emphasizes the eastern-linked process of thinking and praying. Tom's first words of the short commence: "As I write my coming out letter to my mother, I look out from the window of my dorm room and see Mount Hesperus. I ask the Mountain for strength to send this story."[6] As the north is a direction associated with "confidence, assurance, and security,"[7] Tom is indicating that they need great strength to write the coming-in letter and fear rejection from their mother. However, even though Mount Hesperus is the northern direction mountain, its image placement in the beginning of the video with these first words marks it with clear eastern qualities. The prayer to Mount Hesperus represents nitsáhákees, thinking or prayers in the east that begins all action. Beginning all things in the east in daily prayer is a practice that Vincent Werito (Navajo Nation) also shares in memory. Awakening to the aroma of burning cedar and juniper as a youth, Werito recalls following his parents out into "the early dawn light" with his brothers, facing east behind his parents, and listening as they "began their prayers" with "Kodóó hózhǫ dooleeł" (It begins in beauty). In a similar manner to Werito, Tom prays to Mount Hesperus for success in coming in to their mother before taking any action toward that goal. This prayerful thinking in the east then guides the success in this effort through a progression through the subsequent southern, western, and northern phases and teachings of the full circle; as Werito explains, eastern "nitsáhákees" thinking is followed by "Nahat'á (Planning)" in the south, "Iiná (Living)" in the west, and "Siihasin (Assurance)" in the north.[8] Tom's video also demonstrates these directional developments as their story comes to its resolution.

After establishing the eastern teachings of thinking, the story progresses to the south through a process of nahat'á, or planning. Werito further defines “Nahat’á (Planning)” in the south as “achieving critical consciousness through the process of achieving and planning life goals.”[9] Tom’s narrated action, “I send the letter,” can represent beginning the process of nahat’á. The letter is Tom’s plan to come out and find family acceptance, but it is a plan that seems to fail at first, when Tom’s mother does not quickly respond to the letter. Tom’s fears seem justified as they narrate, “Three months go by without a word from my mother.” The small steps of nahat’á have not led to the desired goal of familial acceptance as a lesbian. Tom recounts their road trip with their mother, a chance to finally speak and move beyond the nahat’á (planning) process. As Tom narrates the silence between mother and child intensifying during a road trip, Begaye’s background chant to Tsisnaajiní becomes softer and Tom’s thoughts begin to stray from their original positive orientation. Tom narrates in this middle section, “Usually, she is full of stories along this stretch of road. This drive is silent. . . . My thoughts fill with . . . the dangerous curve that took someone’s life.”[10] The silence and lack of assurance from the mother brings on negative thoughts of spiritual dangers and car crashes. It is at the point that the chant is almost inaudible as Tom begins to stray from their original prayer. They are losing hope at this point, and the prayerful thinking begun in the east seems to be weakening during this process of nahat’á in the south.

Werito explains that “Iiná (Living)” in the west is the direction of completing positive life actions and of “developing an awareness and responsibility to act for self and others.”[11] This iiná phase finally happens during the drive to Page as Tom finds support as a lesbian from their mother. Tom’s mother breaks the silence to explain that she was initially ashamed of having a queer child. The chant volume picks up as her sentiments change. She relates that her new husband recommended accepting Tom, as Diné have always had people like Tom in the community. “We have to love and respect her,” the stepfather concluded. The mother and Tom cry together in emotional release as photos of Tom as a baby on the Navajo Nation’s desert landscape flash across the scene. This image reaffirms the k’e or kinship ties from mother to queer child and within the matrilineal heart of the Navajo Nation. Through Tom’s narration, the mother concludes, “That’s when I realized I have to love you twice as much to make up for all the pain you put up with out there.”[12] The chant really picks up with full strength as the mom comes finally comes around to express her love and support for Tom, reaffirming Tom’s original prayer to find acceptance as a queer child from their mother and resolving the process of iiná. Both Tom and their mother demonstrate a shift to “developing an awareness and responsibility to act for self and others,” in this case, to establish mutual support as a mother and queer adult child in a balanced k’e kinship relationship.

The final section of the digital story is thematically dedicated to "Siihasin (Assurance)" in the north. This direction is also one of reflection on the previous three directions and solidifies what occurred.[13] In the end of the narrative, Tom figuratively arrives in the north with a positive reflection and assurance regarding the process of coming in to their mom with the affirmation of Diné gender traditions. Tom is able to reflect in a positive way upon the whole experience, from east, to south, to west, to north, and from Tsisnaajiní to Mount Hesperus. The car ride restores a kinship rooted in the ancient Navajo oral traditions of gender and sexuality. Including a picture of Naatsis'áán or Navajo Mountain and family photographs, Tom concludes, "Naatsis'áán watches us as we follow the black ribbon of highway into Page. Together my mother and I are reminded of the stories the elders and the mountains gave us to listen to and accept."[14] Here, Tom positions Naatsis'áán or Navajo Mountain as active, watching over both of them along that part of the drive and over the restoration of k'e between Tom and their mother. Even the blackness of the highway could be a subtle reference to the black direction of the north and to the wisdom of elders that traditionally integrates a positive kinship with the nádleehí. With Tom's monologue finished, Begaye's chant returns to full volume, with the chanted eastern mountain name, Tsisnaajiní, falling at the moment that a photo appears of a smiling Tom in a genderqueer presentation wearing blue jeans, T-shirt, and sunglasses and straddling a motorcycle. It is a triumphant moment followed by more family photographs and the succession of the respective southern, western, and northern sacred mountain names, Tsoodził, Dook'o'oosłííd, and Dibé Nitsaa. The final dedication in white letters upon a black background poetically reads

> for mom
> the mountains
> and
> the ancestors

While "mom" refers to a tradition bearer and elder, the mountains and ancestors also reference the Diné north direction of elders. Tom is one of many contemporary nádleehí who are sharing ancestral gender traditions to effect change in Navajo Nation. There is a great need for that. Noting the suppression of nádleehí mixed-gender traditions by settler-colonial Christian boarding schools, nádleehí scholar Souksavanh Tom Keovorabouth (Navajo Nation) argues for "'Coming in' and returning to ourselves" by "reaching back to our traditional knowledges and recognizing Nadleeh and the teachings in Sa'ah naaghai Bik'eh Hozho connects us to our ancestors and to each other."[15] The nádleehí teachings that Tom and Keovorabouth present are an assurance from the northern direction of elders about the sacred place of the nádleehí within Navajo traditions and kinship, despite the recent suppression of the nádleehí genders. In accordance with Keovorabouth, Tom is using clear auditory references to Tsisnaajiní, Tsoodził, Dook'o'oosłííd, and Dibé Nitsaa to make the development of their story align with an eastern-oriented Diné philosophy and spatiality. With Begaye continuously invoking Tsisnaajiní throughout the video, Tom's thinking begun in the east with prayer leads to a positive reflection in the north, completing the full circle and process of "coming in" to their mother.

"Two Spirit—Injunuity" (2013)

Thinking as a Diné teaching of the east direction can also apply to the four-minute "Two Spirit—Injunuity" animation directed by the Hopi Adrian Baker. This short video presents initial two-spirit definitions, a legacy of settler-colonial Christian repression of two-spirit ways, and a reclaiming of two-spirit traditions in urban San Francisco. While an animated version of the Mexica Mica Valdez begins the animation, Nazbah Tom follows Valdez as one of three two-spirit Diné animated presenters who explain their own positive two-spirit experiences. Comedian and drag queen Charlie Ballard (Sac and Fox Nation) is the lone Anishinaabe/Sac and Fox figure in the cartoon. As each speaker tells of their two-spirit experiences and knowledge, the possibility for being two-spirit grows as differently gendered bodies and Indigenous identities multiply as model options. For example, Valdez speaks of two-spirit definitions as a Mexica genderfluid person. Tom recounts the movement from Diné two-spirit historical acceptance and the settler-colonial Christian suppression of those roles. Ballard describes his Anishinaabe/Sac and Fox experience of identifying as two-spirit and finding self-confidence in that choice. Transgender Diné woman Yuè Begay's (Navajo Nation) explanation of thinking can help link these many possibilities to the eastern direction. According to Begay, the Diné eastern thinking process is not only defined by praying, but also by "brainstorming," thinking about the all the possibilities before narrowing down the choices and then truly planning a process of completing initial actions to achieve that goal.[16] In this light, all five "Injunuity" speakers support a thinking and brainstorming process for Indigenous queer youth who are exploring their gender and sexual identities and seeing role models in this media, perhaps for the first time.

Appearing before any of the speakers do, title cards provide a definition for "two-spirit": "A Native American possessing both a male and female spirit . . . An umbrella term used to describe the fluidity of Native American gender identity and sexuality with respect to traditional tribal roles."[17] It's important to note that both gender and sexuality are viewed in fluid terms in that two-spirit definition, something that the LGBTQI identities do not consistently do, as "lesbian," "gay," "bisexual," and "queer" are more often sexuality signifiers while "transgender" and "intersex" are more often gender signifiers. Of course, the Native American aspect of two-spirit is the most unique aspect of two-spirit. Two-spirit is likely a new option to think about for the target audience of Indigenous youth. Whether Indigenous youth identify or disidentify with two-spirit, they can at least think about the two-spirit identity options among many LGBTQI2+ identities that are also possibilities, such as Indigiqueer, cuír, non-labeled, asexual, questioning, and so many others.

Facing the eastern direction is prominent in "Two Spirit—Injunuity," which begins with Mexica Mica Valdez sharing, "Gay and lesbian, bisexual, transgender, it feels like they are all boxes, categories that you have to fit into, and they can't change."[18] First appearing as a puppet hanging on strings amid LGBTQ boxes on a theater stage, Valdez escapes and transforms into a fully human animated form, reappearing in a colorful spring bloom of poppies, bluebells, and California goldfields blooms animated by the Yaqui/Chicano artist Jesse Hernandez. Valdez adds, "When I learned about being two-spirit, it felt more natural to me." Using a Diné directionality, this springtime bloom represents the east of new beginnings, a correlation that one can find within Mexica directionality for the east and spring, when the Mexica new year begins for many.[19] The sunflower heads surrounding Valdez are drawn facing east, as many sunflowers face that direction, especially as they stiffen with age. That both Valdez and the sunflowers are facing east can indicate facing the Mexica direction for new beginnings and "masculinity,"[20] in this case as expressed in the female-bodied two-spirit Mexica person. One could also say that Valdez is positioned facing from the west which represents the complementary Mexica direction of femininity. Thus, Valdez can either represent both genders or neither. In *The Path to Quetzalcoatl* (1977) video, the queer Conchero dance maestro Andres Segura Granados draws upon classic codices and modern physics language to suggest that solar and cosmic energy descends to earth as "positivo, negativo, y neutro (positive, negative, and neutral),"[21] something like a positive proton, negative electron, and neutral neutron. From this modern Mexica perspective, Valdez's two-spirit expression may represent a fractal example of a neutral force in motion throughout the cosmos. This gender-neutral or genderfluid representation is another possibility to add the many possibilities that Indigenous LGBTQI2+ youth can contemplate as they brainstorm possible gender identities. Listing "Mica Valdez (Mexica)" in the credits is also another aspect of giving multiple options to Indigenous viewers who may originate in Mexico and from Nahua communities; including a Mexica presence is another aspect to the brainstorming of different options of gender. Through the prominent announcements of each speaker's Indigenous affiliation in the credits or in visuals, viewers begin to understand that there are different Indigenous traditions of gender. Having speakers from multiple Indigenous areas and languages increases the brainstorming options.

The chimalxochitl (sunflower or "shield flower") hold another subtle meaning of solar energy and protection for a viewer with a Nahua directional lens. However, for Valdez, the protection of the sunflowers isn't about integration into a masculinist military vision of Mexica society.[22] Rather, it is about knowing who you are as a two-spirit person and about connecting with the power of earth and the sun. In a larger context in which 56 percent of Native transgender or gender-nonconforming students initiate a suicide attempt,[23] to protect oneself from gender and Indigenous identity attacks with Indigenous knowledge and connection to earth is a life-saving skill. Symbolically, Valdez offers the protection of two-spirit knowledge like a chimalli (shield) for the target audience of two-spirit youth with all its multigendered potential and high suicide/hate crime rate. Living and thriving as a two-spirit person rather than dying by suicide after experiencing gender and sexuality shame is a key choice that the video wishes the youthful audience to consider. The flowers pixelate and blow away as Valdez's story ends, and Nazbah Tom's narration begins with yet more options to consider.

Figure 2 Nádleehí animated mediation in the Third World in "Two Spirit—Injunuity" (2013), directed by Adrian Baker.

Nazbah Tom offers yet another brainstorming possibility as they narrate the Navajo traditions part of "Two Spirit—Injunuity." As an elder Native American woman elder tells a story to children over a fire, they begin to recount, "What was working before colonization is this practice of passing on . . . stories." The animation switches to a yellowish background with black outlines of two masculine figures in short kilts and braids. Moving like paper puppets, they are arguing, with fingers pointing at each other. Then, a two-spirit figure dressed in a half masculine kilt and half feminine dress appears between them. This figure is animated with two faces seeing both directions. The fighting stops between the masculine figure as Tom's narration explains how two-spirit people taught men and women "to appreciate each other to live in a way that everyone felt like they were safe and belonged." In this dialogue, the two-spirit figure appears to be speaking and gesturing to a pregnant Diné woman as Tom's narration finishes the thought.[24] The clearly gender-mixed clothing is yet another way of conceptualizing gender expression and identity for Indigenous LGBTQI2+ youth. Tom's narrative affirms that two-spirit people were traditionally valued and safe within Diné culture, while acknowledging that the present time is less supportive due to Christian settler influence, which is later animated as a threatening giant priest appears shaking a fist at a Diné traditionalist woman and her relatives.

This animated two-spirit role of mediating between genders recalls the original Navajo nádleehí role of mediator that began in the Third World, when there was a split between male and female camps across a river. The yellow background of the animation, which occurs only in this story, supports the ideas that the animation is depicting the Third World, which was yellow. It is a world the Diné left to emerge in this present Fourth World that is the Glittering World.[25] Elton Naswood (Navajo Nation) relates this story from his elder aunt in greater detail in the film *As They Are: Two Spirit People in the Modern World* (2009):

> I had heard a story from my mother's eldest sister, who played the role of grandmother . . . that long ago when the Navajo world [began], within the Navajo people, there was a separation of the sexes, and that there was an argument between man and woman. And then, at that time, the men went to one side of the river and the women went to the other side of a river. And it was the nádleehí, it was the more effeminate less masculine men, that brought the sexes together, and that because of the nádleehí, our people survived. If it wasn't for the nádleehís, we wouldn't be the people we are today.[26]

While only Diné viewers may understand the oral tradition behind the animated Yellow World images, all viewers will understand through the shadowy figures that the two-spirit Diné figure is bringing harmony to male and female relations and represents a mixture of both genders in a third-gender way. This role of gender mediator is another role that will add to the gender brainstorming and thinking aspect of this animated video.

Like Valdez and Tom, the Diné/Latina spokesperson Esther Lucero also contemplates being both or neither binary genders within two-spirit traditions. As Lucero finishes the four-minute segment, she emphasizes youth empowerment in a gender-neutral way, aided by relatable visuals. Lucero begins her encouragements as a frowning flower is drawn with an animated pencil on lined paper. That image is followed by a neutral face sketched in the middle circle of the male, female, and transgender mixed-male-female-genderqueer signs. Then a weak arm is erased and redrawn as a strong arm. Lucero narrates, "Young people who are just exploring who they are, I want you to remember that there were some tribes out there who didn't even call you a specific gender until you decided what that is."[27] The idea of not labeling oneself by gender or sexuality is an important option within the video's brainstorming of options of gender and sexuality identity. Lucero's concluding video statement neither prescribes a certain transition from one gender to another nor directs youth to identify by a certain gender expression. The possibilities are open and fluid. Lucero's final speech and visuals build upon traditions in which youth are able to define their own gender with the knowledge that there are two-spirit traditions and community that could support that choice even if it does not include the two-spirit identity term. It also allows for youth to simply question or "brainstorm" gender ideas for a time, and says that not choosing a firm gender as a youth also has an Indigenous tradition to it. In this reading, the east is not only a direction of prayer that initiates action but a process of brainstorming of gender and sexuality identities that can help questioning and LGBTQI2+ youth explore their own gender and sexuality identity path.

Drunktown's Finest (2014)

Using parallel editing, the transgender Diné director Sydney Freeland features three Navajo characters: Nizhoni Smiles (Morningstar Angeline, Navajo Nation), an adoptee haunted by deathly nightmares and searching Navajo Nation for her estranged biological family; Felixia (Carmen Moore, Navajo Nation), a transgender woman sex worker seeking intimacy and social acceptance; and Sick Boy Maryboy (Jeremiah Bitsui, Navajo Nation), an army recruit and father-to-be who is mostly failing at quitting his life of addiction and crime. The entire film takes place within the four days of the kinaaldá coming-of-age ceremony for Sick Boy's little sister Max Maryboy (Magdalena Begay, Navajo Nation). Attention to the film's construction of Diné directional spatiality via plot development, camera angle, lighting, dialogue, and mise-en-scène establishes how Freeland directs her young characters to avoid the "hóchxǫ́," imbalances represented by unhealthy activities and a "reeling" disharmony that occur during night, a time represented by the northern direction. According to Watchman, the opposite state to "hóchxǫ́," is "hózhǫ́," which is "best translated as to be in a state of wellness, balance, peace, and harmony, culminating in beauty."[28] Hózhǫ́ is best represented by the film's climactic Diné coming-of-age run toward the east at sunrise. The film evolves from a focus on nightly north-direction struggles to an east-oriented morning kinaaldá ceremony that facilitates overcoming those struggles.

In *Restoring Relations Through Stories,* Watchman adds commentary on the film's opening sequence's sunrise timing with an implicit camera orientation away from an eastern orientation. Commenting on the first pre-title twenty-one seconds, Watchman observes the cultural disorientation in how Freeland's film "opens with a fast-motion, time-lapse establishing shot, cycling from darkness to early morning dawn to daylight," concluding, "Instead of opening with traditional Diné protocol to greet the sun, *Drunktown's Finest* opens with Nizhoni's lament" about the difficulty of living in the fictional Dry Lake. It is a town shot in and modeled on Gallup, New Mexico, a place riddled in the film's first establishing shots with Diné houselessness, gangs, alcoholism, and settler tourism industries. Watchman's book includes an image from the film trailer of that moment in which the sunrise occurs over a cloudy Dry Lake sky, showing that it is indeed a shot overlooking Gallup from its "north side" neighborhood, implicitly looking south, with the southern horizon showing the Tsé Łichíí' (Red Rock) Chapter of the Navajo Nation rising above Gallup.[29] Freeland introduces her film's three characters performing illegal or disturbed actions in the dark of night and out of sync with a traditional Diné progression into reflection or sleep at night. First, Sick Boy is arrested for drunkenly peeing on a liquor store and slapping the investigating Navajo policeman (Ryan Begay, Navajo Nation) making night rounds, an act that disqualifies Sick Boy from joining the armed forces and providing for his pregnant girlfriend. Racked by nightmares that wake her up at night, Nizhoni is shown haunted in bed by nightly reexperiencing a car crash like the one that killed her parents. Next is a cut to an extreme close-up of the beautifully feminine Felixia negotiating for more money from her Diné client, who pays extra to perform oral sex on Felixia's large penis, which is briefly and blurrily shown lit by the night streetlamps. These opening scenes for the three protagonists establish each of their struggles that are intimately tied to the hóchxǫ́ of the potentially dangerous nightly time of north in Navajo cosmology, when people should be home asleep rather than having serial nightmares, being out of the house doing sex work, or getting drunk and arrested.[30]

According to Watchman, a restoration of hózhǫ for the three protagonists culminates at the grounds for the kinaaldá ceremony, the home of Ruth John (Toni Oliver, Navajo Nation) and Harmon John (Richard Whitman, Muskogee Creek Nation), the spiritual leader of the ceremony. First, when Ruth John welcomes in her matrilineal granddaughter Nizhoni on the third day of the ceremony, they begin to restore their "k'é, or kinship . . . determined by the matrilineal Diné clan system," that Nizhoni lost to the forces of her parents' addictions, their fatal car crash, and her adopted white mother's insistence that Nizhoni could never know that her grandparents were seeking contact with her.[31] Second, Felixia resolves to complete the fourth-day sunrise ceremony with her grandparents Ruth and Harmon John and forgo a reliance on sex work to satisfy her need for affection and money. Third, at the sunrise ceremony, Sick Boy begins to sober up and act as a reliable partner to his pregnant girlfriend.

Although valued by her grandparents Ruth and Harmon John, Felixia lacks the erotic intimacy she seeks outside her matrilineal home. Diné men avoid her publicly by day but privately seek her sexual favors for pay by night. Felixia's reliance on nightly sex work to satisfy her needs for self-esteem and money culminates in her decision to allow a lawyer to fly her out to New York for sex. Watchman notes how a retelling of Navajo sacred narratives lays a foundation for Felixia's decision to remain at home. Hearing from her grandfather the sacred narrative that honors her nádleehí place in Navajo traditions,[32] Felixia decides to stay home and complete the kinaaldá ceremony rather than flying to New York for sex work. As the nádleehí were needed in the early history of the Navajo to mediate an early split between men and women,[33] so Felixia is needed as a nádleehí in contemporary times to help both men and women.

Felixia's decision to stay is only announced several scenes later, the next morning, when she helps make fry bread with her grandmother Ruth John at the ceremony for Ruth's granddaughter, Max. Watchmen confirms that it is a vision of "k'e (kinship)" affirmation. In partaking in the ceremony, Felixia forgoes a sex worker trip to New York and begins to integrate herself more into her matrilineal ways. This fry bread scene reorients her actions from sex work at night to sunrise ceremonial preparations oriented toward the east. Watchman notes how the *Drunktown's Finest* protagonists achieve hózhǫ through a coming-of-age ceremonial run to the east in the film climax, explaining, "Max runs toward the East and is supported by family and community who run with her. She is a matriarch in motion, having become Changing Woman, signifying

Figure 3 The kinaaldá Max Maryboy (Magdalena Begay, Navajo Nation) runs east in *Drunktown's Finest* (2014), directed by Sydney Freeland.

rebirth, reel restoration, and hózhǫ́."[34] The kinaaldá running east represents the creatrix Changing Woman, Asdzáá Nádłeehé, who created the kinaaldá ceremony and the first Diné clans. As the first action of the day, Max runs east and is joined by her supporters who aid her in manifesting her positive vision of the future through the power and blessings of the Holy People who appear at dawn in the east. Watchman's analysis concludes that all three protagonists gain the ability to restore hózhǫ́ through thinking and manifesting a positive future by the film's final kinaaldá running scene toward the sunrise.

The film's concluding kinaaldá run to the east scene begins with a slow-motion full shot of the hogan as Ruth John pulls back the blanket door at sunrise so that Max can emerge in her ceremonial regalia as she finishes the ceremony to become a woman. She is followed by mostly children and eventually by Sick Boy, who smiles back at the mother of his child before racing on. In the last scene, the handheld camera follows Max in slow motion as her turquoise jewelry, shiny white blouse, dark skirt, vibrantly colored Pendleton blanket, and dress flap in the wind. The handheld camera emphasizes the personal Navajo connection that Freeland evokes in her film, and the slow-motion filming accentuates the beauty of the running movement and ceremony. The camera at last slows and stops with a full shot of Max running on the dirt desert road lined with sage toward the sunrise on the distant green and gold horizon. The diegetic music is a slow and harmonious guitar instrumental. By stopping in the end, the camera obeys the ceremonial protocol that no one can pass up the kinaaldá. In an interview, Sydney Freeland intimates the significance of the final running scene to the east and toward the Holy People who emerge there. Although there is no sound save for the diegetic guitar music, Freeland fills in the sounds that traditional Navajos would know to occur during that final run:

> Specifically, what she is doing is she is running to the east at sunrise. The way I understand it is that spirits exit and enter the world through the east. She's running to the east to greet these morning spirits. And she has all those people running behind her making noises. They are calling hoo-hoo, hoo-hoo . . . trying to attract the attention of these spirits and deities [as though] saying "Come pay attention to this girl. She's up early and she's working hard and come bless her prosperous and bright future because she's a strong bright woman. Come and shower her with blessings."[35]

These blessings are also communally shared in the dawn orientation to the east, as each of the characters receive their blessings that flow from the grounds of that eastern-oriented ceremony. It is now more possible that, having started with the blessings of the Holy People at dawn, each character can better progress through adulthood and old age and avoid the disorientation of living a life filled with nightly sex work, nightmares, and binge-drinking disturbances. In this way, a life in which hózhǫ́ is rightfully initiated in the east can prevail.

"I Am" (1997)

In the language of her Diné Kinyaa'áanii (Towering House) clan matrilineage, Carrie House (Navajo Nation) identifies as nádleehí and self-identifies with both the masculine and feminine pronouns. In his film "I Am" (1997), House offers artful documentation of HIV/AIDS in the two-spirit/Native LGBTIQ2+ San Francisco Bay Area community of the 1990s. The film begins with the work narratives of Native American butch lesbians or transmasculine people in auto repair and construction work.[36] Halfway through the twenty-four-minute short film, the narrative switches from butch lesbians in traditionally masculine jobs to relatively femme gay Native American men and AIDS. The latter includes narratives of AIDS activism and experiences from nádleehí Dr. Wesley Thomas (Navajo Nation), the stabutz (Northern Paiute two-spirit) and Gay American Indian cofounder Randy Burns (Pyramid Lake Paiute Tribe),[37] and the gay HIV-positive Ojibwe Damien Grey. This chapter section follows eastern direction HIV curriculum connections to emotional balance to understand Grey's emotional HIV-positive experience depicted in "I Am."

Diné like Carrie House often move in and out of Navajo Nation, and so it is important to know how healing practices and directionality can change in urban intertribal settings where most Diné live.[38] For example, urban Diné who use intertribal addictions recovery programs such as the Red Road White Bison Wellbriety may use a medicine wheel reflecting Northern Plains traditions,[39] rather than the Diné-specific T'áá shá bik'ehgo na'nitin, the Sun Wise Path Teachings. Based upon intertribal medicine wheel teachings of addiction recovery, Mattee Jim (Navajo Nation) co-developed a four-directions HIV/AIDS prevention program with Elton Naswood, who implemented it as program coordinator of the Red Circle Project at AIDS Project Los Angeles in the 2000s and 2010s. Because the directional teachings of the various Indigenous nations cannot be encompassed in one vision, Red Circle Project chose a medicine wheel model that was greatly modified to both accommodate secular public health concepts and to be more open to various Indigenous experiences. Red Circle Project offered Native American gay men and transgender women clients workshops in which "the sacred four directions, East, South, West, and North are used as a visual representation of the Mental, Physical, Emotional, and Spiritual parts of individuals."[40] Werito also writes that there is correlation of these teachings within Diné philosophy, noting, "The principles of hózhǫ́ are encapsulated in the cognitive (mental), physiological (physical), psychological (emotional), and intuitive (spiritual) aspects of human development."[41] Following an eastern emotional focus, this final chapter section will consider the emotions of HIV-positive status and stigma as Damien Grey expresses them via House's camera lens.

In House's initial 1991 "I Am" interview, Grey expresses his emotional trauma with his status and experiences with the HIV/AIDS pandemic, for which there were no effective medications at that time. The extreme close-up on Grey accentuates his waxy skin and his short hair, bleached blond on top. His eyebrow piercings punctuate his sorrowful face. He distraughtly describes his gay HIV-positive world near the height of the AIDS deaths in San Francisco, which especially impacted his gay men's community. Responding to House's question about AIDS, Grey replies, "Well, I know quite a bit about it. And, um, I've seen its effects a lot. I myself am HIV-positive and know a lot of other people who are as well, a lot of people who . . . have full-blown AIDS, which means they have diseases which are caused by the weakening of their immune system."[42] In this clip, Grey speaks slowly, as though somewhat weighted by the topic, and he is mostly looking away from the camera directly in front of him to his left, as though speaking to House in that direction. While these words are difficult, they do not yet express the pandemic's personal impact on him fully. Red Circle Project's HIV curriculum draws attention to these kinds of emotions, asking their two-spirit and transgender HIV workshop participants, "What makes you do the things you do on the inside?" and to communicate their "emotions and feelings."[43] Based upon this emphasis on emotional healing within the first eastern direction, it is important to really feel this moment in which Grey begins to open up about being HIV-positive because it can point to the unlocking of emotions that hinder or help in the healing process that must go beyond merely prescribing Western medicines in a two-spirit/Indigenous LGBTQI2+ context.

House makes a radical shift in visual messaging by cutting out the visuals of Grey's affect and inserting a slow-motion sequence of a green grasshopper slowly moving about the leaves of rushes growing up from the water. This insect moves as Grey's voice continues more emotionally, "It's a world I'm all too familiar with. It's been really . . . just incredibly terrible. I can't express the sorrow and devastation I've seen and felt. And it's not easy. It's like living a nightmare to see the people you love like fade away right in front of you."[44] Grey subtly emphasizes the words "sorrow," "devastation," and "nightmare" to make clear the emotional destruction that Grey feels because of the AIDS pandemic deaths. In San Francisco during the early 1990s, an HIV/AIDS diagnosis often included an estimate of months or years to live depending on one's health, a deathly prospect that surely impacts Grey's strong emotions of grief, pain, and vulnerability. He feels for his community that is dying of AIDS. He fears for his own life. Given the many deaths he experienced and his HIV diagnosis, his traumatized reaction is completely understandable. Its expression is also a marker of being able to be emotionally open in ways that are signed feminine within popular culture. This femme openness to sharing emotion is a strength in the healing path because constant suppression of emotions can restrict understanding them, working with them, and eventually shifting them in a healing process. There is a femme health in Grey's openness in sharing his emotions around HIV/AIDS in his personal experience and community. It is brave in a time of high stigma in which silence equals death, as many Queer Nation HIV/AIDS activists noted at the time.

During this most emotionally trying part of the film in which Grey recounts the trauma of having HIV during 1991, a year marked by AIDS deaths, House cut from a close-up of Grey to a bright green grasshopper, and this choice has a several cultural resonances worth contemplating that relate to hope and healing. The grasshopper, which House filmed while salmon fishing in Warm Springs Reservation, refers to an escape from difficult situations within the earliest Diné oral traditions.[45] The Diné emergence narrative tracks movement through three previous lower worlds to emerge into the present surface world. It was grasshoppers and insects who allowed Diné to escape through the roof of the Third World which was yellow. In the published *Diné Bahané* compilation of some of these oral traditions, four grasshoppers, one black, one blue, one yellow, and one white lead humans to the present multicolored Fourth World, which allows humanity to survive and thrive.[46] Even as Grey voices the difficulties of his friends dying of AIDS in 1991, the overt appearance of the green grasshopper is a sign of hope to come.

Indeed, by the 1996 interview, Grey is in much better health and spirits. Part of the emotional impact of the grasshopper cut is to lessen the grief that the audience feels at that moment. There is greater emotional space not having to view Grey's face during this traumatic monologue. This choice is a compassionate move for a two-spirit audience as most in that 1990s time and San Francisco space knew queer friends and loved ones within the community who had died of AIDS.

The second part of Grey's interview comes in 1996, when a cocktail of three medications began to stop people from dying of AIDS. Grey's demeanor and words impart greater hope and health. He is almost unrecognizable, healthier, shot in a close-up unlike the more extreme one that exaggerated his facial worry lines in the 1991 interview. Grey's personal introduction matches basic protocols in the east workshop instructions that read, "Remind everyone that when Native Americans meet for the first time, they try to find out a little bit about them: who their family is, what tribe or community they are from, what they do for a living, etc. This helps us to establish 'relationships' with each other and begin to form a sense of 'community.'"[47] Forming relationships is part of finding emotional support within a social circle that is made of different clans or tribes. And so Grey begins impactfully: "Hello, I'm Damien Grey. I'm thirty-five years old. I'm living in San Francisco, California. I'm HIV-positive. I've been living with HIV for five years now. Up to this point, I'm a survivor. I'm Chippewa, Ojibwe Indian. Here I am, in the flesh!"[48] As Grey identifies himself by tribe and place, he models a Native American simple introductory process of forming emotional bonds with others, including Native American and non-Native film audiences. Giving his name, he delivers the last phrase "in the flesh" with theatrical zest and irony absent in the 1991 interview and wryly identifies as an HIV-positive survivor "up to this point." Virtually assured of longer life on new medications and witnessing the decrease in AIDS deaths, Grey is now able to confront his own mortality and survival with ironic humor. Anishinaabe Lawrence Gross (White Earth Nation) notes how Anishinaabe (Ojibwe) wit and humor is a traditional part of healing, especially in the face of death.[49] This wit, evident in the film, was even noted in Grey's 2018 obituary, which reads, "Even in his darkest hour, he remained gracious, witty, and charming," also mentioning Grey's motto, "We're here to lift each other up, not put each other down." Grey's obituary also reported his theater performances as "the Puppet Fister," a name signaling the unrepentant joys of the gay anal fisting and clever queer word play.[50]

House visually provides the emotional balance that Grey lacks in his reflection upon the Christian stigma of being HIV-positive and gay with his newly reunited sibling. Grey recalls:

> One sister I told that I was HIV-positive after I reminded her that I was gay. Her response was disturbing to me. She said, "I have nothing against *those people* and Jesus teaches us to love everyone." . . . Painful. It definitely made me feel like I can't really be myself with her, that we'll never be able to understand each other because for her I'm one of "them," one of "them" gays with HIV, not her brother or something.[51]

Grey does preface this disturbing story by saying, "two of my brothers and one of my sisters . . . really seem to love me and appreciate me for who I am. And they know who I am in as far as my sexuality goes and HIV status."[52] Yet he lingers on the one sister who cannot accept him, perhaps because she represents the intense 1990s religious hostility of the U.S. society at large. As Grey begins this narrative of Christian stigma, House's camera pans over the nicely painted house, luxurious furnishings, and hopeful visual reminders that serve as an emotional balance during this "painful" narrative. House inserts positive visuals that balance out the pain that Damien expresses. For example, a close-up of a pink embroidered message on blue and white checked satin pillow is stitched with the affirmation, "You are more beautiful today than you were yesterday!" Yet House also films a skull on the wall as Grey announces the word "painful," as if to emphasize the ongoing fear of HIV/AIDS-related deaths that Grey experiences as intense social stigma reflected by his own sister. All is not well with Damian Grey, even as he used his wits and blessings to survive the HIV/AIDS diagnosis that most did not in that place and time. Even so, he finishes his narrative with a comeback, "You know, I told her how I felt at the time, but . . . ," trailing off into a deep exhalation that signals the process of letting go of emotions that overwhelm and linger beyond their time. The loss of a sister's acceptance remains difficult for Grey, even as his overall demeanor with its sweeping femme flourishes and dramatic speech pauses indicate that he has no plan to change being the fabulous gay HIV-positive Ojibwe that he is.

Conclusion

An understanding of Diné eastern directionality can help interpret the four Diné media "Mountain of Stories," "Two Spirit—Injunuity," *Drunktown's Finest,* and "I Am." All four media make sovereign visual, erotic, spatial, and spiritual statements that explicitly or implicitly invoke the Diné eastern direction. For example, the prayer to the sacred eastern mountain Tsisnaajiní in "Mountain of Stories" organizes the Diné progression of events in the coming-out story from Nazbah Tom. The story's plot resolution follows the

Diné T'áá shá bik'ehgo na'nitin, or the Sun Wise Path Teachings of "Nitsáhákees" in the east, "Nahat'á (Planning)" in the south, "Iiná (Living)" in the west, and "Siihasin (Assurance)" in the north. This is to say that video song's prayers to the eastern mountain Tsisnaajiní and to the southern, western, and northern mountains precipitated the positive plans, actions, and reflections in the film as Tom's mom comes to express support for her queer child. "Two Spirit—Injunuity" allowed brainstorming insights into nonconforming two-spirit genders that traditionally balance the Diné masculine and feminine. For the Mexica Mica Valdez, that balancing includes masculinity in the east with femininity in the west. The Diné Lucero and Tom also add their stories as gender and sexual options that can aid youth in brainstorming possibilities to form their own gender identities. *Drunktown's Finest*'s three protagonists learn to reorient themselves from the dangers of the northern night to the eastern sunrise ceremony in order to restore the beauty and balance of hózhǫ́. The transgender nádleehí Felixia in particular makes an important shift from sex work at night to making food for the kinaaldá ceremony in the early morning. Finally, the four directions Red Circle Project's HIV/AIDS medicine wheel workshop, oriented to the emotions of the eastern direction, can aid in understanding the "I Am" film that includes an HIV/AIDS experience of the gay Ojibwe Damien Grey during the height of the pandemic in San Francisco. This first chapter shows how essential spatial directionality can be in the visual representations of Diné nádleehí. To see space as mere background to human actions is to miss the cosmological connections that keep the Diné vibrant, in balance and hózhǫ́.

While political, visual, and gender sovereignties are important notions to pursue, they are also potentially homogenizing concepts to be used strategically and in conversation with culturally specific concepts. However, when Diné historian Jennifer Nez Denetdale (Navajo Nation) originally faulted *Drunktown's Finest* for replacing representations of ongoing Diné Gallup political action with ceremonial tropes, she retained a Diné-specific historical perspective.[53] It is important to note that the Diné Marriage Act of 2005, which limited marriage to biological male and female couples and that Denetdale criticized as discriminatory, is scheduled to be reviewed and potentially repealed by Navajo Nation in 2026.[54] While other chapters take on more of the historical-political sovereignty issues, the strength of Diné directional literature allows for a focused spatial analysis. A more Western linear film history momentarily recounted here is a fine pursuit, but it in no way need supersede the spatial protocols of directionality within film analysis. This book's introduction, which covered the humorous yet dismissive Native American cross-dressing in the Hollwood silent era, the censorship of the classic era, and the opening of visual, erotic, and theological sovereignty in the contemporary, did not detail the amazing leaps in nádleehí representation that have occurred in Navajo national cinema since the 1990s. The films presented here combat a century of queerphobic and settler-colonial tropes that have negatively impacted Indigenous LGBTQI2+ peoples for decades. The rising contemporary political sovereignty of the Navajo Nation empowered the formation of national scholars and cinema that abundantly feature the eastern ha'a'aah representations that radically reoriented this first chapter. These Diné, matrilineal, and nádleehí-inclusive knowledges set a clear directional intention for the remaining six chapters on the Caxcan south, Kānaka Maoli west, Nêhiyawak north, Tongva earth, Yorùbá sky, and personal central direction.

2

SOUTH

Trans*forming Caxcan Xochipilli on YouTube

Reflecting contemporary Caxcan perspectives of the Juchipila River and Juchipila Canyon areas of southern Zacatecas, Mexico, this second chapter touches upon Indigenous southern orientations in Caxcan YouTube videos and makes contrasts with Mexica southern spatiality. The Caxcan connections to the Creation Mountain that Daisy Ocampo describes in *Where We Belong* (2023) help to interpret a southward Caxcan orientation in the YouTube video "Juchipila Zacatecas y el Xuchitl" (2019). Directed by local Juchipilense Alondra Sánchez Medina, this video presents Caxcan celebrations of Xochipilli (Flower Child) called La Danza del Xúchitl (Flower Dance), which occurs in Juchipila for the summer solstice monsoons. After considering the intersex possibilities of the Caxcan Xochipilli, this chapter then considers the monkey-masked, homoerotic, and cross-dressed dancer in the Caxcan Danza de Los Viejos de la Chinana YouTube clips, contrasting a colonial and cis-heteropatriarchal reading of the dance with that of an Indigenous sovereign gender gaze. In fact, this chapter links the southern jungle monkey's ceremonial appearance in the northern Caxcan deserts with colonial Central Nahuas who came from the south, the southern direction toward which the Mexica fled from the north centuries earlier to transform from Chichimeca and Caxcans to Mexica. This chapter's Caxcan, pan-gendered, and transspecies analysis of the Caxcan Xúchitl Dance differs from popular queer Chicano readings of Xochipilli as a god of homosexuality in Central Mexico, a Mexica reading perhaps more correlated instead with a south-direction deity sometimes written as Xochipilli-Macuilxóchitl.[1]

Looking South to the Danza de Xúchitl and Tlachialoyantepec

The Mexican government's official statement on Caxcans does not represent the larger movement to retain Indigenous identity and ceremony in the Caxcan region. The National Catalog of Indigenous and Afro-Mexican Pueblos and Communities states of the Caxcan Pueblo: "Como resultado del fuerte racismo y persecución sufrida, sobre todo con la construcción de la República en el siglo XIX y principios del XX, los caxcanes perdieron el uso de su lengua y su identidad. No obstante, preservan instituciones, tradiciones y formas colectivas de acceder a la tierra" (As a result of the strong racism and persecution they suffered, above all with the establishment of the republic in the nineteenth and early twentieth centuries, the Caxcans lost the use of their language and their identity. However, they preserve institutions, traditions, and collective ways of accessing land).[2] To this modern account of Caxcan identity loss is Ocampo's account of centuries of war, enslavement, and imposition of Catholicism in Juchipila among Caxcans, with the most difficult era being the mid-1500s clash of Spaniards and Central Nahuas with northern Chichimeca Indigenous communities that culminated in the regional War of Mixtón in 1540–42 and extended northward through the 1500s. Yet Ocampo's history is ultimately one of revitalization of Caxcan culture as she writes, "Tepehuan and Caxcan communities alike resisted conquistadors, missionaries, destruction of idolatry, forced labor at encomiendas and haciendas, slavery at the silver mines, and overall loss of autonomy," but emphasizes how the Caxcan Xúchitl Dance was always utilized "to create a resistance movement that advocated for their homelands and preserved sacred sites" to the present day.[3] Key aspects of this Caxcan creation dance have survived with great effort across centuries and fragments of these have made their way onto YouTube videos.

In Alondra Sánchez Medina's YouTube video "Juchipila Zacatecas y el Xuchitl," local Caxcan dancers narrate the history of the Danza del Xúchitl as a celebration of monsoon rains at summer solstice. Xochipilli is the spirit that presides over the dance in Juchipila Canyon. Juchipila is the pueblo name that is just an older local Caxcan spelling of what would be written in Central Nahuatl as Xochipillan, Flower Child Place. In the video, young women dressed in long white dresses decorated with cacaloxóchitl (plumeria) carry the ceremonial elements that are announced as they process down the plaza from north to south toward the Xochipilli statue, their footsteps in rhythm with huehuet (drum), teponazti (slot drum log), and chirimía (flute) music. The young women are accompanied by younger girls, intimating a coming-of-age roots of this ceremony and connecting the blossoming of flowers in the regalia with the blossoming of the girls-becoming-women. As shown in figure 4, the multigenerational families and guests watch from all around as they prepare to place various ofrendas or offerings such as the atecocoli (conch shell) around a carved stone statue of Xochipilli who sits facing north from the south end of the church plaza.

Once the ofrendas are placed, the younger girls leave the circle, and the young women bring in their clay popochcomit (smoke-pots) so that the copal pine pitch burning within can rise as smoke to the sky. Again standing around Xochipilli, they ceremonially invite in the monsoon winds and rain,

Figure 4 Looking south to the Xochipilli statue (*center*) and Tlachialoyantepec, the Caxcan Creation Mountain (*upper right*), during the Xúchitl Dance in "Juchipila Zacatecas y el Xuchitl" (2019), directed by Alondra Sánchez Medina.

offering the copal to the center as an atecocoli sounds. They then turn to the direction to their right in a clockwise fashion as a new atecocoli call marks the next direction. Only the lead dancer begins facing south and she makes a quarter turn west, north, and east each time the conch shells sound, making a final offering toward the center in the end. In this way, winds from all directions are invited to bring rain, as explained in the video. These clockwise movements can replicate seasonal and daily swirling wind movements. For example, the summer's hotter and wetter trade winds blow in from the more southern Caribbean Sea in the east. Southern winds can increase in strength as easterly trade winds give way to the prevailing westerlies from the northern Pacific Ocean. This creates a kind of clockwise east, south, west motion found in the dance. In addition, as winds shift from east in the morning with an increase from the south in the afternoon and a prevalence from the west in the evening, rainfall tends to increase. The clockwise motion of the dancers can match the shifts in winds during a day in the rainy season. Furthermore, eastern and western winds from both the Atlantic and Pacific Oceans often meet in the middle of the continent in Mexico and then make their way north into the U.S. Southwest and the Great Plains. That is the larger picture of monsoon rain patterns in their movement from east, west, and south into the north. Monsoon winds that often come from the southeast, south, and southwest are invoked in this dance along with all other wind directions.

In the figure 4 shot made with a drone camera, the Caxcan Creation Mountain Tlachialoyantepec rises in the southern distance over the store roofs and the ceremonial offerings made to Xochipilli. The Creation Mountain is seen opposite of the cornerstones of the San Francisco church in the foreground.[4] This video shot shows the camera's and lead dancer's orientation south toward Tlachialoyantepec, and that is a powerful orientation in Ocampo's Caxcan analysis. Figure 4 demonstrates that Caxcans are continuing to dance oriented toward the Creation Mountain that stands in the southern distance behind the Xochipilli statue that looks north from the lower center of the frame. The main procession toward Xochipilli is to the south, and the main dancer faces the south and to the mountain that is behind Xochipilli three miles down the Juchipila River. This spatial connection in figure 4 is important because Xochipilli was transformed and resurrected in a Tlachialoyantepec cave and appears as an emissary spirit of the mountain, a palpable spiritual presence over the entire dance and solstice monsoon season. Based on the oral traditions of her Caxcan great-aunt Doña Cuca, Daisy Ocampo recounts that the original tepechi, a Caxcan Nahuat term for "little one," of "Mother Crow" and "Father Snake" was eaten by a jaguar. This caused immense grief, for it was the original death experienced by Caxcans.[5] With lightning bolts from his eyes, Father Snake created caves in Tlachialoyantepec to protect the surviving children at night from this new animal predation. When the Caxcans laid down a bed of cacaloxóchitl flowers for Mother Crow in this cave, the littlest child reappeared amid the cacaloxóchitl, a resurrection that inspired the Xúchil Dance still honored to this day. The summer solstice time of the Xúchil Dance coincides with the cacaloxóchitl flowers that have bloomed in anticipation of the summer monsoons. Cacaloxóchitl are also present in the Xúchitl Dance regalia and offerings in other parts of the "Juchipila Zacatecas y el Xuchitl" video. From the dance area in Juchipila, Caxcans look south to the sacred Tlachialoyantepec mountain, from where Xochipilli and all Caxcans originated from an "underground birth canal, or nautilostot (tunnel)" in the earliest oral traditions.[6] Even from the northern upstream Juchilipa pueblo, Caxcans reconnect south to the Xochipilli's birthplace at Tlachialoyantepec.

Part of the reason for the three-mile distance from the mountain involves the settler-colonial Mexican state appropriation of the Creation Mountain. Seeing the pyramid, ball court, and cliff house as part of the Mexican nation's larger Mesoamerican patrimony, the state archaeological entity Instituto Nacional Antropología e Historia bought legal rights to the mountain and restricted access to it for the Caxcans who are created in that place. Ocampo details how the Mexican state sees the ancestral Indigenous teocali (pyramid), ball court, and cliff house on the mountain as a money-making tourist attraction. Ocampo confirms, "Although Caxcan people today are not physically at the mountain, their dances, prayers, and offerings are there in spirit. The Xúchitl Dance offers Caxcan people an opportunity to experience a renewal of themselves, an assertion of who they are and where they belong." Even when Caxcans were historically enslaved and set to work across the American and the Caribbean, they would turn back toward Tlachialoyantepec in prayerful dance. Ocampo documents, "Enslaved Caxcans danced in silence and oriented themselves toward Tlachialoyantepec while those hiding in the local mountains and canyons made pilgrimages to the cave on Tlachialoyantepec where Xochipilli resurrected."[7] As neoliberal settler colonialism has created economic and refugee migrations of Caxcans away from Juchipila north into Mexico and the United States, diasporic Caxcans have continued to turn south toward the Creation Mountain. Thus, Ocampo's understanding of orientation toward the mountain can invite a sovereign reading of figure 4. Although the Instituto Nacional Antropología e Historia has created separation of the Xúchitl Dance from the mountain summit, the Juchipila Xúchitl Dance orientation south toward the mountain evokes a connection back to Tlachialoyatepec that resonates with centuries of Caxcan struggles to remain at and maintain access to the Creation Mountain.

While the southward orientation toward Tlachialoyantepec shows reconnection during forced separation, the Xochipilli statue was once located on the west and the north sides of the ceremonial dance area in the same plaza that is in front of the San Francisco de Asís Church's doorways. Originally placed in the north looking south and with a back to a ficus tree and the church doors for several years, the icon was moved to the west side of the plaza and placed opposite of the western church doors so that in leaving the church one was immediately faced by the image of Xochipilli and the western Sierra de Morones in the background. Ocampo explains, "In 2014 the Hermandad del Xúchitl decided to rotate its statue of Xochipilli, turning the statue to face the church, symbolizing equal sovereignty, coexistence, and spiritual legitimacy."[8] Ocampo shares that the Hermandad del Xúchitl who have persisted as a Caxcan entity over centuries of war, enslavement, and economic pressures felt especially pleased with that expression of spatial sovereignty and western position. Despite protests from non-Caxcan Mestizos living in Juchipila, the statue remained for a time until the icon found a new home atop a fountain in a reconstructed plaza looking north from the south end of the plaza (fig. 4).

While Tlachialoyantepec is virtually due south of the Xochipilli statue, the Creation Mountain is also part of a western chain of mountains, La Sierra de Morones, which runs parallel to an eastern chain of mountains, La Sierra de Nochistlán, both separated by the Juchipila River and Juchipila Canyon. In Caxcan creation narratives that Ocampo shares, these mountains were once twins, developing in an ancient sea. "Caxcans regard these landmasses as twin fetuses that emerged from an endless body of water much like an amniotic sac." Once they grew and emerged from the water, these became known by the Caxcan as Tlachialoyantepec and Nochistlán, the first being the elder and healthier twin sister who gave life to the Caxcans, the second being the younger and less-developed brother, troubled by illness. Ocampo concludes, "While the sister grew abundant in generosity, her brother grew resentful and bitter. This duality and rivalry framed life on earth for Caxcans and introduced the concept of balance through these storied landscapes. . . . Sierra de Nochistlán represents the brother and is regarded as a place not to visit."[9] While Tlachialoyantepec is the western boundary of the Juchipila River, Nochistlán is found three miles east. Taking these mountains as central gendered entities in the Caxcan landscape, they also mark a gendered directional duality in the landscape, with a sister western Creation Mountain developing opposite of her eastern brother mountain. The western Tlachialoyantepec especially has pacti, or medicine. The San Francisco church blocks sight of Sierra de Nochistlán on the east side in figure 4. Within Ocampo's narrative, the Catholic church's colonial presence could represent a continuity in this masculine power that is ultimately less creative and giving than the power of the feminine Tlachialoyantepec. The power of twins even carries through to human healing practices in which one twin will often have a greater healing power than the other. "Medicine power, or pacti, can usually be identified as more giving because they have a larger source of life, while the other sibling is protective, limited, and cautious," Ocampo explains, with the "pac" or "pah" root of the Caxcan word "pacti" being related to the ancient word for water found in many other Uto-Aztecan languages spread across North America.[10]

Part of the giving nature of pacti includes eroticism of the Danza del Xúchitl, which celebrates the gifts of rain and life in the desert. Some contemporary Caxcan narratives of the Dance of the Xúchitl are fairly cis-heteronormative, but perhaps only in apparent alignment with Catholic teachings. For example, Ruvalcaba Limón comments on the Xúchitl Dance's role in courtship, explaining how the "eldest brother and eldest sister initiate the dance, and the transfer of the tlapaleoliztle to a young person of the opposite sex, and this in turn to a person of its choice, symbolizes the approval of adults to initiate the search ritual to find couple and creation of species [reproduction]."[11] Here Ruvalcaba Limón presents the dance modeling male and female as sexed binaries necessary to produce children across generations. The "Juchipila Zacatecas y el Xuchitl" video shows that the red cloth tlapaleoliztle is indeed alternately handed between the men in white pants and guayabera shirts and the women in white skirts or huipils embroidered with flowers. And yet Caxcan and Tepehuan musician Luis Chávez, who grew up in the Xúchitl Dance ceremony, argues against requiring "indigenous people to fit within heteronormative archetypes of authentic indigeneity."[12] He offers a modern composition incorporating the Caxcan drum in "Xúchil (en vivo/live)," recalling the sound of thunder that especially reverberates within the Juchipila Canyon. Quoting his grandfather who had commented on hearing the thunder in the Juchipila Canyon, Chávez has different family members of various ages and genders repeat the grandfathers' words that link the sound of thunder with life in succession, in both the original Spanish and in its English translation.[13] This composition queers a Caxcan sense of who is included in the Xúchitl Dance as the reference to thunder as the sound of vida/life can include all life, all genders, and all sexualities that are a part of the summer solstice monsoons in Juchipila.

Here, this Caxcan-centered consideration of Xochipilli turns back to the semiarid tropical desert life, exploring the trans*species erotics of the Xúchitl Dance and imagining outside an eastern masculine and western feminine binary. First, the Xúchitl Dance in figure 4 is an invitation for the reproduction of all life in all directions, including the intersex reproduction of the cacaloxóchitl flowers that are central to the ceremony and are intersex in nature, having both male and female reproductive parts. While intersex beings are often outside of popular Western consciousness, they are not in some Indigenous traditions. Consider plant-human relations that are referenced by the Huastecan Nahua term "maxochitl," which literally means hand flower and is a figurative term for a queer person. Jennie Luna and Gabriel Estrada write:

> *Maxochitl* . . . derives from the name of their sacred creator / spiritual manifestation, known as Chicomexochitl, or Seven Flowers, who is the caretaker of all, but especially associated with corn. Within ceremony, Chicomexochitl appears as a sacred, single paper cut-out form that represents a sacred family of various ages and genders. The term *maxochitl* and its understanding are an extension of this cosmogony, acknowledging that those who are "two-spirit" or dual, or who carry multigendered conceptualizations, are connected to the sacred.[14]

Maxochitl is part of the Huastecan Nahua Chicomexochitl (Seven Flower) ceremonies, and this analysis comes from a source statement from Chicontepec Nahua scholar Victoriano Cruz de la Cruz, who documents that his Huastecan Nahua Chicomexochitl corn deity relates to Xochipilli. De la Cruz writes, "Chicomexochitl, la deidad . . . se asemeja mucho a la antigua Chicomecoatl, o con Cintzin, la que evoca a Cinteotl y a Xochipilli. (Chicomexochitl, the deity . . . resembles a lot the ancient Chicomecoatl, or with Cintzin, who evokes Cinteotl and Xochipilli)."[15] In a trans*Indigenous reading, this Huastecan Nahua sensibility of honoring the multigendered spirits of intersex plants like corn could also apply to Caxcans, the plumeria, and Xochipilli. Maize has both male and female reproductive organs—the male tassel above and the female cobs that develop from the body of the plant. Taking seriously the Chicontepec Nahua insight to focus on ceremonial plant gender and sexuality, one can offer that the Xúchitl Dance is also oriented to support all permutations of intersex plants that are found in the desert. Caxcans who tend plants and harvest them in the Juchipila canyons know when male and female plants need to be growing together to pollinate. This is not the case for the cacaloxóchitl, so central to the Xúchitl Dance, which are gathered in the Juchipila Canyon yearly. Flowers have a variety of sexes that may only sometimes resemble human ones, and some like the cacaloxóchitl are true hermaphrodites, having both male and female reproductive organs that can self-pollinate, though often with help of regional moths, butterflies, and other insects.[16] Figure 4's large scope that includes peoples, mountain, plants, and sky can also be an indication that the Danza del Xúchitl is equally large in scope, interweaving all of these erotic elements across many sexes and genders, and going beyond adherence to the primary binary genitalia system of human beings, and out to intersex humans and plants. Instead of portraying creation as an east-direction masculinity and west-direction femininity in a gendered binary, the cacaloxóchitl itself raises questions of in-between or complex genders and sexes that complicate the picture.

With such a broad potential connection across semiarid intersex plant species, the Caxcan Xochipilli is not the same as the rainforest-dwelling Mexica pleasure teotl/spirit Xochipilli-Macuilxóchitl, who is strongly linked with the southern direction and human overindulgences in the Mexica Codex Yohualli Ehecatl (Borgia). While the statue in Juchipila is a modernized replica of the 1400s Tlalmanalco Xochipilli sculpture rediscovered on the famed Central Mexican volcano Iztaccihuatl, both its Juchipila placement and its local Caxcan origin tradition critically complicate a reading of the icon as simply a Nahua god of homosexuality. To understand this last argument at length is to depart from recent queer pop culture readings of Xochipilli in linked Euro-American and Chicano representations. Murky depictions of Central Nahua flowery homosexuality as innately sinful most likely reflect an imposition of Catholic colonial laws reflected in the late 1500s colonial Florentine Codex, which connects the "xochihuan" (possessor of flowers), flower-carrying men, with effeminacy and homosexuality and levies a death sentence against them by torture and burning. But Kimball pens caution when reading Spanish colonial accounts of Mexica laws condemning homosexuality as the Inquisition likely changed those narratives to match Spanish laws of death for sodomy.[17] There is a visual logic in linking the flowery xochihuan with Xochipilli, who is also covered in flowers in the Tlalmanalco sculpture, even though flowers can mean many things beyond gender and sexuality. For example, the flowers of the Tlalmanalco statue include flowers from the consciousness-changing medicines of tobacco, ololiuhqui, and sinicuichi plants and invoke their ceremonial powers.[18] However, contemporary queer history and spirituality books have without great reflection cemented into the online and print records that Xochipilli is the god of homosexuality.[19] The muddled Mesoamerican colonial sources used to queer Xochipilli tend to equate disparate Mesoamerican cultures, gods, and histories as being united in a flowery homosexuality. For example, Antonio Requena's 1945 article links the Maya Chilam Balam account of an earlier Mayan age of sexual abandon and homosexuality with the Toltec La Danza de las Flores (Flower Dance), the Toltec Xochiquetzal, and the downfall of the hedonistic Toltec Age of Flowers in Mexico.[20] Requena is then cited in Murray's casual lumping-in of the feminine Xochiquetzal (Feathery Flower) with the male-bodied Xochipilli and Macuilxóchitl (Five Flower) as deities of homosexual prostitution.[21] In precolonial texts, there is no clear linkage of Xochipilli to male prostitution, contradicting the questionable claims made in David Greenberg's *The Construction of Homosexuality* (1988) that are based upon Spanish and Mestizo histories.[22]

Contemporary queer Chicanos and two-spirit Mexica are reclaiming the Mexica Xochipilli as a representation of the flowery queer Nahua xochihuan named in the Florentine Codex, reworking the homophobic Spanish colonial sources to celebrate queer sexualities. An example of queer flowery reclamations occurs in Luis Salinas's dissertation that considers their two-spirit Xicanx invocation of Xochipilli in their own artwork, a painted retablo of having queer sex in the back of a car. Salinas explains: "This Retablo piece is of my first sexual encounter after 11 years of being celibate due to an abusive relationship. Here I am thanking Mexica gods Xochiquetzal for helping me embrace my sexuality . . . Tlazolteotl goddess of lust and desire . . . and Xochipilli god of the two-spirit men."[23] Salinas explains Xochipilli as an Xicanx Indigenous spirit that helped them in their recovery from relationship violence. They identify with both the feminine Xochiquetzal and Xochipilli, and both appear painted on the retablo along with Tlazolteotl, with the Tlalmanalco Xochipilli statue being the form painted. Salinas's dissertation title, "Yolotl de Papalotl" (Heart of a Butterfly), is in conversation with many other queer Chicano/x art pieces of Xochipilli, whose Tlalmanalco statue base is prominently incised with four butterflies on its four-directions sides. Daniel Pérez's "Toward a Mariposa Consciousness: Reimagining Queer Chicano and Latino Identities" recounts multiple butterfly images of queer Chicanos, including that of Tino Rodríguez's oil painting *Xochipilli's Ecstatic Universe* (2004).[24] The queer image of Xochipilli also made it into the 2020 TV series *Vida* when the queer character Marcos has a quinceañera, dressing in a billowy aqua 1980s dress. Standing in front of a backdrop that reads "Joteriawood" plastered with giant paper roses, "he decolonizes his name, his gender, and dubs himself 'the prince of flowers, song and dance,' before taking on the name Xochipilli."[25]

In contrast to this Xochipilli homosexuality reading, Susan Milbrath concludes that the precontact 1400s Central Nahua Codex Yohualli Ehecatl's eighteen twenty-day months of the Nahua calendar depict Xochipilli "as a solar deity" in the east who rules over the time of summer rains, a period that matches the Xúchitl Dance in Juchipila. She offers that Xochipilli is shown twice in a flowery temple, once on plate 37 at the beginning of the rainy season that marks the summer solstice, and again at the end of the intense rainy season at the fall equinox on page 42.[26] Furthermore, Jose Renteria makes key differentiations between "Macuilxóchitl" and Xochipilli in the Borgia Codex, noting, "The Náhuatl text that describes the hand over the mouth is representative of Macuilxóchitl. This unique iconographic feature of Five Flower, however, differs from what appears to resemble the white butterfly face paint in the final pictorial . . . belong[ing] to Xochipilli."[27] More importantly, Macuilxóchitl represents one of the five Ahuiateotl (pleasure spirits) who represent the southern direction and states of excess or extremes, such as is also the case with Macuiltochtli (Five Rabbit) who represents drunkenness.[28] As depicted in the Yohualli Ehecatl's plate 72 of four spirits in four directions, Macuilxóchitl is clearly a south-direction deity filling the southern quadrant of the page. Page 2 of the Codex Borbonicus depicts the trecena (thirteen-day period) of xochitl (flower), another southern direction sign. It features Macuilxóchitl drumming while Huehuecoyotzin (Old Old Coyote) dances and sings, making even more clear the connection to music and dance. The Ahuiateotl southern direction position of Macuilxóchitl, who can represent the heated joys and excesses in pleasure, does not clearly define Xochipilli, though both are linked to music and pleasure. However, Xochipilli is depicted once in Yohualli Ehecatl plate 13 as presiding over the western direction day of Ozomatli, monkey, a being linked with music, wind, singing, dancing, and excesses or celebrations of all of these things. Nonetheless, the Mexica Xochipilli–Ozomatli connection does not give great insight into the Danza del Xúchitl origin–linked ceremony, in which there are neither monkey impersonators nor monkey symbols. However, there is a closer connection to a Juchipila colonial-era dance brought from the south and that does include a monkey, Los Viejos de la Chinana.

The Old Woman Monkey in Los Viejos de la Chinana Dance

Aside from wind direction and relative direction of the Caxcan Creation Mountain, the south also can represent historical population migrations both away from and returning to the Creation Mountain from many centuries ago. Ocampo recalls that some Caxcans fled in groups when a titanic storm transformed the earth's surface and waters with its strength. She writes of one group that later returned after a variable trade and war history with their origin Caxcan population, sharing, "Some went south into what is today Mexico City and found Lake Texcoco; they came to be known as the Mexica."[29] While the Mexica retained much of the same language in their southward migration, their religion and lifeways changed radically as they went from being the seminomadic high desert Chichimeca of the north to the rainforest agriculturalists Mexica of the south, who quickly intermarried with Central Nahuas and other Indigenous peoples from the south like the Ñuu Savi (Mixtec) and Hñähñu (Otomí). There, the Mexica developed a cultural affinity for the monkey, an animal not found in the semiarid northern interior and coasts of Mexico. Ozomatli is the eleventh of twenty days on the Mexica calendar, in the same eleventh place as Chuen (Monkey) in the twenty-day Maya calendar.[30] Following the rainforest-based calendars of the Olmeca, Maya, Zapoteca, and Mixteca, the Mexica also incorporated the monkey into their understanding of vast solar eras, days, and other divisions of time based on either twenty-day or thirteen-day cycles. When Central Nahuas including the Mexica returned from the south as warriors and settlers of the Juchipila region in the colonial era, they brought that sense of the monkey with them as part of a hybridized Mesoamerican Catholicism that held sway under the growing influence of the Spanish religion. Caxcans in Moyahua interwove both Catholic and Mesoamerican monkey dance traditions into local Caxcan performances for the virtual patron saint of Catholic holy war, Santo Santiago. This figure was credited with spiritually aiding the defeat of the Al-Andalus Muslims who ruled vast areas of Spain from 711 to 1492, just before the Spanish arrival on the Mexican Totonac coasts in 1519. He was linked with the use of military force and all manners of violence as means of Indigenous Christianization in Turtle Island/Abiayala.

While the Xúchitl Dance could be viewed as representing at least a performatively cis-heterosexual moment in human behavior, the Danza de los Viejos de la Chinana is a decidedly queer and trans*species performance, mostly eliciting laughter with the campy cross-dressed monkey wife and her erotic dance. In "Moyahua—Fiestas Patronales 2019," La Danza de los Viejos de la Chinana (The Dance of the Elders of la Chinana) features a monkey-masked cross-dressed dancer in the Santo Santiago fiesta of Moyahua, Zaca-

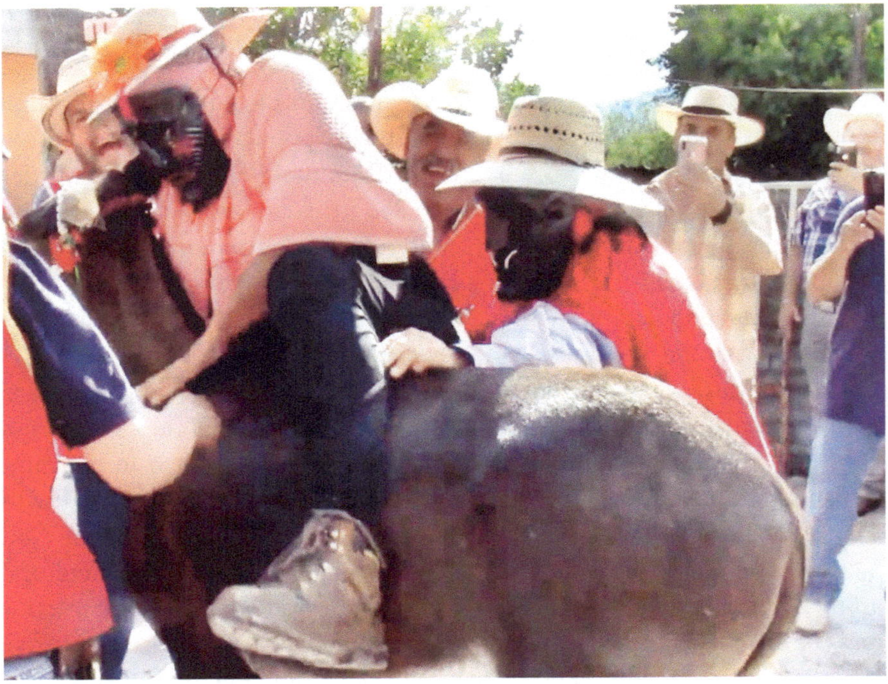

Figure 5 Monkey-masked and peccary-masked Viejos from "Moyahua—Fiestas Patronales 2019."

tecas, a pueblo eleven miles south of Juchipila on the Juchipila River. La Vieja's husband, El Viejo de la Chinana (The Old Man/Husband of the Chinana), is a jabali- (peccary-) masked dancer who accompanies her in the dance, either riding with her on a donkey or dancing with her in the streets (fig. 5).[31] Both Viejos' masks are black and deeply grooved with age lines. Moyahua historian Eleticia Quintero Lara explains how the representations of the peccary and the monkey respectively signal the marriage of "lo bravo y feroz con lo divertido" (the brave and ferocious with the fun), and marks the two as representing Caxcan "curanderos" (healers), "hechiceros" (witches), and respected "ancianos" (elders). Quintero Lara emphasizes that the monkey-masked La Vieja represents the spirit of fun with dance, flirtation, music, and fiesta, while the peccary-masked El Viejo represents the brave ferocity of the Caxcan warriors who fought Spanish and Indigenous troops of Central Mexico in the 1500s.[32] While there are many variations of this dance, a common one is for La Vieja to sing, kiss, dance, and flirt with her husband and the masculine Tastuan (Speaker) dancers in the most exaggerated feminine way.[33] Wearing a shapeless skirt, or even a bra, crop top, or a miniskirt, the obviously cross-dressed and campy La Vieja kisses and vigorously dances with the many throngs of wooden-masked Tastuan dancers who wear leather chaps, serapes (Indigenous/Mexican blankets), layers of towels, and tall headdresses made of cascading cow or horse tails. Many of the tastuanes continuously put their hands on La Vieja's backside as they dance with her. To complicate matters, not all Tastuan dancers are men. Luna and Estrada share, "In a more recent evolution of a few of the regional Caxcan celebrations featuring masked tastoan dancers, women tastoanes don masks with masculine beards and mustaches."[34] So the cross-dressing goes both ways, for female-bodied people to wear masculine beards and for male-bodied people to wear hyper-feminine La Vieja dresses, further complicating the genderqueer nature of the Tastuan and La Vieja dancers.

If the cross-dressed dancing is not queer enough, then the origins of the word "la Chinana" add queer, trans*, and homoerotic impact. "Chinana" in the Caxcan Nahuat variant means something like "puts up the rear," and usually refers to medicinal suppositories to cure hemorrhoids in adults or constipation in children. The entry from Amador's Zacatecas Indigenous place-names book is as follows:

> CHINANA.—Tzinana.—Según Molina, es curar el ano ó las hemorroides. Entre nuestro pueblo bajo se llama chinana á un supositorio de jabón ó queso de tuna que se aplica á los niños para facilitarles la salida del excremento. Algunas gentes dicen, "no me esté chinaneando." esto es, "no me moleste ó no me enfade." (For Molina, it is to cure the anus or hemorrhoids. Among our southern towns, chinana is a suppository made of the soap or cheese of the prickly pear that is applied to children to help them ease the passing of excrement. Some people say, "don't be chinandeando me" that is, "don't bother me or don't make me angry.")[35]

So while the word "chinana" itself really refers to suppositories, the dance performance of a male peccary dancer with one cross-dressed as a woman monkey suggests a celebration of anal sex between a man and his trans, queer, or two-spirit partner and lover. It is literally the dance of putting things in the rear, and the ongoing joke in modern renditions even includes openly simulating penetration between La Vieja and El Viejo. In fact, the video "Moyahua 2009 La Vieja Descarada" (The Shameless Old Lady) begins with El Viejo simulating trying to put his hand up her rear, in effect, approximating entry into his/her anus.[36] Of course, she swats his hand away, only for it to return as the audience laughs at the multiple inversions and reversals of Catholic ideals in the dance. The colonial Catholic church's regional Spanish/Nahuat-language confessional from 1795 explicitly forbids queer anal intercourse, with its Spanish/Nahuat interrogation about it, translated into English by Estrada, as follows: "Quizá has penetrado alguna muger, ó algun varon en la parte posterior? Azo oticuilonti ten zihuat, nozo ten oquichti ipan icuilchil? . . . Perhaps you have been a penetrator of a woman or of a man in their anus?"[37]

Given that monkeys are not native to the semiarid Caxcan region, which only has the coati or cacomixtle as vaguely approximate mammals, the monkey most likely represents a southern Indigenous dance figure migrated into the Caxcan region during the early Spanish colonial-era settlements of Christianized Indigenous populations in Zacatecas. In marked contrast, there is no monkey in the Juchipila Xúchil Dance, and none in Ocampo's *Where We Belong* account of Caxcan animals that take part in creation like Hummingbird and Elderly Bat.[38] Arguably, the Chichimeca-turned-Mexica bring Xochipilli south to Central Mexico, with the wild cacaloxóchitl flowers central to the Xochipilli creation narrative being available for gathering even before the rise of Mesoamerican agricultural cities. While it is possible that monkeys were brought as pets along with pyramid building and urbanization at the Chichimeca Tolteca settlements of Chalchihuites and Chicomoztoc/La Quemada in northern and southcentral Zacatecas, respectively, there seems to be no evidence of monkeys in Zacatecas art as there is in the Codex Yohualli Ehecatl of Central Mexico, where one of the nahualli, or spirit/embodied forms, of Xochipilli is Ozomatli (howler monkey). Jaime Echeverría García notes that the Codex Yohualli Ehecatl also presents Ozomatli blowing a conch shell and drumming a tlalpanhuehuetl, a stand-up drum. While Ozomatli also has strong association with wind instruments like the conch shell and Quetzalcoatl, the spirit/deity of wind, the musical association is why Ozomatli is likely shown paired with Xochipilli in a representation of the eleventh Nahua calendar day of the monkey.[39] In addition, howler monkeys can call across long distances. Given the likely Central Mexican origin of the monkeys who prefer the steamy jungles of southern Mexico, Central America, and the Amazon, it makes sense to understand what the monkey means to Central Mexican Indigenous peoples including Nahuas, especially in the context of colonization.

Jaime Echeverría García gives explanations of the monkey-masked dance figure of Central Mexico that can apply to the Caxcan Los Viejos de la Chinana Dance. He writes of "el desarrollo," or evolution of the child to adult, as replicating the evolution of Indigenous peoples from hunter-gatherers to city-dwellers, a city life that eventually required for most the acceptance of the far-flung Spanish empire's Christianity.[40] Echeverría García's analysis is historically complicated. On one hand, he describes how Central Nahuas felt about their hunting and gathering Chichimeca ancestors of northern Mexico. While they did not necessarily reject this ancestry, some felt that Chichimeca represented a stage of simplicity that they were eager to discard for the riches of the city, sedentary agriculturalism, and political dominance in Central Mexico. When Spaniards arrived in the 1500s, the Chichimeca who had resisted Spanish colonization and Christianity for decades were once again deemed to be clinging to a past that could not be maintained. In effect, Echeverría García argues that northern Chichimeca are shown to be childlike in two cases, first for not having evolved the urbanity of southern Nahuas, and second for resisting the colonial Christianity that came to typify the Mexica center after its fall to Spanish and Tlaxcalteca invasion. In fact, monkey-masked or even gorilla-masked dancers are common in many Catholic Indigenous dances in Zacatecas. They can represent music, dancing, and the sublimation of these carnal desires and pleasure along the Christian path of Spanish colonization. Of course, for Chichimeca, the monkey can also simply represent someone who just wants to have fun, to dance, to sing, and to experience love, without taking to heart Echeverría García's and Central Nahua's historical and colonial meanings.

But the dance is not simply a displacement of Caxcan culture. Daisy Ocampo sees the tastuanes in terms of the sacred nature of their wooden masks and the cathartic aspects of the violence in the battle, and these insights also apply to the Viejos' wooden carved masks. Writing of her own Caxcan community of El Remolino, she states, "La Mesquitera reject the Catholic narrative and use the dance to heal internal community conflict." As with many other Tastuan dances, El Remolino Tastuan tesguino (corn beer) is imbibed in order to allow the healing to occur.[41] Tastuan dancer Jordy Ocampo confirms, "While this may seem like a violent dance, it is actually meant to bring peace and is a day to honor our place in this world." Emphasizing a sovereign Caxcan spirituality, Daisy Ocampo concludes of the Tastuan mesquite tree masks, "The tree is sacrificing a piece of itself for the healing of the people through the mask." Here, Ocampo signals an insight regarding "historical trauma" from the Hunkpapa/Oglala Lakota Maria Yellow Horse Brave Heart. Because the of the ongoing consequences of colonial Spanish and Mestizo Mexican government suppressions, Caxcans have great reason to continue to heal from the centuries of wars and cultural impositions that came from the south, and the Tastuan Dance is one part of that healing. In this light, the actual mesquite wood that forms the Viejos' de la Chinana masks is doing healing work. A literally darker meaning for the black color of the masks could originally recall the black cremation ashes used during mourning. After a year, human ashes were returned by the wind to Tlachialoyantepec, according to one colonial source. Caxcan tribal member Ruben Ruvalcaba confirmed of the Creation Mountain in the west, "Our ilamazi [ancestors/grandmothers] return here when our time is up."[42]

Trans*gendered violence is another paradoxical issue in the Moyahua version of the Tastuan Dance. One common Moyahua version of La Danza de los Viejos de la Chinana includes the violent tearing-off of La Vieja's clothing. Yet this could be a critique of colonial cis-heteropatriarchal violence rather than an advertisement to attack cross-dressing, two-spirit, or transgender peoples. This critique would give new meaning to Moyahua Tastuan dancer Ismael García Ávila's statement, "We've never accepted what [the Spanish] told us, that the conquest was clean. . . . They said they were the saviors—not at all."[43] A second Tastuan dancer, Ramiro Durán-Rentería, states, "Santo Santiago isn't a figure free from contradiction. . . . [The allegory of the tastuanes] continues to be a hypocritical discourse. But it's still a hugely moving manifestation for me, because of the paradox." The violence of the dance counters myths of Spanish kindness and civility in colonization that goes from south to north in northern Mexican and southern U.S. history. B. Ruby Rich's take on complicated images of contemporary Mexican film drag can aid in rethinking the violence against La Vieja de la Chinana. Citing Arturo Ripstein's 1977 film *El lugar sin límites* (The Place Without Limits), she notes how the film's ending, in which the transgender woman La Manuelita is brutally murdered by her macho dance partner, subtly condemns the macho for giving into the conflict of his desires for La Manuelita and his desire to appear heterosexual to his male small-town peers. She cites Chicano film scholar Sergio de la Mora, who writes, "it is 'the first Mexican film to take homosexuality seriously,'"[44] although perhaps bisexuality, queer, and trans sexuality might update that sentiment. It is the same tastuanes who dance and flirt with her who eventually disrobe her. Because the Tastuan Dance contains many ironic critiques of violence, the stripping of La Vieja could also be an ironic statement on the violent nature of colonial wars in which the place of Indigenous spirituality, women, animals, and trans* peoples are subject to disruption and attack. As Esselen and Chumash lesbian Deborah Miranda showed in her accounts of missionary rapes and suppression of queer Native Californians, an account of settler-colonial regimes and Indigenous sovereignty is incomplete without queer, gendered, and sexual considerations of settler-colonial violence.[45] From a critical Indigenous perspective, the violence of the Tastuan Dance is just such a record of the northern Chichimeca historical trauma and its gender and queer components that call for healing. One can see the "Moyahua—Fiestas Patronales 2019" YouTube video dance as a northern Caxcan warning about the perils of Spanish Catholic violence toward the spirits of any kind of transformation, whether that be from human to animal or man to woman.

Conclusion

South is not only a direction of monsoon winds, or a relative direction toward the Creation Mountain at Juchipila, but also a cultural marker dividing northern Chichimeca of Aridoamerica from the Nahuas of Mesoamerica to the south. In the first case, this chapter opened up possibilities of the intersex plants impacted by monsoon rains from the south and other directions. Facing south toward Tlachialoyantepec (fig. 4), one sees the spatial reconnection back to the mountain despite state barriers that do not honor Indigenous perspectives of their own ancestral spaces. Finally, this analysis looked at the monkey as a Nahua signifier of a southern direction excess that includes the trans*gender and trans*species monkey mask dance. Even with the Indigenous and Spanish influence in colonial Catholic conversion, Caxcan dance seems to lampoon conversion violence and question the narratives of condemnation of queer sexualities. This monkey critique is more complicated than the popular narrative that Xochipilli is simply the god of homosexuality. With the increasing conflict between human and nonhuman ecologies during a global climate crisis, it may be that a pan-erotic inclusion of Xochipilli's relationships to intersex plants and all life's queerness is a bigger picture needed as much today as it was in the beginning.

3

WEST

Filming Kumu Hina, Aloha 'Āina, and Māhū in Hawai'i

This chapter is a trans-Indigenous take on how media from Hawai'i would look from a directional perspective that is more common on Turtle Island. It does not directly reflect Kānaka Maoli culture and spatiality even though Kumu Hina and other Kānaka Maoli are cited in the chapter. Kānaka Maoli scholars have not made great use of directionality, including west directionality, as a main framework for viewing their own culture in the way that is done in this chapter. In a 2019 personal interview, Hinaleimoana Kalu-Wong (Kumu Hina) makes her support for Hawaiian sovereignty: "I would love to see our people politically free from the United States of America, and that we would have a relationship of international cordiality and respect versus us being subject to the whims of the United States." Separatist Kānaka Maoli increasingly strive toward an aloha 'āina that ideally includes "control of one's own lands and resources—for Native Hawaiians, that would be the Hawaiian Kingdom Crown and Government Lands."[1] A Kānaka Maoli (Native Hawaiian) mele composer, filmmaker, and kumu (teacher), Kumu Hina, also shared understandings about the Indigenous western direction of Hawai'i. In light of west-oriented afterlife journeys, healing east–west practices, and western femininity, this chapter considers western spatiality in Hawai'i as well as the related healing themes involving sovereign gender, politics, and HIV/AIDS activism in Hawai'i. In this third chapter, west-direction feminine spatiality and ancestral healing themes are detailed in the films *Ke Kulana He Mahu* (2001), in which appears Kumu Hina as one of several māhū spokespersons; the animated "Kapaemahu" (2020), co-directed by Hinaleimoana Wong-Kalu, that recounts the ancient four māhū honored for their healing feats at Waikīkī; and the documentary *Kumu Hina* (2014), which documents Hinaleimoana's marriage and her teachings of mele, aloha, and hula to youth at the K-12 Hālau Lōkahi Public Charter School.

Māhū as Combination of Kū in the East and Hina in the West

As the opening credits of *Ke Kulana He Mahu* appear across the black background, Kumu Hina chants mele at the ocean's edge in Waikīkī, O'ahu, eventually becoming visible with a fade to her image. Wearing a flower-patterned

Hawaiian dress, a flower in her right ear, and with her long black hair tied behind her, the tall Kumu Hina presents her beautiful mix of Kānaka Maoli and Chinese features. As she chants to the watery horizon at Waikīkī, Oʻahu, the afternoon sun strongly shines from above on her face as it begins its westward descent. In that establishing shot at Sans Souci Beach, she turns from facing south to face west and makai, toward the ocean, the "moana" she names in her chant.[2] Given Kumu Hina's Hawaiian and English directions, "Hikina is east. Komohana is west. ʻĀkau is north. Hema is south,"[3] the ocean in this shot of Waikīkī is komohana (west), with waters visible to the west and north behind Kumu Hina.[4] An understanding of the name Hina itself relates to the komohana directionality of this scene. First, Kānaka Maoli scholar Marie Alohalani Brown shares that the name Hina is linked to komohana and femininity. Noting how Hina and Kū are both akuas (deities) paired as siblings or as mates, Brown elaborates that "kū" personifies "male-generating masculinity" linked with the east and rising sun while "Hina" signifies "female fecundity" and the west direction in which the sun declines and sets.[5] Molokaʻi Kānaka Maoli Nālani Wilson gives further Hina insights, stating, "Everything that controls tides or life always has Hina in it. The moon that actually controls the way our cycles move, the cycles of the tides and water. . . . She is the Mama of the water sources . . . whether it's inside a woman's body, in the ocean or in the sky."[6] Of course Hinaleimoana's full first name with its "Hina" and "moana" (ocean) parts exactly highlights that relationship to water, reconnecting the Hina figure that was curiously missing from the Disney animation *Moana* (2016). Furthermore, Kū in the east and Hina in the west represents a complete cycle, and Brown represents these as the eastern and western sides within a diagram of four directions within a circle, perhaps analogous to a medicine wheel familiar to many in Abiayala/Turtle Island. In light of this komohana association with Hina that Brown describes, the afternoon light on Hina's face can reference Hinaleimoana's very name with its komohana relationship to a solar downward movement into the ocean.

As the sun transitions from the ʻākau masculine akua Kū to the komohana feminine akua Hina, so Kumu Hina also transitioned from a more youthful masculine gender expression to a more feminine gender expression as she became fully adult. As a wahine-kāne (woman-man), Hina retains both Hina and Kū aspects of herself, and *Kumu Hina* documents that visual gender expression transition. Kumu Hina in masculine Hawaiian clothing is shown in older footage chanting mele during a 1990 Kamehameha competition three years before making her gender expression transitions. Kumu Hina's voiceover explains, "When I was in high school over twenty years ago, I had a very rough time." A cut to Hina pictures her with three flowers in her hair and adorned as a wahine-kāne in a dress. "I was teased and tormented for being too girlish," her voice continues as the image cuts back to Hina finishing the mele and walking off the stage. In the cut to a modern Hina wearing a hibiscus flower, flower shirt, makeup, and up-do, she concludes, "But I found refuge in being Hawaiian, being Kānaka Maoli. My purpose in this lifetime is to pass on the true meaning of aloha, love, honor, and respect. It's a responsibility that I take very seriously."[7] Part of this refuge is in the māhū mixed-gender traditions of ancient Hawai'i.

According to the several centuries of mo'olelo (story), the four pōhaku (stones) that stand at Waikīkī Beach honor famed māhū healers who sailed to Hawai'i from Tahiti before the 1400s. To honor these māhū, Hinaleimoana Wong-Kalu co-directed the 2020 "Kapaemahu" short animation with the gay Euro-Americans Dean Hamer and Joe Wilson. The first lines of the eight-minute animated short highlight the mixed-gender nature of the māhū. Amid animated images of the ancient sea voyage from Tahiti to Hawai'i from seven hundred years ago, "Kapaemahu" begins with Kumu Hina speaking in 'Ōlelo Ni'ihau, an Indigenous language still spoken in Hawai'i. The English translation occurs in subtitles:

> Long ago, four extraordinary individuals voyaged across the ocean from their home in Tahiti to Hawaii.
> They settled at Ulukou in Waikīkī.
> The visitors were tall and deep in voice, yet gentle and soft-spoken.
> They were not male nor female.
> They were māhū—a mixture of both in mind, heart, and spirit.[8]

As Kumu Hina speaks this last line in 'Ōlelo Ni'ihau, the animation shows kāne and wahine figures as energy forms that swirl and combine into the shape of a tall māhū in feminine dress. The short film then beautifully elaborates upon the māhū's feats of healing. Incredibly, centuries of Kānaka Maoli oral traditions preserved their names and abilities that are drawn, narrated, and subtitled in the film:

> The Gods favored the four visitors with skill in the science of healing.
> Kapuni possessed great spiritual power.
> Kinohi was all seeing.
> Kahaloa could heal from afar.
> Kapaemahu healed by laying on hands.[9]

The film's accompanying animation here shows the soft-spoken māhū generously helping all ages and genders at O'ahu.

Kū and Hina, masculine and feminine, east and west, are also a part of the healing practice of prayers at sunrise and sunset that the animation depicts in its own imaginative way. Kumu Hina shared in her interview with the author, "When you pray for healing, you must pray to the rising of the sun and to the setting of the sun, the new life coming from the rising of the sun and the illness slipping away to the setting of the sun."[10] Since healing can incorporate both Kū masculine and Hina feminine attributes, this healing incorporation of both can exemplify the balance that the māhū represent internally as both masculine and feminine figures. Lynette Kahekili Paglinawan, "a Living Treasure of Hawaiʻi and hoʻoponopono practitioner," discusses the Hawaiian philosophy of duality, in which there is "a Kū and a Hina, a hard and a soft, a male and a female" in each person,[11] with the historical Kapaemahu being an early māhū example of a great healer with mastery of certain Kū and Hina attributes and of traditional medicine.

After healing many Kānaka Maoli in the 2020 "Kapaemahu" short animation, the four māhū prepare to depart. Motivated by their thanks, and at the request of the four māhū, the Kānaka Maoli of Oʻahu honored the māhū by laboriously dragging four huge pōhaku stones down a hill at Kaimukī in a ceremony for the healers at Waikīkī Beach. The film's animation that shows the sun rising in the east at Waikīkī is an artistic imagining, as Waikīkī Beach looks out komohana, not east, as it curves south in the Kona or leeward dis-

Figure 6 Four māhū and the pōhakus at Waikīkī in "Kapaemahu" (2020), directed by Hinaleimoana Wong-Kalu, Dean Hamer, and Joe Wilson.

trict of Oʻahu. In fact, the sun's later placement komohana above the ocean horizon and behind the four māhū on the shore makes more sense to indicate a setting of the sun in the west. As day turns to night in the "Kapaemahu" animation, the full moon goes through its various phases, and its placement low above the horizon at Waikīkī indicates a komohana placement, if the animation were compared to the actual Waikīkī Beach. With this understanding, the full moon is prepared to set in the west as it shines above the four māhū on the shore and on the glimmering ocean. As with the appearance of Kumu Hina at the western shore horizon at Waikīkī, the prominent full moon over the Waikīkī ocean and the narration that "the ceremonies lasted a full moon" invokes Hina and her life-giving abilities. The māhū act of putting their healing mana into the four pōhaku on the Waikīkī sand is seen in figure 6.

Komohana as the Path of the Deceased

The animation's climactic final scene (fig. 6) is an example of "moʻolelo ea," or story sovereignty, and the moʻolelo's ability to go "beyond the Western binary of fact versus fiction."[12] Having completed their task of imbuing their mana into the pōhaku, the four māhū vanish, their sparkling mana disappearing into pō, the night darkness over the moonlit ocean, as they complete their ceremony.[13] While the moʻolelo does not say that the māhū died, that their mana leaves their bodies on the western horizon is reminiscent of the departure of souls into pō linked with the sunset in the west and the "setting of the sun on one's life," as Kumu Hina mentioned. Kumu Hina elaborated, "The jumping off point of an island for a soul to go onto its next world is always in the west, the western tip or more westernly region of an island . . . when one refers to the road that spirit of the deceased must travel, it is the red chiseled path started by Kānaloa . . . Kānaloa who is deity of the sea, the great ocean."[14] In agreement, Laurel Mei-Singh retells a moʻolelo of the westernmost "Kaʻena Point" on Oʻahu, writing of "Leina Ka ʻUhane, a large, flat rock from which spirits leap into the next dimension after death . . . into pō, the darkness where the universe originated."[15] Because the disappearance of the four māhū is mysterious and ceremonial, it leaves open possibilities of travel through pō and its own association of other worlds. With an understanding of komohana as the entryway to the afterlife, one can look back with spatial insights at Kumu Hina's chant at Waikīkī in *Ke Kulana He Mahu* mentioned above in which she invokes Kānaloa's name. In invoking "Kānaloa" in her opening mele along that western-facing beach, she subtly references ancestors, including māhū who have long made their komohana journey on the path of Kānaloa.[16] The moʻolelo does not say where the four māhū went; it only states that they left their mana in the four pōhaku before vanishing.

Returning to the sense of the komohana direction and the kūpuna's western afterlife journey gives more understanding to *Kumu Hina*. While Louis and Kahele explain the ocean and western path of Kānaloa,[17] Brown shows how iwi kūpuna leave part of their mana in their bones as "bones are imbued with the *mana*, or 'spiritual power,' of the deceased."[18] Understanding the importance of iwi (bone) in the Hawaiian language and identity helps explain why Kumu Hina is so motivated in her governor-appointed role as chair of the Oʻahu Reburial Council in the *Kumu Hina* film. Citing Pukui and Elbert's *Hawaiian Dictionary* definition of iwi-related words, Brown explains, "kula iwi means 'land of bones,' with the understanding that 'here my bones began' and thus 'birthplace.' ʻŌiwi, which includes the root word iwi, or 'bones,' means 'native son; native of the land.' . . . Native Hawaiians continue to revere the ʻāina and hold sacred the bones of our kupuna. . . . Mourning the damage to or loss of land and the desecration of burial sites is unsurprising."[19] In overseeing the respectful treatment of ancient and often unmarked Kānaka Maoli burials uncovered in Oʻahu construction sites, Kumu Hina literally protects iwi kūpuna's mana imbued in the bones. In the mālama i kūpuna section of the film, in which heavy equipment digs at a Honolulu Rail Project site, a Kumu Hina voiceover explains, "To turn one's back on one's ancestors is to sever oneself from one's future. And I will do everything that I can to prevent that." *Kumu Hina* shows that the living Kānaka Maoli demonstrate aloha for iwi kūpuna, whose mana remains very much alive on the islands.[20]

The death and mana of ancestors ultimately support the living. Suzanne Woodward notes, "Hina's life stories are presented in ways that suggest a more cyclical understanding of temporality. Through this non-linear construction, identity is portrayed as a complex process of reaffirmation."[21] *Kumu Hina* demonstrates a cyclical sense of being, that the living Kānaka Maoli reconnect with the language, traditions, and hula of the ancestors, despite the assimilation barriers that the occupying forces of U.S. institutions erected to prevent this reconnection from happening. Kumu Hina embodies the knowledge of the kūpuna (ancestors, elders) and teaches her students to do the same. When Jozie Kamai, mother of Kumu Hina's star kāne-wahine student Hoʻonani Kamai, explains, "I want my children, my girls to learn the hula and learn Hawaiian culture because I never did,"[22] she is speaking for a majority of Kānaka Maoli who are no longer fluent in their own native tongue as a result of assimilationist Western youth education. As a kumu, Hina puts her philosophy into action by teaching the youth at the K-12 Hālau Lōkahi to show aloha to their kūpuna through Hawaiian language, mele, and hula.

In a climactic confrontation at the Hālau Lōkahi school, principal Laara Allbrett speaks at a pualu school assembly. She starts frankly by reporting,

"Kumu Hina was more upset than she has been in a while," referring to the high school students who aren't participating in school functions. Motioning to Hina beside her she affirms, "This is a cultural icon in Hawai'i. . . . Do you guys all understand?" Stepping forward, she continues, "Hina is trying to hold on to what is *left* of Hawaiian culture." A cut to several rows of kids in blue school shirts shows them in a long shot looking around worriedly. The cut back to Allbrett shows her growing indignation. Her voice begins to break as she shouts, "To say the word *kumu* means what?" "Teacher" respond students from off-camera. "But what does it mean?" she pleads as a soft strumming of diegetic guitar begins. "If you say aloha to anybody, where's it coming from? Your mouth?" she testily queries the assembly. "Your heart," say several kids as the camera cuts back to the kids lined up in assembly. She charges, "It's supposed to be! Or don't say the word!" This cut back to Allbrett shows her speaking with a voice breaking with passion and wiping tears from her eyes. "When you sing 'Hawai'i Pono'ī,' what flag do you have on your chest?" she continues. "Hae Hawai'i," say kids in the reaction shot. In the cut back to Allbrett, the principal continues, "We didn't get to sing that stuff in our schools. We had to pledge allegiance to the flag that took over our Hawai'i. Do you get it?" Several reaction shots show Hina and the student assembly now crying as well. In the return shot to Allbrett she concludes, "There's a reason you were born in Hawai'i or came back to Hawai'i. There's a reason. It's a divine energy that runs up through the lava. Do you guys get it? You are the warriors of today." The reaction shots to the children shows that many are crying, including the usually unflappable kāne-wahine Ho'onani as all begin to slowly sing "Hawai'i Pono'ī."[23] It's an intense scene, and part of why the children cry is because they are at some level realizing their lost connection to the culture of the kūpuna, those who have departed into the west on the road of Kānaloa.

But in this scene the ancestors also motivate the political reclamation of a sovereign Hawai'i. While Kumu Hina defines aloha as "love and respect" in *Kumu Hina,* part of that respect goes to the ea of the stories themselves and the places they describe. Stressing a related push for linguistic decolonization, Noelani Goodyear-Ka'ōpua emphasizes the Kānanka Maoli philosophy "ea," which signifies interconnected "life," "breath" and "sovereignty."[24] Ea is the larger philosophy within which Wong-Kalu's directionality is rooted. Aloha 'āina is another Hawaiian language concept that brings together place and story in powerful ways. Le'a Malia Kanehe states, "The heart of the movement to resist biocolonialism in Hawai'i is aloha 'āina (love for land)—a core value and practice underlying all Hawaiian movements." The front cover of the anthology *A Nation Rising: Hawaiian Movements for Life, Land, and Sovereignty* features Kumu Hina with several of her students in a successful protest to stop the genetic modification of the hāloa (kalo/taro) plant, held sacred within Kānaka Maoli origins. In *Ke Kulana He Mahu,* Aiona links Kānaka Maoli family structure to the firstborn Kānaka Maoli child who was stillborn and became the taro/kalo: "Hāloanakalaukapalili, the first kalo, is the elder brother sibling of the Hawaiian people," the first and primary food of the Kānaka Maoli.[25] The book's front cover image acknowledgment includes the terms "aloha" and "ea" as it reads, "Mahalo me ke aloha to Kumu Hina Wong-Kalu and Hālau Lōkahi Public Charter school for gracing the cover of this book and for your steadfast commitment to aloha ʻāina and ea."[26] This aloha ʻāina activism counters the "aloha" marketed in U.S. settler-colonial neoliberal tourism, a critical difference noted by Kānaka Maoli scholar Stephanie Nohelani Teves in her analysis of Hawaiian tourism, media, and māhū performances.[27]

At a celebration with Kumu Kauaʻiʻiki Olores and Kumu Hinaleimoana Wong as two Lā Hoʻihoʻi Ea 2022 māhū honorees, Kaʻiminaʻauao Cambern, Kanoa Cleveland-Lagareta, and Keawe Parker lead a Zoom roundtable film review of the 2001 *Ke Kuluana He Mahu* film produced more than twenty years earlier. They included guest panelists Kaliko Aiu, Maddalynn Sesepasara, Keahi Johnson, and Tehina Kahikina. In the "*Ke Kulana He Mahu* Talkback," Sāmoan trans activist of Honolulu Maddalynn Sesepasara recounts māhū reconnections to the kūpuna through aloha ʻāina protests against the construction of the eighteen-meter telescope on the sacred peak of Mauna Kea on the Big Island of Hawaiʻi. She shares:

> Being there with our Kānaka Maoli folks, and people that were not also māhū or Hawaiʻi out there on Mauna Kea, embracing the māhū folks that came up there to show their respects and to show their love and compassion for our community was beautiful. This is our moment. This is where we knew we have a place because our kūpuna knew that we needed to be there, knew we needed to be in this space.[28]

Several agreed how aloha ʻāina experiences have irrevocably shaped many Kānaka Maoli and māhū identities. The "kūpuna" that Sesepasara mentioned and their eventual westward journey are the foundation of these aloha ʻāina movements as culture carries from the past forward.

Queer Kānaka Maoli wahine scholar Jamaica Heolimeleikalani Osorio's work on indigenizing queer genders in Hawaiian history is an example of politics, history, and poetry founded in aloha ʻāina movements at Mauna a Wākea. The film *This Is the Way We Rise* (2021) by Kānaka Maoli director Ciara Lacy documents her protests at Mauna Kea, a passion that fuels her poetry. The Big Island is also famous for Pele and her role in volcanic activity at Kīlauea. Osorio points out her role in queer Hawaiian mo'olelo. Pele's lava brought the regeneration of land through the powers of her younger sister Hi'iaka, "the one who plants lehua groves to flourish after Pele's lava flow." Osorio recounts how in a fit of jealousy, Pele used her lava to kill Hi'iaka's female lover and 'aikāne Hōpoe, who was linked to the lehua and the making of lehua lei. She defines the same-sex 'aikāne relationship of Hi'iaka and Hōpoe as one of utmost "emotional and physical intimacy," writing of their "great reciprocal commitment, and that boundless loyalty. Through these qualities, we witness aloha between 'aikāne."[29] Since the 'aikāne are related in the earliest mo'olelo oral histories told by the kūpuna, their formative presence in Hawai'i predates the rise of modern queer movements by many centuries. This means that not only are the protestors at Mauna a Wākea both queer and multigendered, the very landscape of Hawai'i is as well. While Kumu Hina's marriage to Hema is erotically celebrated in *Kumu Hina* with scenes of open affection between the two, the masculine female-bodied Ho'onani does not have any examples of romance from an adult kāne-wahine or a woman with an 'aikāne. At school, Ho'onani is teased a bit at Valentine's for not receiving any love letters, a reflection of his/her mixed gender that is otherwise appreciated by her schoolmates.

As the film progresses, only the kāne-wahine Ho'onani Kamai of the men's high school group consistently uses the Hawaiian heart and teachings from the kūpuna to excel in the hula and mele that Kumu Hina demonstrates to all. Throughout the film, Kumu Hina is the omnipresent affirmer of Ho'onani as a student "in the middle," with both kāne and wahine gender attributes. In one scene, Kumu Hina allows Ho'onani to wear both the boys' yellow and girls' white lei as a sign of "both" genders, of having strong masculine kū in a wahine body. As a kāne student in *A Place in the Middle* later says, "She does have more laho (balls) than all of us here."[30] Ho'onani earns the spot as the main chanter in their production at the end of the school year by virtue of a truly resonant and powerful voice and command of the Hawaiian language. As the students practice the "'Ai Kamumu Kēkē" mele, Kumu Hina brings back the lava teachings that Allbrett previously mentioned:

> What this piece is saying is that like the lava flow coming from Kīlauea, the magma itself is like the mu'umu'u, doesn't have arms or legs but it consumes everything in its path. And slowly but surely, it will continue until it reaches its destination to the ocean. But, in the wake of the destruction, there is rebirth and new growth and new place for new life to exist which is what I believe you have availed yourself to.[31]

In these words, Kumu Hina again references the cyclical nature of being Kānaka Maoli and the close connection to aloha ʻāina and the ancestors. The lava represents the process of death and destruction that is sometimes represented by the western direction, but death is not a final state. Death provides the momentum for life and rebirth. In this case, it is the rebirth of the Hawaiian Kingdom and its ancient integration of all genders including the māhū, after a time of U.S. occupation, English-language hegemony, and violence toward māhū.

The schoolboys accept Hoʻonani as one of their own, as a kāne-wahine of the pronoun "he," especially as Hoʻonani excels in the final performances of the "ʻAi Kamumu Kēkē" mele, after which many of the boys thank Hoʻonani for providing the masculine leadership they needed. After many flubbed sessions of the young men's high school practice sessions in which Kumu Hina can only hold her head in exacerbation, the group pulls through in the end with Hoʻonani front and center at the school presentation. With the lava-red lights highlighting their figures in traditional Kānaka Maoli clothing, the group makes an impressive show of "ʻAi Kamumu Kēkē" to which the audience of parents and community applaud loudly. At the final performance, Kumu Hina commends the boys and the kāne-wahine for his excellent mele. Through this performance, the students were able to embody the lava that creates new life after its destructive cycle of expansion to create even more land at the ocean's edge. In a historical sense, the youth's use of Hawaiian language represents a political, māhū, and cultural rebirth after more than a century of suppression of the Indigenous language, gender, and nation that their ancestors knew so well.

Māhū legacy is part of the larger aloha ʻāina movements that are strongly rooted in the ancestors. The four healing stones recounted in all of Kumu Hina's films were respectfully named "Ka Pōhaku Kahuna Kapaema-hu" (the Healing Stones of Kapaemahu) in the 1907 Hawaiian-language newspaper *Ka Nupepa Kuokoa*. Kumu Hina reports stories that Queen Liliʻuokalani's sister, Princess Likelike, and her daughter Princess Kaʻiulani "would place seaweed or flower lei on the stones and offer a prayer when entering or leaving the water."[32] However, the respect for the Healing Stones of Kapaemahu waned from the public awareness as Hawaiian traditions faced increasing suppression from U.S. settler colonialism in the 1900s. As shown in the animated "Kapaemahu," the four pōhaku were even buried beneath a bowling alley in the mid-1990s, to the protest of Kānaka Maoli at the time. Rising Hawaiian sovereignty movements motivated the Kānaka Maoli to again honor and "mālama (take care of)" the large boulders at Waikīkī in 1997 in accordance with the correct lunar cycles and under the spiritual supervision of Papa Henry Auwae, a "poʻokela (master)" of "laʻau lapaʻau."[33]

Yet, even when restored to a place of honor, the signage at the four pōhaku was incomplete in terms of gender. The public English rendering of the māhū as merely "four healers," "four wizards," or "Hawaiian healers," masked the mixed-gender māhū nature of the healers. In a personal interview with the author, Kumu Hina elaborated that the pōhaku Waikīkī plaque only mentions "four healers" because "George Kanahele['s] . . . articulation of that little parcel of our history was clearly influenced by his religious background and upbringing. He is a staunch member of the Church of Latter-day Saints."[34] In other words, the idea of mixed genders within each person, especially as represented by the māhū, was too great a conflict within conservative Christian perspectives.

In the 2001 film *Ke Kulana He Mahu*, Kumu Hina affirms the correct māhū nature of the healers that was silenced within Christianized Hawaiian signage and history. One scene's cinematic fade from a contemporary drawing of the four māhū into the image of Kumu Hina indicates Kumu Hina's role in revitalizing ancient Kānaka Maoli culture, gender, hula, and language. The discussion of the Healing Stones of Kapaemahu begins with a shot of the four imposing boulders at Waikīkī Beach, an image that cuts to a contemporary charcoal sketch of the four māhū as muscular, bare-chested, long-haired, and somewhat androgynous beings arriving by boat on O'ahu shores. This image fades into a contrasting image of a strong and beautiful Kumu Hina sporting

Figure 7 Ancient māhū and Kumu Hina fade from *Ke Kulana He Mahu* (2001), directed by Kathryn Xian and Brent Anbe.

feminine attire including a long dress, dark purple lip liner, pink lipstick, carefully drawn brown eyebrows, large gold earrings, and a pink hibiscus flower in her pulled-back long black hair. This fade from past to present indicates the direct relationship that Kumu Hina maintains with the kūpuna in general and māhū traditions in particular. She indicates that the pōhaku's name Kapaemāhū indicates that māhū arrive to heal. She continues in the film, "We are not freaks. We are healers. . . . These māhū brought with them the arts, the knowledge of healing, and the knowledge of their pule, their prayers. And the wisdom that they brought was so influential that it gave merit to them marking this place, marking the pōhaku, marking the stones that they came with."[35] That the Healing Stones of Kapaemahu persist in being venerated for their mana after several centuries is an impressive testament to their māhū healing power indeed.[36]

The impact of *Ke Kulana He Mahu* and "Kapaemahu" in educating about the māhū nature of the four healers was augmented by the installation of a new plaque at the Healing Stones of Kapaemahu site in Waikīkī, an area ironically now the main hub of Hawaiian tourism. In October 2023, Kumu Hina helped to install a new stone and signage at the Healing Stones of Kapaemahu site in Waikīkī that reads:

> Aloha Mai
> E hō'ihi i kēia wahi pana a me ona mau mana
> mo'olelo o nā kahuna ho'ōla 'ehā o Kahiki a
> me ko lākou kuleana lapa'au a ho'ola kānaka.
> Please respect this cultural site of reverence.
> There are many stories of these four healers from
> Tahiti, known for their duality of male and female
> spirit and their wondrous works of healing.

After this text, there is a Quick Read code for the www.Kapaemahu.info site that includes a longer one-hour "The Healer Stones of Kapaemahu" version of the much shorter "Kapaemahu" film with animation, interviews, and historical photographs. The website also contains a link to a holographic image of Kumu Hina explaining the māhū legacy of the four pōhaku. On a smartphone, one can take a picture of Kumu Hina hovering about whatever background the camera sees as she details māhū healing history. This information is meant to prepare people to visit the actual Healing Stones of Kapaemahu.[37] The Healing Stones of Kapaemahu represent one mo'olelo of the ancestors who have long taken their komohana journey toward where the sun sets into the waves of the moana.

Modern Māhū Healing and HIV/AIDS in *Ke Kulana He Mahu*

In terms of the larger theme of healing, the necessity of aloha in healing is one that *Ke Kulana He Mahu* clearly affirms with narratives of the original four māhū healers, the ʻohana resolve to show aloha to their family in the worst of the 1800s plagues, and the modern drag confrontation of HIV/AIDS illness with acceptance and aloha. Kānaka Maoli of all time periods show aloha as central to the support one needs in the process of healing. This healing theme reflects an east-west healing practice in Hawaiʻi. Kumu Hina deftly explained a practice of healing from sunrise to sunset that involves the western direction, sharing, "When we face the east, it's where the sun rises. Face the west, it's where the sun sets. . . . When you pray for healing, you must pray to the rising of the sun and to the setting of the sun, the new life coming from the rising of the sun and the illness slipping away to the setting of the sun."[38] This healing aloha could represent what is welcomed in at sunrise. The social illness that the movie *Ke Kulana He Mahu* seeks to release as though releasing illness at sunset is that of a lack of aloha for māhū who struggle to heal from HIV and stigma today. To let the social disease of withholding aloha from māhū and Hawaiian LGBT "slip away" into the sunset is the complementary half of the healing cycle that this film successfully puts forward.

Through its final section, *Ke Kulana He Mahu* argues that gender and sexual discrimination today go against the aloha that Kānaka Maoli traditionally have for each other as demonstrated during the early contact times of sickness and plague. Noting in the film the disastrous impact of European-brought diseases for which Kānaka Maoli had no natural immunity, Lilikalā Kameʻeleihiwa details the horrific genocide that occurred as the Kānaka Maoli population declined from one million at the James Cook contact date of 1778 to forty thousand by 1893. The title cards note how healthy Kānaka Maoli family members would join their sick relatives even in quarantined areas, where they also became sick and often died. The last card reads, "the bonds of family far outweighed the fear of any disease."[39] The solidarity of Kānaka Maoli during the 1800s epidemics is especially meant to engender acceptance for HIV-positive Kānaka Maoli, especially the māhū, queer, and drag culture populations of Honolulu most infected by percentage with HIV. The unity during 1800s time of death and sickness contrasts to the specter of AIDS and māhūphobia that arises in the narratives of modern Honolulu.

Ke Kulana He Mahu focuses on Honolulu's drag scene and HIV, with most attention given to the HIV-positive drag mother and performer Sami L. A. Akuna a.k.a. Cocoa Chandelier. Between fabulous performance scenes in which Cocoa fuses Hawaiian movement, dance, and Madonna club songs, Sami appears out of drag and dressed in masculine clothes. In one interview scene, Sami confesses, "I was first diagnosed with HIV in ninety-one. . . . My mother found out by accident." That Sami could not tell their own mother about their HIV status speaks to the intensity of homophobia, HIV/AIDS stigma, and the breakdown of the ʻohana's unconditional support. Until the 1996 advent of HIV-resistant drug combinations, an HIV diagnosis was a virtual death sentence and those diagnosed required even greater understanding. Sami's mother Debra Akuna recounts, "When I heard about it that's the first thing that I thought . . . gosh, I'm going to lose my son soon." When Debra recalls asking Sami if he's taking their medicine, she reports that Sami only answered with a short "Yes." The terse response indicates that HIV support and reassurance is hard to come by, either because of the lack of communication about being HIV-positive or because of a complicated heterosexist family history. Debra admits, "My ex . . . he called Sami fag a lot when he was a child. . . . I mean, he was very abusive. He was very abusive to my family and myself. So when Sami came out for me, it was no big thing."[40] The childhood suppression of being māhū also suppresses Sami's ability to trust their family with news of their HIV status that ended in AIDS and death for most during the early 1990s.

However, Sami does show appreciation for both family and friendly support in their life through their drag performance choreography. One Honolulu bar dance practice scene is particularly telling. Moving to a slow beat in billowy white shorts and shirt, Sami practices choreography with slow, ritualistic dance steps on stage while many behind them silently follow their lead. They explain that the people walking behind them represent "the support of my friends and my family and how they help me, you know, stay on my path of life."[41] For Sami, drag is a key component of their healing as an HIV-positive person. For Teves, Cocoa Chandelier both offers "a performance of aloha . . . that can be recognized by other Kānaka Maoli and locals," and "asserts her Hawaiian indigeneity" by masterminding the critiques of cultural appropriations of aloha.[42] Sami later shares that they pray every day for their family to accept and understand them and that they look forward to sharing that understanding with newer generations to come. However, for those who miss "the path of life" by chance or by poor choices, death awaits. Sami later details the queer hate crime murder of "Ian," who went off with a particularly "shady" character from a gay bar. Debra Akuna warns that homophobia in Hawaiʻi is very dangerous: "I give a lot of positive energy to my children. I am afraid."[43] While Debra shows aloha for Sami, the kūpuna's aloha for the māhū is clearly lacking in a context of 2001 anti-LGBTQ hate crimes and AIDS-phobia.

In the 2001 *Ke Kulana He Mahu* film, the Reverend Darrow Aiona explains how māhū are traditionally integral to all Kānaka Maoli life:

> Nobody was discriminated against. It was all a family. . . . That's what the ʻohana was. . . . That's what aloha spirit is. . . . Family, that's what ʻohana means. What does the word ʻohana come from? It comes from the taro, the ʻohā. When you break that down, the taro has many shoots. It's strong . . . But even the word hā is breath, breath of life. . . . Religious-wise, breath . . . hā is very important. . . . That word is encompassed in . . . ʻohā, ʻohana, aloha. So hā is very important, breath, but that breath is shared.[44]

Here Aiona keeps to the teachings of the kūpuna, resisting the internal colonization in which the historically honored māhū now face internal discrimination from their own family, a situation worsened by HIV/AIDS stigma.

Conclusion

While many film analyses primarily look at dialogue, this chapter also works to make central the Hawaiian spatiality of the western direction through a trans-Indigenous application of Turtle Island directional concern for the west that is not central to current Kānaka Maoli media interpretation, though briefly mentioned by Brown. In doing so, it hopes to refract from afar in a method distinct from Kumu Hina's sense of moʻolelo ea, which includes a story's sovereign "genealogies, spirits, and relationships to specific places and peoples."[45] As a Kānaka Maoli, Kumu Hina related place-based moʻolelo ea and aloha throughout her three media, *Ke Kulana He Mahu* (2001), *Kumu Hina* (2014), and "Kapaemahu" (2020). In this limited western directional reading, *Kumu Hina* exemplifies the aloha for the ancestors who are known traditionally for their homokana path of Kānaloa also linked with Hina, femininity, and sunset in the west. At the charter school, the renowned māhū teaches Kānaka Maoli boys, girls, and those in the middle with aloha as they learn to reconnect with the Hawaiian hula, mele, and language of their kūpuna. Finally, the east–west path illuminates a theme of healing present in *Ke Kulana He Mahu* (2001) and "Kapaemahu" as māhū heal with aloha in ancient, early colonial, and modern HIV/AIDS contexts. However, the Kānaka Maoli directionality in which the ocean can be more easily found in all directions from the islands differs from that of the many on the western edge of Turtle Island for whom the ocean only lies to the west and who traditionally never access the north, east, and south sides of Turtle Island. If anything, Kumu Hina's films are most oriented to the south in their retelling of ancestral journeys to Hawaiʻi from the South Pacific centuries ago.

4

NORTH

Healing Kamloops with Two-Spirit and Nêhiyawak Jingle Dress Video

This northern fourth chapter completes the circle that began with the east in chapter 1. It will begin with northern direction teachings from Stoney Nakoda, Pelican Lake Cree, and Saddle Lake Cree perspectives. The Nêhiyawak (Plains Cree) northern teachings of elders and healing especially help interpret the two-spirit media in which intersect issues of abuse, gendercide, and genocide that mark the 215+ graves reported by Tk'emlúps te Secwépemc First Nation at the Kamloops Indian Residential School in 2021.[1] Directed by Frog Lake Cree Sharon Desjarlais, "First Stories—Two Spirited" celebrates the elders' spiritual guidance of a Stoney Nakoda two-spirit Jingle Dress dancer to participate in the annual Kamloops Powwow despite community resistance. The film is a special testimony of cultural and two-spirit resilience given the powwow's location at Kamloops. The chapter then covers the two-spirit dance by Woods Cree choreographer René Highway and his Cree nephew actor Billy Merasty within a context of two-spirit-phobia and healing from residential school abuses. Next, the Teslin Tlingit elder and director Duane Gastant' Aucoin offers a prayer for the Kamloops children in a 2021 video. As a longtime representative for 2SLGBTQIA+ issues, Aucoin also shares digital insights on two-spirit suppression and sexual abuse in Indian residential schools and visions for healing from that gendered and cultural violence. While Aucoin's two-spirit Tlingit film "My Own Private Lower Post" offers Raven story healing from the intergenerational trauma of Canada's Indian residential school program, his other media also demonstrate Teslin Tlingit two-spirit well-being.

Both Stoney Nakoda and the Nêhiyawak people connect directionality with the sacred peaks of the Rocky Mountains bordering what is now claimed as British Columbia and Alberta in settler-colonial mapping. In restoring treaty 7 land rights in Alberta, Chief John Snow documented his Stoney Nakoda people's larger ancestral presence "along the foothills out onto the prairies to east and deep into the Rocky Mountain country to the west," including Rocky Mountain regions now largely encompassed by the Banff and Jasper National Parks. He also recalled that a spiritual leader of a "vision quest" sacred pipe ceremony in the Rocky Mountains "would offer a prayer using the sacred pipe and offer it in a circular manner beginning in the east (from where the sun rises), then to the south, then to the west, and concluding by holding the stem of the pipe toward the north."[2] The Nêhiyawak whom Snow mentions as neighbors and sometimes adversaries also connected to sacred mountains in the Rocky Mountains with their own pipe ceremonies.

Nêhiyawak and Two-Spirit Kamloops Healing

In two videos, the medical doctor James Makokis (Saddle Lake Cree Nation) connects the pipe direction of the north with sacred mountains in the Rockies. In the larger version of the video, "Keynote: Two-Spirit Rites of Passage" from Summit 2019: Queering Healthcare Access and Accessibility held in Vancouver, Makokis shared a slide of a mountain as a one of the "Nehiyô spiritual teachers, Kiskwekanskwew—Tornado/Happy Woman," related to the northern pipe direction and a caretaker of two-spirit people.[3] This mountain comes up again in the video "The Indigenous Doctor Helping Trans Youth," as Makokis sits in his medical office on the reserve with a Nehiyô transmasculine patient Alec who had reached a point of a suicide attempt as a result of a lack of transgender support. Makokis goes beyond simply prescribing testosterone to Alec. He also teaches him about the two-spirit landscape within Nêhiyawak culture. Motioning to a picture of a Kiskwekanskwew's mountain's face hanging on the wall by his office computer, Makokis explains to Alec and Alec's mother Janet Whitstone, "This mountain, you see there? There's a face in there. This is one of the spirits that helps to look after two-spirit people, and also men. Our people always accepted diversity. That's why these places are so important because Creator wrote those on the land for us and we can read them." This link back to the northern pipe direction and Kiskwekanskwew's role in supporting two-spirit people is an important aspect of healing the erasure of two-spirit people in residential schools. The oral tradition surrounding two-spirit sacred places that Makokis shares is a gift from the Nêhiyawak elders, the northern direction, and part of the cultural knowledge that complements the Western medical hormone treatment that he is giving to the trans youth. Outside a two-spirit family meeting held later in a tipi, Makokis instructs Alec about how to "smudge" the pipe over a fire by demonstrating how to turn it "always going clockwise" as part of Nêhiyawak ceremonial protocols.[4] In doing so, Makokis resists limiting this task to biological men, earlier noting how the two-spirit way that was hidden when settler-colonial institutions obscured Indigenous multigender acceptance is now returning out to the open.

Across the Plains Cree lands to Saskatchewan, Nehiyô elder Mary Lee (Pelican Lake Nation) shares teachings about the east, south, and west, concluding, "we'll finish in the northern direction, which is our journey . . . as older people in that direction."[5] Also of Makokis's Saddle Lake Cree Nation, Francis Whiskeyjack offers a similar teaching to Lee's medicine wheel progression with babies in the east, youth in the south, adults in the west, and elders in the north.[6] This chapter returns to the northern direction of elders in order to better understand two-spirit media and the healing from Indian residential school repressions, most prominently exemplified in world news by the Kamloops reporting. Although writing in a U.S. and Native American context, Alicia Carroll's statement on two-spirit repression in boarding schools broadly applies to the Canada's residential schools: "Colonial school policies and procedures imposed an alien heteropatriarchal Euro-American sex/gender binary construct onto Native students to dismantle Indigenous social structures, including matriarchy, relationality, communalism, and expansive, multiple, or non-binary gender systems."[7] The repression of two-spirit genders was part of the larger repression of all Indigenous languages, dancing, and beliefs in the Christian-run residential schools of the 1800s and 1900s. Although historical trauma of the Indian residential schools transmits across generations, it is the elders of the late 1800s to the mid-1900s featured in this chapter's videos who directly experienced this trauma as the schools were largely phased out in the decade after the Canadian government, and eventually more First Nations, took control of those institutions en masse in 1969. The Truth and Reconciliation Commission of Canada reports that Indian Affairs then operationalized its plans for an "integration policy" in which Indigenous children would find schooling while living with their families and going to "provincial or territorial schools."[8] While most Indigenous students went home, their memory of the place of two-spirit people within their kinship was altered and often erased. To understand gendercide of two-spirit people that took place in these religious and government institutions is part of the path of healing that many two-spirit people like Rodney "Geeyo" Poucette (Stoney Nakoda Nation) are sharing in their media presence through films like "First Stories—Two Spirited."

Filmed at and around the Kamloops Indian Residential School, the six-minute 2007 "Two Spirited" short produced within the National Film Board of Canada's First Stories series features a male-bodied Jingle Dress Dance that certainly would not have been allowed during the early Catholic maintenance of that school. Elders play an important role in "First Stories—Two Spirited," directed by Frog Lake Cree Sharon Desjarlais and starring Geeyo Poucette. In the short film, Geeyo narrates being stripped of his Jingle Dress prize at the 2001 Kamloops Powwow when judges were made aware that he was a "guy" in a "women's category: Jingle Dress." The loss is deep for Geeyo, and he begins to stray from healthy living. Says the elder Valentina Fox (Stoney Nakoda) in the film, "But all he was doing at that dance, when he was dancing, jingle dancing . . . was honoring the female spirit in him. There's nothing wrong with him dancing as a jingle dancer."[9] Geeyo recalls the shame he felt when his championship title was revoked at Kamloops and how he began to doubt his ability to dance as a two-spirit person. This self-doubt lasted for years. But in the 2007 film he recalls, "My grandma told me a whole bunch of stories about two-spirited people way back in the past. Some two-spirited people became holy people. Two-spirited people was a blessing for the people. They were the persons . . . who look after for the camps and, and I guess back then two-spirited people . . . were respectable people." This grandmother's teaching about the traditional positive value and sacred roles of two-spirit peoples is important because it motivates Geeyo to keep dancing. A teacher of Nakoda language, Fox also affirms, "We all had names for our two-spirited people. We call them Weeyantay for a male and Weechuntay for a female."[10] Fortunately for Geeyo, enough oral tradition from his Stoney Nakoda elders survived to ultimately help him to affirm his place as a two-spirit Jingle Dress dancer at Kamloops Powwow.

Encouragement from elders in dreams and support from living elders convinces Geeyo to return to dance the Jingle Dress category once again

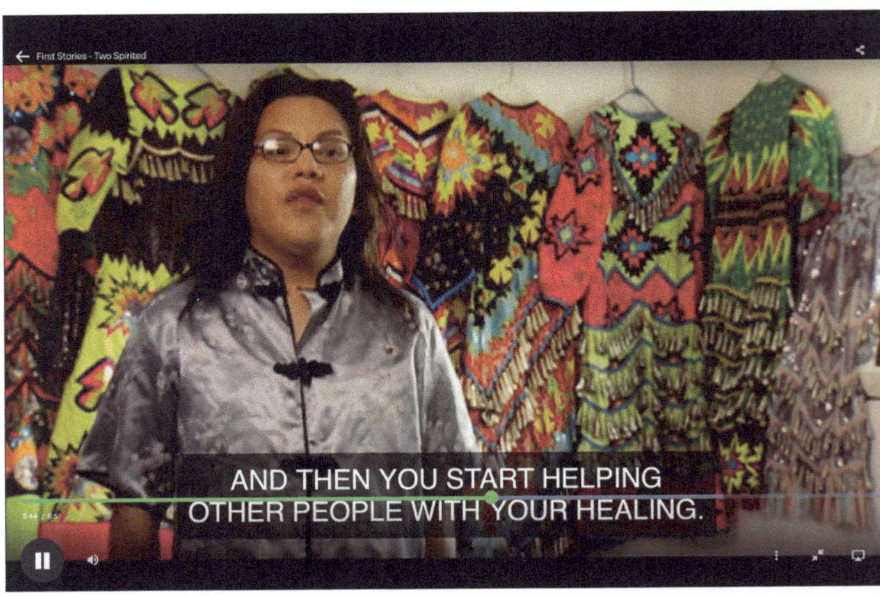

Figure 8 Geeyo's dream of elder Jingle Dress dancers from "First Stories—Two Spirited" (2007) directed by Sharon Desjarlais.

at Kamloops five years later. Geeyo shares a dream of elders from the spirit world who direct him to return to his Jingle Dress dancing. He recalls:

> In my dream . . . it was this big powwow and these two older Jingle Dress dancers came up. They told me that the creator put you on this earth to use that gift. They told me that I was going into the wrong path and then they told me that if you dance to this, you're going to be healing yourself. And then she said . . . when you start healing yourself . . . then you start helping other people with your healing.[11]

What the dream elder said is proven true in the film. Toward restoring himself with good health and spirits, Geeyo kept up with the dancing and helped his younger relatives to dance too. In film, Geeyo introduces two adolescent girls, Tomasina Poucette and Trish Chiniki, to whom he has taught the Jingle Dress for many years. They share that Geeyo has taught them the "jingle dress . . . the sewing, and the healing" that come along with real cultural responsibilities as they dance for others.[12] That Geeyo received the elders' spiritual guidance surrounding the Jingle Dress relates the creation of the Jingle Dress Dance over a century ago, as several people including "Maggie Wilson, a Scots-Cree visionary," at Manitou Rapids and especially "Maggie White" of the White Fish Bay Ojibwa helped originate the Jingle Dress Dance that came as a result of dreams and visions.[13] Led by his dreams, the film ends with Geeyo returning to Kamloops as a Jingle Dress dancer entering the arena. He recalls the experience at the film's conclusion, saying, "I guess six years ago after that incident happened, I guess half of my spirit didn't come home with me. And so last night when I walked into the arena, I called my spirit and I told, I told my spirit that I was back. . . . I felt happy that I came back here and danced." The gendered shaming that Geeyo experienced at Kamloops is healed by his return to dance there and to call back his missing spirit in that Kamloops arena. In the end, Desjarlais shows Geeyo sewing a purple and green Jingle Dress to represent luck and healing, explaining, "I'm preparing for my healing journey for the future."[14] Through listening to his elders, Geeyo affirmed two-spirit hope for the future at Kamloops Powwow.

While Desjarlais consciously made an uplifting short film, many will now also view the film and its quick shots of the Kamloops Indian Residential School against the viral news reports of the 215-plus burials there in May 2021. In the film, Valentina Fox appears and observes, "Since contact we have learned to judge and condemn our two-spirited people," as a cut from Fox shows a photo of a redbrick building engraved with the words "Kamloops

Indian Residential School A.D. 1923."[15] Although there is no further commentary, Desjarlais gives this clear visual cue that Indian residential schools were central in teaching this judgment and condemnation of two-spirit people. At the time of the film's making in 2007, acknowledgment of the cultural genocide perpetrated by the Indian residential school system was already circulating, with accounts of child deaths, molestation, and chronic negligence documented at Kamloops by many survivors. Indigenous dances, along with singing and language, were abusively prohibited at Kamloops during the heyday of its 1890–1978 history.[16] So it is with this larger narrative that audiences can appreciate the incredible resilience of Geeyo as a Stoney Nakoda Jingle Dress dancer.

Without a doubt, the major responsibility of healing at Kamloops lies with the Tk'emlúps te Secwépemc Nation, whose mission statement reads, "To promote & ensure the physical, mental, emotional and spiritual well-being of our people and community."[17] The Tk'emlúps te Secwépemc Nation has long used the old residential school to teach Indigenous language and culture, reclaiming the space on their own land. It is they who reported the 215-plus "Le Estcwicwéy̓ (the Missing)," have fielded Indigenous and international inquiries, and built "a Healing House for Survivors and intergenerational Survivors."[18] It is their political leadership of Kúkpi7 (Chief) Rosanne Casimir who stated "that with the goal of fostering healing and reconciliation and countering targeted skepticism and denial, Tk'emlúps chose to work with Catholics and allow Church leaders to publicly acknowledge past wrongs, particularly arising from the Catholic Church's role in administering many of the Residential Schools."[19] It was from within the Tk'emlúps te Secwépemc Nation that the Kamloops Powwow bylaws specifying "correct gender" were changed in 2022 to allow for more Indigenous 2SLGBTQIA+ participation, thanks to Kamloops Powwow Society president Deyla Daniels and her two-spirit brother Jeffrey McNeil-Seymour.[20] In fact, McNeil-Seymour was honored at the 2022 powwow before a two-spirit round dance special among other residential school survivors and two-spirit people, the grand entry prominently including the "Every Child Matters" flag and a 2SLGBTQIA+ flag. Kukpi7 Doug Thomas of Splatsin First Nation carried the 2SLGBTQIA+ flag and said, "When I mentioned I wanted to carry the flag to support not just my family but every Two-Spirit person, the chiefs were all on board."[21] Years before he transitioned to the spirit world in June 2023 after battling cancer, McNeil-Seymour shared his concerns for his nation's environment and for two-spirit people at a TED Talk. Speaking on the importance of water sovereignty and the collapse of the salmon due to climate change, he said:

> Our social justice initiatives as two-spirit people matter just as much as the ability to get married and to adopt children. . . . Our protection of our lands and our waters and our sovereignty are just as important. . . . Two-spirit youth in this country are the most at risk of colonialism, the most at risk of homelessness, are the most at risk of substance misuse, and they're also the most at risk of committing suicide. These children matter.[22]

Here McNeil-Seymour explains that the national LGBTQI2+ campaigns for marriage rights and adoption rights do not eclipse the particular importance of two-spirit peoples whose issues of sovereignty complicate the common LGBTQI2+ issues of homelessness and suicide.

While McNeil-Seymour's two-spirit activism was key in changing Kamloops culture, Indigenous powwow guests on the Tk'emlúps te Secwépemc Nation land like Geeyo also have their part to play in healing the larger two-spirit/LGBTQI+ powwow community. The Christian-based two-spirit-phobia that Geeyo experienced and transcended at Kamloops showed that there is still much healing to do in terms of gender, culture, and sexuality in the larger Indigenous community. Other youth community activists also had impact in pushing the issue of gender-inclusivity at Kamloops. As a two-spirit winkte and Cree TikTok creator with more than 230,000 followers, Kairyn Potts (Alexis Nakota Nation) has raised popular awareness around changing this Kamloops gender regalia rule. The pressure to change came from inside and outside of Tk'emlúps te Secwépemc Nation. At a Trans Summit talk, Kairyn shared oral traditions surrounding the winkte from Dakota/Cree Paulette Petra of the Muscowpetung First Nation about the word "winkte" coming from the "in-between" space of the bison's hump that originally was a gift from Wakan to help keep the bison's coat off the ground.[23] This in-between space represents the in-between gendered spaces that winktes also occupy. Kairyn also loosely translated the meaning of winkte or wiyankte as "somebody who moves through the world like a woman."[24] Youth two-spirit advocates like Potts who operate between genders are grounded in oral traditions and modern technologies and build upon the efforts of those like Geeyo and McNeil-Seymour to change the two-spirit-phobia at Kamloops and internationally.

Plains Cree Healing from Residential Schools

Desjarlais, of course, was not the first Cree to make a film that references two-spirit dance and healing in the context of the Indian residential schools.

Métis June Scudeler makes important interventions in this direction, documenting the life, video record, and choreography of gay Woods Cree René Highway in the film *New Song . . . New Dance* (1988). She writes, "While key moments in the performance address sexuality and abuse, *New Song . . . New Dance* uses humour and Woods Cree traditions to show Highway's mamâhtâwisiwin." While the filmed *New Song . . . New Dance* performance intimates the sexual abuse at residential schools, it also transcends it by returning to the source of Indigenous life and movement and celebrating homoerotism among the male dancers. Scudeler translates "mamâhtâwisiwin" from Cree as "spiritual power, talent, and magic," and she also recounts an early experience that Highway had of encountering a running migration of caribou in which he may have acquired that mamâhtâwisiwin before entering into the captivity of the Indian residential school system. Highway once wrote, "It was an overwhelming feeling to watch this mass of thundering hooves and flashing antlers rush past me. . . . This energy seemed to stir something within me. . . . The energy I had seen and felt was, and still is, within me."[25] Scudeler argues that this reindeer medicine is part of what motivates Highway to dance and relate the power of reindeer bodies with human dancing bodies that can express two-spirit being.

Mohawk Shelley Niro (Mohawks of the Bay of Quinte First Nation) directed *Honey Moccasin* (1998) featuring a male-bodied two-spirit Jingle Dress dancer character named Zachary John, played by Billy Merasty, Cree, the queer nephew of René Highway. In the film, Merasty dances in stolen Jingle Dress regalia in a basement, which functions as the two-spirit "closet." While Niro's two-spirit representation is sympathetic, the fact remains that the two-spirit character is a thief and the antagonist of the campy film. Zachary's motivation for stealing seems to be to wear women's regalia in secret. In a key scene, Zachary steals away from his Inukshuk Café, dons a Jingle Dress, and says to his reflection in a dirty mirror, "I'd drive all the men wild if I was a woman." Turning on a tape recording of powwow music, he furiously dances with feather fan before abruptly stopping to address an invisible gentleman, saying, "No sir, I do not go into strange tents with strange men." He then takes Polaroids of himself in the regalia with big pouting lips, to the protagonist detective Honey Moccasin's (Tantoo Cardinal, Cree/Métis) laughter outside as she sits viewing his exaggerated performance of femininity.[26] The collection of selfies posted to the wall recall the basement selfies of the white cross-dressing serial killer Jame "Buffalo Bill" Gumb (Ted Levine) in the transphobic 1991 *Silence of the Lambs*. The selfies in both films are a desperate attempt at representation in a world in which binary cisgender expression is the norm and transgender expression mostly illegal or taboo. They also index a level of self-obsession that leads to violence. In Zachary's case, however, his campy attempt to stab and kill Honey Moccasin to avoid public exposure is comedically foiled. The elders in the fictional Grand Pine Reserve require Zachary to go on TV and return the regalia to the proper owners, once Honey Moccasin catches him in the act of Jingle Dress dancing in all the stolen regalia. Honey Moccasin announces, "Zack here is giving out the stolen articles part of the penalty imposed by the elders and if this shirt is yours call us."[27] Lacking from *Honey Moccasin* are the serious intention to heal that Geeyo represents as well as the presence of elders to say that two-spirit Jingle Dress is culturally appropriate. The lack of two-spirit support from elders has led Zachary to take matters into his own hands, though underground and illegally.

There are two Indigenous films within the main *Honey Moccasin* film that feature key moments of northern direction visuals from Mohawk, Delaware, and Cree perspectives, and with two-spirit connections. The first film within a film is called "Fever," and its fictional director is Mabel Moccasin (Florene Belmore, Métis), daughter of Honey Moccasin. In that short film, Mabel sings, "When you put your arms around me, you give me fever," with her head protruding from a tipi while historical black-and-white images of nuns holding stolen Indigenous children in Indian residential schools are screened across her tipi body.[28] Niro and Monani also report that "there are quick shots of a person with smallpox" at this line as well.[29] The original sultry "Fever" penned by Black Americans Eddie Cooley and Otis Blackwell and popularized by white pop legend Peggy Lee changes meaning from that of sexual excitement to that of an Indigenous indictment, recalling the findings that the Kamloops school's shoddy conditions and negligent care led to mass deaths by various fevers,[30] and that deadly epidemics were originally brought to the Americas by Catholic and Christian white colonial settlers. While there is never a direct connection of Zachary's two-spirit isolation and the queerphobic legacy of the residential schools made in dialogue, the connection exists as the first short film speaks to the second film on urban Indigenous and two-spirit alienation. This rejection of two-spirit people in *Honey Moccasin* is an unspoken result of the very Indian residential schools that forced Christian cis-heteropatriarchy onto Indigenous children and forbade two-spirit genders from being supported as the generations went forward.[31]

In *Honey Moccasin* a second film within a film restores Zachary's standing as a two-spirit protagonist and a part of the cinematic Grand Pine Reserve community.[32] Screened at Honey Moccasin's bar a year after the stolen regalia fiasco, Mabel Moccasin introduces the film, saying, "The piece was developed through the words of Daniel David Moses," as the two-spirit Delaware poet Moses (Six Nations of the Grand River) stands and tips his hat to the audience, acknowledging his poem "Inukshuk."[33] The poem that is read by Honey Moccasin as the only dialogue of the film refers to inukshuk, piled stones often made to look human in the Arctic regions. In the short film, Zachary become fused in meaning with the inukshuk as he stands and spreads his arms and legs wide like the stone figure inukshuk shown just before him. The poem details the invasion of northern inukshuk space by settler-colonial narrative from the south of Canada where most settlements are. Zachary's lonely walk through the black and white space of Toronto indicates that the solitude of the inukshuk in this case could also refer to Zachary's time living off the reserve in the town Pluto, which sounds as cold and distant as the Arctic. Catherine Higginson notes the "somber" and oppressive feel of that Toronto cityscape that features Zachary looking out from behind bars and a settler-colonial statue of the "Mohawk chief Joseph Brant (Thayendanegea)."[34] One section of the poem and film could also have eerie homoerotic connotations. Honey Moccasin poetically narrates, "They keep singing about / the Great Blue Whale the world / is, how it swims through space / having nightmares about / hunters who only hunt their brothers / each after the other's snow-white face. / How beautiful frozen flesh is! Like ivory, / like carved bone, like the light / of Polaris in hand. / So it goes on and on, / the hunting refrain. Dead / silence would be better, / the Pole Star overhead."[35]

Given that it is Zachary's two-spirit body that moves the film, the line "hunters who only hunt their brothers" could have a homoerotic subtext of gay cruising for sex in urban areas such as those in which Zachary is first shown. It could also refer to white men who kill each other and spread this violence in the Indigenous Artic, where Indigenous men would appear frozen and white in the icy environment when dead. "The Pole Star overhead" would only appear to be so in the very far northern polar regions, as the North Star usually appears to the north of most viewers in the Northern Hemisphere. The line "Dead / silence would be better" refers to the peace before settler ideologies and language begin to predominate even in the northern reaches of Canada and the Indigenous nations there. When this last line is read, Niro points the camera up toward the blue sky and a bare winter tree and spins the camera around counterclockwise so that it replicates the counterclockwise rotation of sky around the North Star Polaris when viewed from the polar region. As the main film figure, Zachary's tie with the inukshuk is one that validates his indigeneity, even as he wanders the Toronto streets, like the migrating geese briefly shown. While Zachary is originally rejected by the community for being an outsider and for being two-spirit, the filmic representation as integral to indigeneity restores Zachary's place in the community, even after stealing the regalia. Wearing earrings and red lipstick, Zachary hugs his father after the film ends as a sign of family and community support for Zachary as a two-spirit person and community member who has survived the ongoing queerphobic, anti-Indigenous residential school alienations, and deadly histories that Kamloops and other Indian residential schools have come to represent in Canada and worldwide.

Two-Spirit Teslin Film and Residential Schools

For over a decade, Duane Gastant' Aucoin has been both the Yanyeidi executive councilor of the Teslin Tlingit Council and a media spokesperson for the two-spirit/queer Indigenous community. The current chair and Yukon representative, Assembly of First Nations 2SLGBTQIA+ Council, Aucoin mentioned the two-spirit hate crime murder of Dolan Badger and a two-spirit history of residential schools. He shared:

> The Crown and the churches did a very good job of brainwashing our people and indoctrinating our people in intolerance and hate. When I was gay bashed, it was by other indigenous people, but where did they learn that from? They learned that in the residential schools when we had the priests telling that the two-spirit people are evil and then they'd be raping the kids at night. So, our people have got it mixed up. It's through trauma, misunderstanding of and a forgetting of what it means to be two-spirit. I think our people are remembering that once more.[36]

When the 2021 news of the 215 burials was released by the Tk̓emlúps te Secwépemc Council to worldwide Anglophone reception,[37] many Indigenous people also began the healing process of uncovering their own local Indian residential school histories and survivors. Living in Ontario at the time while taking care of his Acadian French Canadian father Cyril Aucoin, Duane Gastant' Aucoin (Teslin Tlingit First Nation) created his own short "Tlingit Prayer Song" video, filmed on his cell phone, to aid in this process. First thanking the Algonquin peoples on whose land he is standing, he recounts that his mother was also a survivor of the Indian residential school system and names his grandfather's Deisheetaan (Split Tail Beaver) Clan from Teslin. Then he shares, "When I heard the news today of those over two hundred children and babies found in the Kamloops residential school, it broke my heart, but didn't surprise me because we as First Nations we've heard these stories of babies and children being buried in every residential school. So, I thought I'd come down here to the river with the cedar bow and say prayer that they rest in peace, pray for their families, pray for their people, that we all can have some healing."[38] In the video, Duane locates himself on the land holding a cedar branch by the river. He sings his prayer in four directions, each time turning to face a new direction as each verse is sung. Beginning in the east and ending in the north, he added the text words in translation below his chest with the directions that he faces added above his Wolf crest on his headdress. The prayer cycle is coupled with directions each time he turns to face a new direction: "Spirits of the East: Our Father, My master, Daakeeaankowu," "Spirits of the South: Have pity on us, Daakeeaankowu," "Spirits of the West: Help us, Daakeeaankowu," and "Spirits of the North: Thank you, Daakeeaankowu" (fig. 9).[39]

Figure 9 Duane Gastant' Aucoin's "Spirits of the North" prayer, from "Tlingit Prayer Song" (2021), directed by Duane Gastant' Aucoin.

This same Teslin Tlingit song prayer in his own English translation from another video, "2-Spirit Blessings," is very similar: "Our father, our leader, Have pity on us. Come to help us. Thank you for all that you've done for us."[40] The last northern direction, thanks, is an affirmation of the life that is already gifted to the world and is a balance to the act of asking for something more. In "2-Spirit Blessings," Aucoin encourages two-spirit people to be honored for being mediators, "to be a peacemaker and to help bridge communities and bring them together."[41] He again sings the prayer as a way to uplift the two-spirit community. Acknowledging the 2011 passing of his Yanyeidi mother, Vicky Bob, he again recalls the historical trauma he faced as a two-spirit person in which the Christian religions imposed "beliefs . . . values that called us evil as two-spirits, evil and sinful and we were punished and persecuted for it and many of us just learned to be quiet and hide it. . . . Each of our communities has beautiful teachings on how us two-spirits fit within the community and we're once again realizing that and we're taking a role in our community."[42] He ends this video with the same blessing ending in "Gunalcheesh ho ho," though this time he does not turn directions as he does in "My Own Private Lower Post."

Aucoin begins his 2009 "My Own Private Lower Post" video with his own drumming and singing voice. This beginning marks the high visual, theological, and erotic sovereignty value of the film, as the entire cast and crew is Teslin Tlingit, and the final Raven story is acted out entirely in Teslin Tlingit by Aucoin, who identifies as two-spirit in the film. When the richness of Aucoin's Tlingit singing stops the film's opening, it marks the cultural interruption in Tlingit narrative and language use that occurred through the restriction of Tlingit language in residential schools. In this silence, black-and-white photographic images of Indigenous residential schoolchildren begin to fade in and out as Canadian Prime Minister Stephen Harper stridently states, "Mr. Speaker, I stand before you today to offer an apology to former students of Indian residential schools. . . . These institutions gave rise to abuse or neglect and were inadequately controlled, and we apologize for failing to protect you."[43] This apology, formally offered by Harper in 2008, was a cornerstone of the Settlement Agreement and the Indian Residential Schools Truth and Reconciliation Commission that attempted to address cultural genocide and Indigenous child abuse. However, two-spirit scholar Dian Million (Tanana Athabaskan) notes how the settler-colonial state rhetorically situates Indigenous people as officially recognized "victims" of a failed past state policy in order to increase Indigenous dependency upon the settler state's anti-Indigenous therapeutic and policing programs as the mode of therapy, noting Harper's choice to battle the domestic violence that resulted from residential school trauma by increasing state police and state social work centers while defunding Indigenous women's programs to serve their own communities of abused women.[44] Even so, this moment was a victory for many Indian residential school survivors such as Chief Robert Joseph of the Gwawaenuk First Nation, who explained that "when the apology came, I was so happy, so liberated; I suddenly recognized that it wasn't our fault these misconstrued policies that were intended to destroy our Indianness. When you discover that attempt, then you're not ashamed anymore."[45] This moment of apology is an Indigenous victory that Aucoin includes with emotional triumph.

In "My Own Private Lower Post," Aucoin travels with his mother Vicky Bob to the now-defunct Lower Post Indian Residential School to make peace with her culturally and physically abusive school and work experiences there. Once back home at Teslin, both smudge with protective sage and sing a prayer in Tlingit before discussing the difficult Catholic Lower Post memories that include the normalization of physical abuse that led to an abusive marriage to a French Acadian Canadian. She tearfully narrates her own subsequent alcoholism, her grief due to the death of a child who was injured during delivery, and her eventual sobriety, apologizing for her behavior as a mother. After Aucoin and his mother enter the mother's Teslin home similarly dressed in blue jeans, button-down shirt, and distinctive embroidered and shell-beaded vests with the highlighted Wolf crest, Aucoin lights sage on an abalone shell and explains, "Ha Kus Teyea, Our Tlingit Way, has the medicines that will cleanse and protect us." As both begin to bless themselves with the smoke, he explains, "We smudge with sage to purify our spirits and to lift our spirits up to the spirit world. We sing our song so our voices will be heard in a good way. The truth needs a safe place to be heard." Both Aucoin and Bob smudge and pray with the spirit to help with the speaking and healing of traumas. As Aucoin sings, both he and his mother face east and then turn clockwise three times to the next direction as Aucoin completes the song and the scene fades to black.[46] This is the same sung prayer as in the "Tlingit Prayer Song" and "2-Spirit Blessings" videos, translated as "Our father, our leader / have pity on us / come to help us / thank you for all that you've done for us," and ending with "Gunalcheesh ho ho." To follow Tlingit healing protocol before looking through the potentially triggering black-and-white family photographs of Lower Post is significant. It demonstrates how "Ha Kus Teyea, Our Way" is at work decolonizing and healing Aucoin's family and community. Reencountering the historical trauma of domestic violence and alcoholism could retraumatize Aucoin, his mother, and the audience who watches. For a Tlingit and Indigenous audience especially, this visual rhetoric of singing, smudging, and finding safe spaces in confronting residential school experiences is an important reminder of how to begin to safely heal from historical traumas. In his "Truth and Reconciliation" essay, Aucoin expresses how he was angry at his mother most of his life because he never understood how residential school history and policy shaped her hurtful behavior. Aucoin then cites his own drinking and lack of parenting skills with his male partner as a direct result of the abuses that were normalized at Lower Post Indian Residential School, exemplifying how historical trauma travels across generations. In the end, Aucoin thanks his now sober mother for trying as best she could to parent, and returns to the idea of facing the four directions to improve parenting, writing "Parents, the most important thing we can say to our kids is within four directions. 1) I did my best for you. 2) I made mistakes. 3) I'm sorry. 4) I love you."[47]

To make the point clear about Tlingit health, visual, and linguistic sovereignty, the conclusion of the film is a transformative and genderqueer Raven story of creation that is performed in Tlingit with English subtitles. Aucoin plays the lead role Nashakaankowu as he retells the release of the sun, moon, and stars by Raven. Raven is played by the two-spirit ally and celebrated performer Sharon Shorty (Teslin Tlingit First Nation), who is herself of the Teslin Tlingit Kùkhhittàn (Raven Child) Clan, further establishing the importance of clan-based knowledge and how gender and species transformations are alive and well within Tlingit culture as originally taught by Raven. In the Raven story, the world begins in darkness and shadows, "as dark as the wings of the Raven himself," narrates Aucoin as he spreads his arms out like Raven wings in a shot above Teslin Lake. As he takes on the role of the Tlingit leader Nashakaankowu, he explains that Raven desires the sun, moon, and stars and that Nashakaankowu kept them in boxes as great treasures. In the story, Raven transforms into a spruce needle, is ingested by Nashakaankowu's daughter, and is born nine days later as a fast-growing human child. The Raven-grandchild receives the treasured three boxes only after crying for them incessantly. The following English subtitles accompany Aucoin's completely Teslin Tlingit–language narrative of what happens once Raven freed the stars, moon, and sun from their boxes into the sky:

> Raven regained his true form and flew away happy.
> . . . Nashakaankowu was sad over what he lost.
> . . . But then a ray of light shone down on him. He felt its
> warmth and it felt
> good.
> And, he finally accepted and understood.

Aucoin concludes that just as Raven improved the world by releasing the luminaries that were once locked away in boxes, so must residential school survivors share their once-hidden stories to heal their respective nations and clans. He prefaces the story saying, "The legend of Raven stealing the sun teaches me something new every time. Like Raven, I was tired of the darkness. And like Nashakaankowu, I didn't want to share my light. But in the end, the box is now open and everything is made clear. My hope is that Raven's light will shine down upon you, too."[48] Both Raven and residential school stories tell of recovery after incredible theft. Here Aucoin shows how these stories can shift in meaning depending upon one's perspective, as Lawrence Gross would predict about the Indigenous rhetorical reception of Indigenous stories.[49]

Northern Cheyenne Two-Spirits in "The Roof"

In the fifteen-minute Disney+ Jingle Dress short film "The Roof" by two-spirit Tsitsistas writer W.A.W. Parker (Northern Cheyenne Tribe), Anishinaabe Phoenix Wilson (M'Chigeeng First Nation) plays the part of a youth, Ray, who is sent to his Grandpa Nick's (Wes Studi, Cherokee Nation of Oklahoma) house when they have trouble at school surrounding their gender expression. When Ray doesn't want to talk about their school problems, they challenge their grandfather for criticizing them for leaving school since Nick also left school, saying, "Mom said you ran away from boarding school, and you never talk about it." Nick abruptly leaves in anger. However, after Ray tries on their deceased grandmother's Jingle Dress and rips it, Grandpa Nick invites them to a fire outside. Grandpa Nick explains, "Ke'eehe was hetanémáné'e," that the grandmother was "two-spirit . . . like . . . ," pausing for Ray to fill in the rest. "Like me?" obliges Ray, surprised to find commonality with their ke'eehe, their grandmother, played by Lakota two-spirit icon Beverly Little Thunder (Standing Rock Sioux Tribe).[50] This scene challenges the idea that two-spirit people cannot have children and grandchildren. In fact, Little Thunder's biography proudly details her role as a grandmother, along with the lesbian sexual abuse she experienced by a nun in a Catholic girls' residential school, and overcoming the challenges of rejection for being two-spirit within the Sun Dance of her Lakota community.[51] Grandpa Nick's revelation is a key moment. Bringing up the boarding school trauma, Grandpa Nick tersely explains, "They tried to erase us . . . especially things they didn't know anything about, probably a lot like the kids at your school. I wish you could have met her. I see her in you."[52] This dialogue that privileges family two-spirit traditions over boarding school repressions is a testament to two-spirit resurgence and family support. That the respected Oscar-winning Cherokee actor and elder Wes Studi would lend his talents to the project gives this dialogue and two-spirit affirming message even more weight for a key audience of Native Americans with two-spirit youth relatives.

Figure 10 Grandpa Nick (Wes Studi) drums for two-spirit grandchild Ray's (Phoenix Wilson) Jingle Dress Dance at home on the Northern Cheyenne Reservation in Montana in "The Roof" (2023), directed by Alexander Bocchieri, with screenplay by W.A.W. Parker.

After another day of bonding, both Grandpa Nick and Ray go to a two-spirit powwow. Ray's mother (DeLanna Studi, Cherokee Nation of Oklahoma) brings an amazing yellow Jingle Dress for Ray with a Tsitsistas morning star pattern in white, blue, and pink transgender colors and LGBTQ rainbow ribbon colors on the sleeves and skirt. This morning star is also on the Northern Cheyenne Nation's flag and its presence in the regalia mark it as a national statement of two-spirit, gay, and transgender support. Both the mother and Grandpa Nick embrace Ray once they don the Jingle Dress. Flanked by two-spirit Jingle Dress dancers played by Chiricahua Apache John Sneezy (San Carlos Apache Nation) and Travis "Buffalo Barbie" Goldtooth (Navajo Nation), Ray dances with several Jingle Dress dancers in a "coming-in" ceremony recognizing Ray's special gifts as a two-spirit person. While raising their fan during an honor beat, Ray smiles at Grandpa Nick while dancing and Grandpa Nick smiles back. The final shot of the film shows Grandpa Nick playing a hand drum in front of his house while Ray dances in front of him in their new Jingle Dress. In this shot (fig. 10), Studi faces south with his back to the north in front of his home; Wilson faces the grandfather from the opposite direction. In this way they could be said to be respectively looking at each other from the northern elder and southern youth directions of the medicine wheel. Although Ray is older than a youth of past ages, Ray can still be considered a youth in some contemporary understandings. The coming-in ceremony can mark a transition from youth to adulthood and adult choices in gender identity. Yet, as is so often the case, queer, genderqueer, and trans folks often make the transition into a fully realized adult identity later in life as it may take them time to find the space and support to make that shift. The presence of the two-spirit ke'eehe (grandmother) who built the roof of the house framed in this scene between the two figures is also part of what brings the two to understanding. This scene then marks the elder helping a youth make a transition into a two-spirit adult gender that can still evolve over time. This story shows the full support that an elder can give to a two-spirit youth, and it is an example to the many Indigenous nations of what is possible to counter the two-spirit gendercide instilled in the boarding and residential schools as mentioned in the film dialogue.

Conclusion

The Nêhiyawak northern direction of elders guides this analysis of healing from residential school cis-heterosexism in two-spirit film. "First Stories—Two Spirited" foregrounded the supporting roles of two-spirit Stoney Nakoda peoples via Geeyo's grandma, the dream elders, and the elder Valentina Fox. Highway's two-spirit dance showed holding onto the mamâhtâwisiwin power that gave life to his Cree people from the earliest times, a power gifted from the reindeer that he retained even through residential school abuses. René Highway was elder and uncle to Billy Merasty, who played the lead as a covert two-spirit Jingle Dress dancer struggling to find integration into his community after taking the wrong road in his moments of alienation in *Honey Moccasin*. Through his numerous films, Duane Gastant' Aucoin relayed healing from the queerphobic residential schools as a two-spirit Teslin Tlingit, showing intergenerational healing as a two-spirit child of a mother interned at Lower Post Indian Residential School and giving blessing for the loss of 215-plus residential school children at Kamloops. Finally, Parker's Tsitsistas short film on Disney+ demonstrated an elder who knew to fully support his two-spirit grandchild with a Jingle Dress that also honored his deceased two-spirit wife. All films show how to overcome the incredible two-spirit-phobia learned in residential and boarding schools with two-spirit vision, dancing, education, and prayers that end their cycles with the northern direction of elders.

II

Seeing Trans*Indigenous Time/Space

Down, Up, and Center

5

DOWN

Unsettling Hollywood Eras with Tongva Two-Spirit Video

Through postmillennial videos, two-spirit Tongvetam/Ajachmem/Rarámuri artist L. Frank affirms contemporary Tongva land connections, gender, and language. Their images and songs unsettle the "extinction," "assimilation," and "vanishing Indian" tropes of silent and classic Hollywood that render queered Native Southern Californian lands as tragically emptied and irrevocably settled.[1] To affirm Tongva land relationships and the downward direction to earth, this chapter first considers L. Frank's contributions in "L. Frank Manriquez Oral History" (2008), "Queer California: Untold Stories" (2019), and *City of Ghosts* episode 4, "Tovaangar" (2021). Next, it contrasts Native Californian and Spanish colonial understandings of earth, with reflection upon Theodor de Bry's late 1500s Flemish print of a Spanish two-spirit massacre in Panama. Third unfolds Indigenous criticisms of Carewe's 1928 *Ramona*, Clark's 1964 *Island of the Blue Dolphins*, and Mackenzie's 1961 *The Exiles*, which respectively represent queered silent, classic, and new Hollywood depictions of Tongva and Native Californian lands. Finally, the film readings return to L. Frank's 2000s–2020s videos "Common Ground: L. Frank Manriquez" (2008), *Two Spirits* (2010), and "Opening Blessing: Indigenous Pride LA" (2020). These videos unsettle the cis-heteropatriarchal Catholic Californio savior tropes of silent and classic Hollywood films by integrating visual, spiritual, and erotic sovereignty grounded in Tongva culture. In contrast to the suppression of queer Native American images in Hollywood films set in Los Angeles, L. Frank's videos affirm contemporary Tongva two-spirit presence on the Tongva lands called Tovaangar.

L. Frank affirms Tongva time and space in the "L. Frank Manriquez Oral History" (2008) video filmed by queer Norwegian anthropologist Paul Christiaan Klieger for the California Museum. In the film's medium shot (fig. 11), L. Frank presents themself in semiprofile at the Tongva village of Yaagna at downtown Los Angeles. While noted for their butch aesthetics evident in their military jacket, L. Frank elsewhere explains that their prominent "111" Tongva chin tattoo seen in the video is "a way to hold hands with my sisters through time."[2] Though pó does not announce themself as a butch two-spirit in this video, their mixed-gender expression of tattoos and military gear are also not constrained

Figure 11 L. Frank Manriquez explaining the Tongva village Yaagna near Olvera Street in Los Angeles in "L. Frank Manriquez Oral History" (2008), directed by Paul Christiaan Klieger.

by rules of masculinity and femininity, like their Indigenous pronoun pó. L. Frank introduces Tongva settlements: "They were here since the beginning of time when the Creator put them here, these villages, and sent the people to them."[3] Pó faces away from the power, water, jail, and courthouse buildings of Los Angeles that frame the shot. While the power and water institutions mark the state's appropriation of Native Californian resources, the jail and courthouse demonstrate the prison-industrial complex's targeting of Indigenous and de-indigenized populations.[4] Facing northern San Gabriel Mountains, L. Frank instead focuses Tongva traditional hunting practices in the nearby "foothills" and concludes that "all the buildings . . . will pretty much go away, and the land will be what the land needs to be again." In their vision, the thriving green plant regeneration evident at the rare open field at Yaagna behind her will spread throughout Tongva lands as the intensive urban cycle of Los Angeles settler colonialism completes itself. Because L. Frank's Tongva continuous ancestral and futuristic gaze isn't based upon a linear settler-colonial sense of time, pó is not simply hoping for distant green Tongva utopia. Instead, pó expresses a Tongva way of being in which "it's all one space and time."[5] Introducing a Tongva sense of fused time and space, their presence at Yaagna draws from the original power of that village. Defying the settler-colonial history that divorces contemporary Tongva land from living Tongva people, L. Frank simply affirms Tongva presence and futurity rooted in ancestral land. However, formerly featured on the Tongva Taraxat Paxaavxa Conservancy web page that documents a successful "receiving and managing land back" campaign, L. Frank also presses for the return of Tongva lands in the present.[6]

The composition in figure 11 shows contrasting spaces that help to convey this decolonial message of Tongva futurism in Klieger's video. The video's deep focus lens shots and intense color compositions add to Tongva presence at Yaagna. Filmed on the left side of the shot, L. Frank's figure is a mere one-third of the total image space, shifting the center to the green lot at Yaagna. The image's saturation of L. Frank's navy blue coat, blue-green face tattoos, and Yaagna's green grass mark an organic contrast with the gray street and pale concrete of "postmodern" architecture.[7] The slightly low-angle camera perspective creates a larger and more imposing silhouette for L. Frank, who dwarfs the washed-out power, water, and prison-industrial buildings of the background. Their message, like their image, dominates the Tongva landscape. The framing, camera angle, and saturation choices visually reinforce the vision that Tongva presence will outlive the postmodern city of Los Angeles that is built upon appropriated Tongva lands.

In the Yaagna video, L. Frank explains how Tongva spiritual communication on Tongva land is central to cultural survival. Pó interjects, "This is our place and we know how to talk to it. Even if we don't use the language, we still know how to talk to it. And even beyond that we know how to listen to it. . . . The way we feel and love our homeland, that gives power for this land to thrive." While L. Frank always had communication with the spirits of Tongva land, pó did not grow up being able to articulate it publicly, even in their childhood home. L. Frank overcomes their family's Tongva cultural suppression in which "you learn not to say that you heard the trees talking."[8] Yet pó never ceased listening to land even as the other human beings discounted these voices. In a 2002 journal interview, L. Frank elaborates on this communication. Pó recalls how the raven taught pó Tongva words in a dream but that it took eighteen years to really understand the significance of this dream and the words they were saying. Pó recounts, "in the dream[,] the raven spoke . . . laughing, 'She's the slowest person we have ever taught!'"[9] Tongva language, ancestors, and knowledge never left Tovaangar; they just became harder to hear, share, and understand after waves of Spanish, Mexican, and U.S. settler colonialism. But Tongva like L. Frank are reviving their ancestral communication within their own lands and sharing their community learning on media.

Two-spirit Tongva spokesperson Craig Torres echoes the importance of acknowledging and hearing Tongva ancestors and earth in the animated Netflix series *City of Ghosts* episode 4, "Tovaangar" (2021), directed by the Japanese/Hispanic Ako Castuera. In the cartoon, he talks to a group of animated Los Angeles kids that includes a Tongva child, Jasper, who hears ancestral voices and songs. Jasper is voiced by Honor Calderon, who is Tongva and Chumash, in the following dialogue:

CRAIG TORRES: Well, people have voices, you know, but so do animals, water, rocks, and plants . . .

THOMAS (BLUE CHAPMAN): Plants have voices?

JASPER: Do you talk to them?

CRAIG TORRES: I do. All the time. You know, everything that we see in nature has a personhood. There are plant people. There are animal people, rock people, or human people. . . . And for us, the Tongva . . . we also consider . . . these nonhuman people, our ancestors as well. To help us survive . . . they . . . became the landscape, the animals, the plants. Some of 'em went up into the sky and became the constellations. Some of 'em went underground. . . . We, in turn, owed them . . . to never remove ourselves from nature and to always take care of it . . . for the next generation.[10]

In this dialogue, Craig confirms Jasper's experiences by adding his own practices of talking with Tongva spirits. He explains this practice as conversations between people within a Tongva cultural understanding that people include plants, animals, stars, and other natural beings. These conversations among human and more-than-human peoples are a foundation for Tongva connections to ancestral spirits, ecological traditions, and ethics of reciprocity. They are a reminder of how Tongva are connected to Tongva lands, despite the presence of the Los Angeles megalopolis.

The animation ends with Craig Torres and the Tongva/Chumash/Yoeme family Honor Calderon, Jessa Calderon, and Tina Calderon singing L. Frank's song, "Wee totaa 'ooxoram wee totaa xamee'evet horuura' xaa heteek 'eyooyook,"[11] words that Jessa Calderon had only partially translated for Jasper earlier in the animation. While the lyric translations appear in "Artist Talk: L. Frank Manriquez" (2022),[12] they are more subtly present in the "Queer California: Untold Stories—L. Frank" (2019) video filmed at L. Frank's outdoor home workshop in Santa Rosa, where pó hosted the building of a ti'aat, a Tongva sewn-plank canoe. In the "Queer California" video, the camera pans around across the ti'aat canoe paddle, abalone shells, coming to rest on Tongva words for two-spirit genders, and then lyrics written in white chalk. On one wooden panel, the Tongva song lyrics are written:

Wee totaa
'ooxoram
wee totaa
xamee'evet
horuura' xaa
heteek 'eyooyook

On the next wooden panel is the English translation written with an alternate enjambment:

> Every pebble
> a
> planet
> every stone
> a
> grave
> time is the
> universe
> birther to us
> all[13]

This song invokes the Tongva ancestors in the Tongva language. The "every rock" words of the song gain new meaning given Craig Torres's "Tovaangar" monologue. Every Tongva rock really is an ancestor within his understanding of how the Tongva world formed. His narrative affirms why the settler-colonial transformations of greater Los Angeles urban spaces do not erase the underlying Tongva creation from ancestral spirits from time immemorial. Time is the creator universe in the song's expression of Tongva thought, and that creation has never stopped. By invoking "horuura," time, and "wee totaa," every stone, in the *City of Ghosts* episode, L. Frank, Torres, and the Calderons affirm that the Tongva have never ceased to feel Tongva time on their own lands. Amid the many layers and centuries of settler-colonial urban impositions, Tongva stories, time, and space persist in Tovaangar.

That both Craig Torres and L. Frank are two-spirit Tongva speaks to the ability of two-spirit Tongva to give back to their people. In fact, while the "Wee totaa" lyrics and its translation are shown in the "Queer California: Untold Stories—L. Frank" video, L. Frank explains, "To some, two-spirit is strictly a spiritual thing. We permeated the sacred and the profane parts of life. To me, my two-spirit is . . . part of my service. We two-spirit have always been those who can do what others cannot do but needs to be done."[14] This idea of two-spirit exceptionalism or simple difference in gender role comes up in the literature on two-spirit people. In her reflection on L. Frank's revitalization of coastal Native Southern Californian two-spirit traditions, Chumash and Ohlone Esselen lesbian writer Deborah Miranda homes in on the relationship of two-spirit genders and earth. Miranda explains how Chumash two-spirit people, the 'aqi, demonstrated an ability to bridge gendered earthly and heavenly levels during death ceremonies. She writes:

> The *'aqi*, with their male-female liminality, were the only people who could mediate these experiences. Since the female (earth, abundance, fertility) energies were so powerful, and since the male (Sun, death-associated) energies were equally strong, the person who dealt with that moment of spiritual and bodily crossing over between life and death must have specially endowed spiritual qualities and powers.[15]

Embodying a balance of both masculine and feminine energies enabled the 'aqi to find a respected place among the Chumash. In other words, the 'aqi could offer their families the ability to access the feminine energy of earth and the masculine energy of sky to allow passage of deceased spirits. Extending these two-spirit roles that the Spanish called "joya" to the Tongva and other coastal Native Southern Californians, Miranda names L. Frank Manriquez as a "Tongva/Ajachmen" revitalizer of traditional two-spirit roles of caring for the dead.

To consider these Chumash and coastal Native Southern Californian relationships to earth, it's helpful to again review how Anne Waters differentiates Indigenous nonbinary thought from Western either/or binaries. Waters explains that within Indigenous "nonbinary dualism," both parts of a system "act together in such a way that one would remain oneself, and also be a part of the other."[16] This means that a Chumash feminine earth and masculine sun space can complement each other without great conflicts. Within the colonial Western oppositional binary system, in contrast, the masculine heavenly forces are at war with life on the feminine earth. Miranda shows how balanced vertical relationships that supported the two-spirit Chumash 'aqi contrast with those of the Catholic colonial Spanish who were convinced they followed heavenly law in killing or punishing any two-spirit people they could find. In light of Waters's and Miranda's writing, de Bry's etching of a Spanish massacre of forty two-spirit people (fig. 12) doesn't depict simply a clash of peoples but a clash of Indigenous and Spanish Catholic understandings of earth and sky vertical spaces.

Because colonial 1500s cis-heterosexist violence sets in motion the erasures of two-spirit peoples that impact the images of 1900s silent, classic, and new Hollywood eras, it is important to briefly consider the gendered spatiality of de Bry's image. Drawing upon Pietro (Peter) Martyr d'Anghiera's 1516 *De orbo novo* travel accounts of Central America, Flemish-born Renaissance artist Theodor de Bry depicted Vasco Nuñez de Balboa's 1513 massacre of forty two-spirit people in the *Darién* Province of Panama almost a lifetime later, in the late 1500s. The location of this massacre is on or near what is now the treaty-defined Indigenous land of the Embéra-

Figure 12 Theodor de Bry, *Balboa Throws the Indians Who Have Committed the Abominable Crime of Sodomy to Be Torn to Bits by Dogs*, in *Collected Travels of the East and West Indies* (1594).

Wounaan, likely descendants or relatives of the massacred Cueva. In Richard Eden's English translation of the narrative of the Balboa army's massacre of six hundred warriors and two-spirit peoples, the remaining Quarecua or Cueva survivors "lift their hands to heaven" in praise of the Spaniards' massacres, as if testifying to the universal moral superiority of colonial Spanish cis-heterosexism and welcoming their deliverance from "sodomy." De Bry's etching portrays a Eurocentric vertical spatiality in which the nearly naked Indigenous figures either flail or rest in pieces upon the earth while attacked by dogs.[17] This lower-half Cueva and animalistic space is diametrically opposed to the upper-half space of heaven that frames the fully armed Catholic Spaniards who look on from above while striking statuesque Renaissance poses. This vertical spatiality demonizes the Indigenous spiritual practices in which the earth and two-spirit people are revered. These images were used as justification for the Spanish colonization of the Pacific, from Chile in the south to California in the north.

Miranda connects Cueva two-spirit or "joya" suppression to that experienced in coastal Southern California missions, writing, "By the time the Span-

Figure 13 Omeggids sewing molas at HIV workshop in "Descubriendo nuestra identidad . . . !" (2014), directed by Duiren Wagua.

iards had expanded their territory to California, the use of dogs as weapons to kill or eat Indians, particularly joyas, was well established."[18] However, in visually tracing the Spanish mission colonial roots for Chumash and Tongva two-spirit violence, it is important to not disappear today's strong two-spirit and Indigenous presence of the Darién. The settler-colonial cis-heteropatriarchal violence that began in the 1500s continues in internalized forms among some Embéra, but not so among the Dule, also known as Cuna, Kuna, and Guna. For example, Maloney recounts that some transgender women are shunned within the Embéra communities in Colombia.[19] However, the Dule inhabit what was once also Cueva lands and mark an Indigenous presence in the Darién through their Comarcas of Guna Yala, Guna Madungandí, and Guna Wargandí, as well as their border Dule populations in the middle of the Darién that extend into Colombia. Guna Yala is where Balboa met his own death by Spanish political rivals at Acla in 1519 and it is Balboa's early Spanish colonies that have disappeared into the Dule jungles and coasts of Panama, not the Indigenous presence. Since the 1925 Dule revolt, the Dule have been very active in maintaining their treaties, land, art, tourist-market, and intellectual sovereignty, as well as an honored place for their two-spirit people.[20] In Duiren Wagua's (Dule) largely Dule-language HIV-prevention documentary "Descubriendo nuestra identidad . . . !" (2014), contemporary omeggids (two-spirits) prominently assert their spatial cosmology and femininity by making and selling molas, a role the Dule women fill and men do not. In figure 13, an omeggid with the Dule feminine black line drawn down her nose that replicates older tattoo patterns sews her reverse-appliqué mola of what appears to be a rainbow-colored butterfly.[21] She is sewing at an HIV-prevention program that responds to higher rates of HIV among Indigenous populations, especially those of the omeggid.[22] This mola represents not only financial gains and health sovereignty for the omeggid but also a spatiality that resists the Eurocentric verticality that condemned earlier two-spirits to death as the worst representatives of a feminine earth. Dule scholar Sue Haglund offers insights into Dule duality that includes feminine mola traditions, tattoos, and spatiality that can help one to understand Dule space as depicted in the molas. Haglund explains that these tattoos Dule women once wore on their faces and exposed torsos and bodies were transferred into mola designs to wear their as mola blouses:

> Dule artwork's movement from body to cloth represents . . . creating a link between two physical layers. . . . A correlation of layers emerges within a variety of worlds; for instance, the physical and spiritual or the heavens and earth. The layers of the space and place, in both physical and spiritual realms, are not separated but rather synchronous spheres.[23]

For Haglund, both the omeggid mola-maker and the butterfly mola design itself act as media between interrelated worlds, fusing earthbound human and airborne butterfly spaces. In light of Haglund's Dule writings and Wagua's Dule HIV video, de Bry's depiction of Balboa's slaughter of forty two-spirit Cueva should not lead contemporary readers to falsely surmise that the Indigenous peoples of Panama have either abandoned their sense of vertical space or failed to resist Balboa's cis-heteropatriarchal rule. Even so, Miranda is correct to note a continuity of two-spirit and Indigenous erasure that follows the Spanish into Native California lands and representations, including those of the Hollywood occupation of Tongva lands.

Unsettling *Ramona* (1928) and Silent Hollywood

Silent Hollywood played up Native American stereotypes of savagery and of disappearance even as Native American directors became more engaged with the possibilities of expressing visual sovereignty as actors and directors. Edwin Carewe (Chickasaw Nation of Oklahoma) did both acting and directing in his career. In *The Snowbird* (1916), directed by Edwin Carewe, Carewe plays the rugged frontiersman Jean, who whips a woman dressed as an adolescent male (Mabel Taliaferro) when "he" will not shine Jean's boots. The visually masculine couple seems to experience attraction for each other in this scene, an effect that Horak suggests intimates "sadomasochistic and pederastic" desire. Only once the passed-out "boy" reveals her long hair as a sign of the woman's cisgenderness does the dark Jean allow his "wild" frontier nature to be tamed by her. One 1916 reviewer remarked that the Chickasaw Carewe was especially suited to play this whipping role that called for "passions . . . elemental in force," naturalizing brutality and primitivism for Native American actors.[24] Some of this coding for Native American wild passions also came to define his own Native California–themed film *Ramona,* but with important visually sovereign insights on the violence of settler colonialism in Southern California.

Based upon Helen Hunt Jackson's 1884 popular romance novel *Ramona,* Edwin Carewe's cinematic 1928 *Ramona* dramatizes the genocide and displacement of Native Southern Californians by land-and-gold-seeking Anglo-Americans shortly after the 1848 Mexican-American War. Although Carewe's *Ramona* expresses key scenes of visual sovereignty, the film also makes use of established cross-dressing humor tropes as it ultimately embraces a late 1800s tragic assimilation of Native Californians into Catholic Mexican Rancho culture. While the screenplay, written by Edwin Carewe's brother Finnis Fox (Chickasaw Nation of Oklahoma), condemns Native Californian genocide, it nonetheless features a Californio assimilation resolution that leaves unproblematized key aspects of the Native Californian legal, gendered, spiritual, and cultural alienation from their own lands. Played by the striking Mexican icon Dolores del Río in partial redface, the adopted Ramona learns from her dowager stepmother, Señora Moreno (Vera Lewis), that her biological mother was an "Indian" and her father "white." She leaves her wealthy Spanish Californio Moreno family and identity to elope with the Luiseño chief's son, Alessandro, played by the Euro-American Baxter Warner in redface. After the couple settles at a Luiseño village near Temecula Valley, her only child dies, her Luiseño community is massacred by white settlers, and her husband is murdered as a result of violent racism. Felipe Moreno (Roland Drew), Ramona's stepbrother, childhood admirer, and would-be lover and husband, brings the catatonic Ramona back to the Moreno ranch where she begins to regain her speech and childhood memories but retains amnesia about her adult traumatic experiences. Thus, ignoring the severe Spanish-era abuses, the *Ramona* film plot situates its Californio rancho as a pastoral haven from the U.S. genocides that plague Native Californians.

Ramona's black-and-white establishing shots of the Moreno ranch emphasize a benevolent Catholic pastoralism. While the hit romantic orchestral Ramona theme plays in the background, an intertitle card states, "Early California ~ ~ In the colorful days of the Spanish Dons ~ ~." The *Ramona* orchestral theme continues as three Moreno Hacienda chapel bells silently ring in their mission adobe arches. Likely based upon Rancho Camulos in the Santa Clara valley, these bells mark the highest vertical point in the film's rancho setting and make clear the rancho's dominant Catholic morals and social structure.[25] A cut to Franciscan monks pacing in their brown robes while contemplating scriptures is followed by Californios and Native Californians, most likely Tataviams, gathering to worship at the chapel in answer to the bells' call to Catholic mass.[26] One Tataviam/Native Californian woman momentarily demonstrates her servant position as she bends down to the earth to feed the chickens in the foreground. Most Tataviam/Native Californian women wear braids, full-length calico rancho dresses, bright woven serapes, and long seed or shell necklaces. In contrast, the Californio women who walk by wear flouncy full-length lacy skirts, and their high peineta combs hold up their hair under their lace mantillas. Their Californio men sport embellished suits with short bolero jackets, black hats, and colorful sashes. The next intitle

Figure 14 Ramona (Dolores del Río) in Californio men's clothing and Native Californian braids while riding a donkey with Felipe (Baxter Warner) in *Ramona* (1928), directed by Edwin Carewe.

card reads, "When adventurous pioneers panned the mountain streams for gold ~ ~ ~," introducing an image of an exalted white forty-niner holding up a gold nugget midriver among other toiling men.[27] The pastoral Californio Catholic Moreno Rancho contrasts to the motley crew of sweaty forty-niners who extract Native Californian land resources without Christian moral law. However, both Californios and Euro-American gold-panners are depicted with mastery over Native Californian lands as the subservient Native Californians meekly go to church and tend ranch animals.

Ramona first appears riding a donkey and wearing dark braids and a Californio men's shirt, sash, and pants (fig. 14). Signaling the impending clash of a dual European and Indigenous heritage, Ramona is signed as a mixed-race by the contrast of her Indigenous braids and her inappropriate use of masculine Californio clothing. The youthful Rancho Moreno heir, Felipe, mopes behind her and wears similar masculine clothing. An intitle card reads: "There was a mystery in the dark eyes of Ramona ~ ~ in her birth and in her adoption by Señora Morena." When Felipe jumps up on the donkey at Ramona's request, he begins to embrace her from behind. Ramona elbows him, kicks her donkey, and leaves Felipe in the dirt. Felipe gets revenge by tickling the donkey with a stick, which causes the donkey to buck Ramona off into the dirt. When Ramona falls and skins her knee, Felipe dries her tears and carries her home on his back.[28] Ramona's fall foretells that her proximity to Native American earth will lead to pain and that her future escape from Felipe's romantic interests will only lead her back to Felipe's desirous arms.

An intertitle card announces Felipe's mother Señora Moreno as one who rules "with an iron hand" over her vast coastal Californio hacienda "with a feudal grandeur." Filmed in black and white, Señora Moreno's pale skin contrasts with her heavy black floor-length dress that marks her as a widow in her Catholic faith. When Señora Moreno finds Ramona, an intertitle card interjects, "Señora: Where have you been ~ ~ and what are you doing in that outfit!" Although britches would make limited inroads for women playing sports in turn-of-the-century United States, Californio dress codes did not allow women to wear trousers. Señora Moreno soon reveals that her perennial lack of love for Ramona stems from a settler-colonial distaste for Ramona's "Indian" mother, whom she identifies as a "low common woman" in an intertitle card. She also reveals that Ramona's father is a "white man."[29]

Understanding queer settler colonialism allows for new insights regarding the meaning of Ramona's initial cross-dressing. The settler Jewish American Mark Rifkin might note how Ramona queerly falls outside the norms of the national ideals of the "heterosexual nuclear family."[30] Ramona in masculine clothing represents the Indigenous subject destined to fade away into a nonreproductive future within the logics of queer settler colonialism. With no land upon which to safely regenerate her Native Californian line, Ramona's initial cross-dressing signals a lack of Indigenous futurity in which Spanish/Mexican assimilation and genocidal amnesia is her only viable option. The subsequent massacre scene realizes this vision of Indigenous absence as Manifest Destiny and California law claim land for white settlers in California.

Eloping with the marriage blessings of Father Salvierderra (John T. Prince), Ramona and Alessandro escape to the pastoral bliss of Alessandro's village, presumably the Rancho Little Temecula deeded in 1845 to Luiseño Pablo Apis.[31] Anti–Native Californian sentiment quickens the plot. When Ramona and Alessandro's daughter becomes ill, a white doctor refuses to help their child, who soon dies, foreshadowing the impending massacre. Carewe graphically depicts invading Euro-Americans shooting unarmed Luiseño women, children, and men at the village. A title card reads, "Marauders, motivated by hatred and greed, descend upon the defenseless Indian village." The card for cowboy 1 says, "Burn the houses take the cattle." Another cowboy card states, "Anyone who stands up to us ~ kill them." Luiseños are shot immediately, some by their adobe houses and some as they run away. One woman is killed by a statue of the Madonna and another is shot down while running away with a baby on her back. The cowboy first shoots the mother and then shoots the baby. Cowboys set fire to everything. Dressed in an embroidered Mexican-style blouse and a long rancho dress, Ramona grabs her Catholic statue of Mary and flees with Alessandro before the cowboys can set fire to their house. As Alessandro and Ramona narrowly escape from this massacre, the camera offers a wide shot of their cottage in flames with smoke thickly billowing many stories above the house as dark horsed men circle around it.[32] Hearne terms this sequence as an "ethnically-reversed massacre scene" in the context of the Western genre.[33] Carewe replaces the attacking Plains Indian horsemen circling the burning wagons of the presumably innocent Euro-American pioneers with greedy white men circling the innocent Ramona's burning home. A clear Choctaw indictment of Native Southern California genocide, this is Carewe's strongest moment of visual sovereignty as he clearly condemns the violence of the Gold Rush era dispossession of Native Californian land.

When a white settler shoots and kills Alessandro for borrowing a horse and leaving his own in its stead, Ramona blindly flees through the mountains. In the 1928 film conclusion, Felipe finds Ramona in a coma and takes her home. When Ramona wakes up back at the Moreno Hacienda, she has no memory of her tragic losses. Dressed in an opulent jeweled necklace and wavy hair that symbolizes her renewed Californio identity, she is impactful in a white lace dress that references her childlike state of mind. The loss of her California Native dress accompanies the loss of her memory and Indigenous family. Although she was married to Alessandro in the Catholic faith, she is denied the black dress of mourning, a sign that Felipe wishes to make her his wife. Felipe restores the first traces of her memory by playing his guitar for her as she dances. The intertitle card registers a spark of memory saying, "Ramona ~ You, are you Felipe?" As he presses his face close to Ramona's lips, she turns from him at the last second, affectionately resting her head on his chest and saying via an intertitle card, "Why ~ Why, it is just as though I had never been away."[34] Although Ramona appears to finally recognize Felipe and the Moreno household staff, she still does not register the loss of her daughter and husband. Her final words invite the audience to also forget the Native Californian massacres in favor of a romanticized Californio happy ending. Hearne correctly notes that this finale "melodramatic plot device" facilitates Ramona's subsequent "assimilation" back into the racial privilege, wealth, and safety of the Moreno Californio family household. Ramona's amnesia also represents the general suppression of "traumatic frontier history."[35]

There are alternative Native California interpretations and insights regarding the implications of this finale. Craig Torres shares that many Tongva did come to identify as Mexican during the late 1800s and early 1900s in order to avoid massacres, enslavement, and legal attacks. In a Puvungna video made via the UCLA Mapping Indigenous LA website, he reports that one of his grandmothers would not identify as Tongva even when she had the tattoos that marked her as such.[36] His own lighter chin tattoos recall this lost legacy regained, though perhaps across gender categories. Ramona's amnesia could represent the generations of Tongva descendants whose knowledge of their Native Californian heritage was suppressed within a racialized Mexican and Californio hegemony. While the film Ramona only knew her Indian/white race and not her exact people, Hunt's book crudely specifies that Ramona's mother was a "squaw with several Indian children," who came from the "Indian" community at "San Gabriel Mission," while Ramona's alcoholic father, "Angus Phail," was a "Scotsman."[37] Given that mostly Tongva settled at San Gabriel Mission, along with some Tataviams and Serranos, the implication is that the film and book Ramona is most likely Tongva, with some chance of being from any mix of local Native Southern Californians. The cultural amnesia that afflicts Ramona in the film finale therefore begins with her adoption by Californios who racialize the narrative of her mother's exact Native Californian Nation. Torres's narrative confirms that Tongva descendants can reclaim identity even after many decades of state repression and legal silencing.

Tongva, Tataviam, and Pechanga tribal website histories call for a political, visual, spiritual and cultural sovereignty that eludes *Ramona*'s melodramatic conclusion. For example, the Gabrielino-Tongva history webpage marks the 1928 year of *Ramona*'s release as the authorization year of "the California Attorney General to represent the Gabrielino Tribe, among others, and to bring their land claims before the U.S. Court of Claims."[38] Their website notes how the eighteen Native California "lost treaties" of 1851–53 were never ratified by Congress, leaving many Native Californians to fight for recognition across the centuries and into the second millennium. As the Moreno rancho most likely represents the Tataviam village Camulos in what is now reckoned as the Santa Clarita Valley, it is important to note how the Fernandeño Tataviam Band of Mission Indians online historical timeline states how the 1797 Spanish era "marks the beginning of recruitment and enslavement of Indians to Misión del Señor San Fernando Rey de España (San Fernando Mission) [in which] . . . more than 80% of the Indian population in California decreased in a 60 year period due to traumatic change to lifeways, harsh conditions, and foreign diseases."[39] Their website highlights the Tataviam protests over the Santa Clarita Valley being deeded to a Californio in 1839, also documenting their continuous campaigns to regain their lands into the 2000s. Finally, the Pechanga history webpage recounts, "Author Helen Hunt Jackson was instrumental in securing reservation land for the Pechanga people."[40] After the violent eviction of the Temecula Luiseño people at gunpoint during September 20–23, 1875, Helen Hunt Jackson visited Temecula while working for the Bureau of Indian Affairs and reported what had happened to the Pechanga people to the U.S. government. Her reports helped to convince Congress to set aside land for the Pechanga Reservation, which was established by executive order on June 27, 1882, by President Chester A. Arthur. A century later in the 1990s, the Pechanga became a very well-to-do gaming tribe as Carole Goldberg and Duane Champagne (Turtle Mountain Band of Chippewa Indians) recount in their article pointedly named "Ramona Redeemed? The Rise of Tribal Political Power in California."[41] In light of ongoing struggles and successes for Native Southern California sovereignty into the 2020s, *Ramona*'s romantic assimilation resolution was by no means a final political solution.

Spanish scholar Carolina Fernández Rodríguez's critiques of Ramona's erasure as a mixed-race Mestiza are also worth noting. Within Hunt's settler Anglo-American logics of racial purity as norm, the mixed-blooded Ramona must either assimilate into purely white Spanish or purely Native Californian racial categories. In emphasizing Californio whiteness, Hunt erases that early Californios were largely classified as Afro-Mexicans, Mestizos, and Indians and often hailed from Sonora and Sinaloa, not Spain. For example, at a time when Mexican California land claims extended from California's Pacific coasts to the Rocky Mountains, the last Mexican Californio governor, Pío Pico, was of mixed-race Afro-Mexican and Mestizo descent. Fernández Rodríguez argues that Hunt wrote Ramona as mixed-race and lighter skinned as way to gain the sympathy of white readers. Similarly, having Anglo-American actors play the Californio Morenos and the Luiseño Alessandro was intended to draw financial and political support from white audiences. The lightening of Ramona also compromises the specific Native Californian women's histories who were the basis for Ramona's tragedies. For example, the Cahuilla Ramona Lubo, whose husband was also shot for taking a horse, was likely the model for the fictional Ramona's loss of Alessandro.[42] By displacing full-blooded Native Californian women's stories with Ramona's mixed-blooded assimilation resolution, Hunt and Carewe limit depicting the repercussions of genocide and removal upon the surviving Native Californians.

LGBTQI2+ Native American Censorship in Classic and New Hollywood

Replicating the silent Hollywood settler-colonial tropes evident in *Ramona*, classic Hollywood of the 1930s–1960s prominently queered representations of vanishing Native Californians restricted to 1800s film settings. For example, set off the coast of Los Angeles on the southern Channel Island of San Nicolas in the mid-1800s, the *Island of the Blue Dolphins* (1964) film plot evolves as a Russian and Aleut crew kill off most Nicoleño island inhabitants in a sea otter hunting territory war. This classic Hollywood film is faithful to the "vanishing Indian" trope that Goldberg establishes for the film's source children's novel, written by Scott O'Dell.[43] The film's surviving Nicoleño flee by boat to the Santa Barbara Mission. The remaining Nicoleño survivor, Karana (Celia Kaye in redface), hides herself and her brother Ramo (Larry Domasin in redface) from discovery on the island. After Karana's brother is killed by wild dogs, she befriends Tutok (Ann Daniel in redface), an Aleut female member of the Russian crew. Alone for years, the young Karana necessarily adopts the male hunting roles once sternly forbidden to her by her chief father, effectively acting in a cross-gendered manner throughout the latter half of the film. As in *Ramona*, this cross-dressing signals a failure of sovereignty within the character's Native California peoples that will end in assimilation into the mission system. After Tutok declines to stay on the island with Karana, Karana decides to join her Nicoleño family in the last scene and openly approaches the ship sent to retrieve her to Mission Santa Barbara. Karana's retreat to the mission marks Nicoleño land as permanently vacated, cementing the settler-colonial logics that claimed Hollywood and the surrounding region free of any contemporary Native Californian presence.

The film's Mission Santa Barbara was no haven for the historical "Juana Maria," the last Nicoleño to be taken from San Nicolas Island and inspiration for *Island of the Blue Dolphins*. She died within seven weeks of her 1853 resettlement at Mission Santa Barbara.[44] Although disease-ridden California mission settlements were colonial death traps for her and many other Native

Southern Californians, some Nicoleños survived, and their legacy is not forgotten within Native Southern Californian oral traditions.[45] Scattered records indicate that Nicoleños settled with mostly Southern Channel Island Tongva at the Ranchería de los Pipimares at Yaagna in 1835. Records of an "1842 . . . mourning ceremony" at the rancheria report that the Pipimare "participants threw chia seeds, juniper berries, pine nuts, as well as cloth and other items belonging to the deceased Indians, into the fire."[46] L. Frank reports that the island is also known within Tongva oral tradition as Minar, the island navel through which Tongva are born into the world.[47] A Tongva map names the island as Xaraashnga, what the ethnographer Alfred Kroeber documents as the Gabrielino name Haraasnga and Chumash name "Xalashat ('Ghalas-at') for San Nicolas Island."[48]

Neither the 1960 novel nor the 1964 film predicted the establishment of the Native American Graves and Repatriation Act (NAGPRA) of 1990 that would enable legal intervention to unsettle the "vanishing Indian" film and novel tropes of San Nicolas. Pressing for NAGPRA consideration, "the Pauma, Rincon and Pechanga bands of Luiseño, as well as the Santa Ynez Band of Chumash were all deemed to be culturally affiliated with the island," and the remains from San Nicolas were finally reburied on the island after strong tribal interventions.[49] Although the film is set in the Chumash "Ghalas-at" village at San Nicolas Island, Juana Maria herself appears to have spoken a Nicoleño language Cupeño-Luiseño activists claim is most similar to their own language.[50] Even though the non–federally recognized Tongva letters for NAGPRA legal claims for reburial could not supersede those of the federally recognized Chumash and Luiseño bands, Tongva narratives of the importance of San Nicolas remain. The legal actions by Tongva, Chumash, and Luiseño people demonstrate a persistent care for their ancestors and relatives' remains at San Nicolas Island, a clear contrast to the film's queer settler-colonial concluding images of eternal Nicoleño abandonment of the island.

With the rise of new Hollywood, gay images emerged from the classic Hollywood censorship. Filmed by British director Kent Mackenzie, *The Exiles* (1961) was an early new Hollywood outlier that momentarily exceeded gay film censorship in its depiction of relocated Southwest and Oklahoma Native Americans in Los Angeles out drinking, fighting, and singing. Filmed in 1958–60 in the general Tongva (Gabrielino) Yaagna area then known as Bunker Hill in downtown Los Angeles, *The Exiles* includes a mixed-race gay dance scene at a largely Native American bar. There, an effeminate gay white man drunkenly screams as he embraces and then dances with his Asian American male lover. Seeming to curse the campy gay white man under his breath, the film protagonist Homer (Homer Nish, Hualapai) attacks another Native American man who is harassing a Native American woman. It is as if

Homer is proving his masculinity within the unscripted context of the intense gay carousing. While the gay couple could have been arrested for sex perversion by the white policemen who are filmed prowling outside the bar only minutes before, the pair freely leave the bar. Mackenzie marketed the early new Hollywood outlier *The Exiles* as an authentic account of urban Native American life, but Tsitsistas/Hinono'ei scholar Ho'esta Mo'e'hahneh (Cheyenne and Arapahoe Tribes of Oklahoma) notes how Mackenzie scripted the constant scenes of late-night Native American drinking, dating violence, and fighting in the tradition of European "pseudoethnography." Mo'e'hahneh observes how Mackenzie included the gay couple in the film as "Indigenous" to LA as a way to queerly dislocate Homer's urban Native American identity and the Tongva at Yaagna. It also displaces two-spirit Native Californians such as the queer Kumeyaay/Barona Band of Mission Indians Kenny Ramos, who was featured in Pamela Peter's (Navajo Nation) 2014 remake of *The Exiles*.[51] In other words, the queer settler-colonial fiction is that the white gay man is the true "Native" Angeleno who renders the strictly heterosexual Native American diaspora and the Tongva as the true outsiders and "exiles" to modern Euro-American-dominated Los Angeles.[52] Although Mackenzie's independent film skirted the anti-LGBTQI2+ suicide and death mandates of Motion Picture Production Code censorship evident in *The Outsider*'s (1961) gay-coded story of Ira Hayes, it never found a national distributor that would have required homophobic edits to screen nationally.

The militarization of the Southern California coasts during World War II brought new masculinist representations to classic Hollywood, with all of its homosocial and homoerotic undertones in some films. Classic Hollywood representations of queer Native Americans were tragically homoerotic in the case of the World War II film *The Outsider* (1961) in which Jewish American Tony Curtis acts in redface as the Pima (Akimel O'odham) war hero Ira Hayes. The white fellow trainee Private James B. Sorenson (James Franciscus) overcomes a racial divide to befriend Hayes in the film. However, the bisexual Jewish American screenwriter of *The Outsider*, Stewart Stern, later admitted that he wholly fabricated the Sorensen character.[53] Only the nationally celebrated Hayes was an actual historical figure, one whose photographed action in raising the U.S. flag at Iwo Jima became iconic after World War II ended in victory for the USA and Allied forces. After Sorenson and Hayes have slept off a drunken night together on a San Diego beach in Kumeyaay territory, Sorensen warns Hayes: "If you are about to kiss me, banjo-butt, I can tell you are the wrong type!" In the film, Hayes later recalls his intimate combat sleeping routine with Sorensen, saying: "You sleep closer than you ever did before. And you make yourself breathe in time with the other person because it makes you know that there is somebody else in the world."[54] After

Sorensen and Hayes help raise the iconic American flag at Iwo Jima in the film, Sorenson dies in combat. The celebrated Hayes returns home to the Gila River Indian Reservation at Sacaton and drinks himself to death as he laments his lost love for Private Sorenson. To even hint at affection and intimacy between men in combat was to incur the Motion Picture Film Production Code's death sentence, a common ending for coded homosexual characters in classic Hollywood film. Richard Barrios intimates that the homoerotic war-buddy film made it through censorship because "Hayes' [Native American] outsider status permitted somewhat more candor than the Production Code normally allowed."[55] Although *The Outsider* modernized Native American images, it also promoted the "drunken Indian" stereotype, adding a subtextual homoerotic suicidal twist mandated by classic Hollywood censorship.[56]

Hollywood films from 1968 to 1980 occasionally broke with some of the Hays Code queer censorship. When the new Hollywood *Little Big Man* (1970), directed by Jewish American Arthur Penn, featured the first openly transgender Tsitsistas (Cheyenne) hemaneh/two-spirit figure Little Horse (Robert Little Star), along with sororate polygamy, these queer arrangements end with the graphically filmed 1864 Sand Creek massacre. Once her comedic role was completed, the two-spirit transfeminine Little Horse is killed without further mention. The protagonist white character, an orphaned youth renamed Little Big Man (Dustin Hoffman), opts to assimilate back into white settler-colonial society once his adopted Cheyenne family is massacred. His final appearance as a solo elder housed in Los Angeles' old Veterans Hospital on Wilshire Boulevard replicates the trope of coast-to-coast Indigenous disappearance. Trans hemaneh Adrian Jawort (Northern Cheyenne Tribe) critiques *Little Big Man*'s comedic diminishment of the honored two-spirit hemaneh role and links it to the silent era's comedic tropes for cross-dressed characters and persistent Hollywood transphobia, a pattern highlighted in the trans film documentary *Disclosure*.[57] Margo Kasdan and Susan Tavernetti anticipate this sentiment in a 1993 critique of *Little Big Man*.[58]

Reflecting the relaxation of censorship and rise in pornography and San Fransico/West Coast hippie culture, the gay independent 1970 *Song of the Loon* film directed by the non-Indigenous Andrew Herbert idealized frontier gay masculine Native Americans as back-to-the-land models of gay white male freedom. Based on the eponymous classic 1966 gay liberation book by Richard Amory, *Song of the Loon* features the fit young blond protagonist Ephraim MacIver (Morgan Royce), who learns to accept his homoerotic desires and settle down with his even more muscular and older Euro-American lover, Cyrus Wheelwright (John Iverson), in Oregon in the late 1800s. In the film's beginning, Singing Heron (John Kalfas in redface), a generic Native American man, makes love to Ephraim, who thereafter overcomes his trauma of being gay-bashed by the closeted frontiersman Montgomery (Jon Evans) and his scoundrel companions. The film later features a beefy "Indian shaman," Bear-Who-Dreams (Lucky Manning in redface), who leads Ephraim through a "golden mushroom" psychedelic soft gay porn vision quest by intoning the Nichiren Japanese Buddhist chant "Namu-myōhō-renge-kyō."[59] Managing to combine appropriations of West Coast cultures including Maria Sabina's Mazatec mushroom healings and Japanese Buddhism, the oddly mixed Japanese, Native, and Mexican Indigenous practices illicit a kaleidoscopic homoerotic vision in which the older Cyrus penetrates Ephraim in a psychedelic river setting, setting Ephraim free of his fear and shame. After this vision, Ephraim faithfully returns to Cyrus at his ranch and even confronts the evil Montgomery, who himself confesses his homoerotic desires for other men. *Song of the Loon* appropriates gay American Indian images in a way artistically lampooned by Cree artist Kent Monkman (Fisher River Cree), who inserts queer erotic cowboy and Indigenous figures into his purposefully ahistorical 1800s landscape paintings.[60] *Song of the Loon*'s several nude and seminude redface Native American caricatures seem more inspired by acid trips and 1960s beefcake magazine pornography than the Western Oregon tribes from the Confederated Tribes of the Grand Ronde Community, Siletz Indians, and Cow Creek Band of Umpqua Tribe of Indians, on whose traditional lands the book is likely set. Its homoerotic Native American caricatures merely exist to teach the white gay protagonist about the hippie ideals of rural gay sexual liberation, offering no real critique of U.S. white settler colonialism in the Pacific coastal states.

Restoring Two-Spirit Tongva Earth with L. Frank Manriquez's Videos

Only after AIDS activism funding combined with cheaper video production in the late 1980s would Indigenous visual, erotic, and spiritual sovereignty combine. *Her Giveaway: A Spiritual Journey with AIDS* (1988) by director Mona Smith (Sisseton-Wahpeton Oyate) is one such multiply sovereign example.[61] It isn't until the 1991 documentary "Two-Spirit People" filmed in San Francisco on Muwekma Ohlone lands that Koyangk'auwi Maidu Janice Gould announced herself as a Maidu poet "lesbian," contesting a century of Hollywood's erasure of lesbian and two-spirit Native Californians.[62] L. Frank would continue representation for two-spirit Native Californians in the 2000s, 2010s, and 2020s. While L. Frank does not announce their two-spirit identity in the "L. Frank Manriquez Oral History" (2008) video filmed at Yaagna, pó directly advocates for two-spirit issues as a Tongvetam/Ajachmem artist in "Common Ground: L. Frank Manriquez" (2008), directed by Santa Clara Pueblo Zakary Naranjo-Morse. Filming themself in an extreme close-up against a white background, L. Frank appears in the one-take four-minute short. In an opening statement, Manriquez says:

> There are two challenges. One is being "extinct" in your own homeland. The other is being a two-spirit-person in your homeland. The challenge of extinction—I guess we can procreate as much as we want, but we're not going to be deemed viable by the United States government and I don't look for that. I refuse that extinction. . . . My people are still heavily Catholicized. . . . Being a two-spirit in pre-contamination time meant . . . something, powerful and good. And in these times, it's something to be ashamed of and hide away. And I resist that by just simply being.[63]

Here, L. Frank quickly negates narratives of Native Californian genocide and two-spirit gendercide. Pó uses irony to emphasize that pó is still active on their ancestral land, even though some settler-colonial sources render their cultures as "extinct." Acknowledging the histories that prevented federal recognition, L. Frank commits to being Tongva regardless of that legal status. Here pó also recounts the ways in which two-spirit people are distanced from other Native Americans due to the impact of cis-heteropatriarchal settler colonialism. Pó simply resolves to continue being two-spirit in a "powerful and good" way, despite Catholic missionary attempts to eradicate two-spirit people within their Tongva/Ajachmem "homeland" and communities. Here, L. Frank's narration of Tongva two-spirit place is an example of Tonawanda feminist Mishuana Goeman's sense of "narrating geographies that unsettle the heteropatriarchal institutional structures."[64]

In an interview with Euro-American director Lydia Nibley in *Two Spirits* (2010), L. Frank again emphasizes how being two-spirit and Tongva are completely integrated. Filmed at the International Two-Spirit Gathering in Minnesota, Manriquez recalls learning a Tongva gender-neutral from the ravens that have remained in Tongva place. Returning to raven teachings, L. Frank explains the two-spirit land connections she "got from ancestors" while growing up in rural "LA":

> I roamed all of that land and I talked to that land and it talked to me, you know. I thought everybody did this. I thought this is how, that everybody heard things, you know. And I had the ravens who are my—I like the Hawaiian term of 'aumākua,—my spirit guides. They taught me a neutral. So, it's because my people were so rubbed out so quickly. But creator made a way for me to understand, and for me to know.[65]

Here, L. Frank affirms that even in the face of gendercide and genocide, pó learned a gender "neutral" through speaking with "ravens." The spirits of the land talked to pó to explain their Indigenous connection to land and their two-spirit being. For L. Frank, two-spirit gender is an integral part of their connections to their Tongva land. In the animated Netflix episode "Tovaangar," L. Frank voiced the crow Aawkut, who comes singing to the Tongva child Jasper and his friends. There by the concrete Los Angeles River upstream from Yaagna, Aawkut explains:

> This river is life, even though quite a bit of it is now closed up with concrete.
> But the river is still there at the right times, in the right ways.
> So it's still taking care of the people who can hear it.
> All these people you meet and all the lessons that you learn about how the world really works and who lives in it—that's your gift for the future, that you can never forget who you are.
> When times change, you will never be lost because you will always know what holds you and who holds you.
> And that will be your ancestors and the people around you, more than you've ever known, that you are not alone.[66]

Not being alone as Tongva is a great lesson, as Tongva make up such small parts of the Los Angeles population. Aawkut's emphasis here is also to learn the Tongva language, in which no one has remained fluent, and to not feel bad for not knowing. In this "Tovaangar" scene, L. Frank completes the circle of their life. While pó had long dreamed of crows speaking to pó in Tongva and only slowly learned enough language to understand what they were saying to pó, pó appears to the Tongva youth Jasper in the animation as a crow singing the "Wee totaa" song that pó themself had composed. Pó has become the crow to reach a new generation, just as the crows had reached pó when pó was young.

In order to correct myths of Indigenous and two-spirit extinction, L. Frank is consistent in their protocol of naming themself and their tribes at the beginning of their talks. For example, in the "Queer California: Untold Stories—L. Frank" (2019) and *Opening Blessing for Indigenous Pride LA* (2020) videos, L. Frank first identifies as Tongva, Rarámuri, and Ajachmem before addressing the two-spirit topics of the videos. Not only is their additional inclusion of the Rarámuri of Northern Mexico an important decolonization of Native American and Indigenous transborder identities, the naming of their tribal affiliations is part of Indigenous protocol that pó confirms in their videos. In the *Opening Blessing for Indigenous Pride LA*, L. Frank affirms that the invitation for pó to open the Indigenous Pride LA event is appropriate and "in keeping with protocol." In other words, as Los Angeles is mostly on Tongva land, it is appropriate for L. Frank as a Tongva two-spirit person and elder to fulfill that opening welcome. L. Frank finishes that video by saying, "I'd like to say welcome, special welcome to the LGBTQAI Two-Spirit community, by whatever name carries your spirit. . . . Welcome to Indigenous Pride LA."[67] As welcoming two-spirit spaces in LA are few, these statements are deeply needed. It is also true that most Angelenos and online audiences are unaware of contemporary Tongva presence. L. Frank's tribal affiliation protocol educates the audiences that two-spirit Tongva people do exist and traditionally support their multigendered communities.

Conclusion

Through their videos "Common Ground: L. Frank Manriquez," "Artist Talk: L. Frank Manriquez," and "L. Frank Manriquez Oral History," and their interview in *Two Spirits,* L. Frank restores Tongva connections to earth as a two-spirit person. Both L. Frank's and Craig Torres's two-spirit Tongva images and words unsettle Hollywood cis-heteropatriarchal timelines that begin with once-sovereign Tongva villages and terminate with Spanish missions, Mexican ranchos, and post-1849 U.S. California Gold Rush violence. Silent films such as Carewe's *Ramona* (1928) made visually sovereign inroads in condemning the U.S. genocidal violence against Native Southern Californians. Its fault was its inability to also critique Spanish and Mexican cis-hetero-settlerism and Hispanic assimilation narratives, a failing also evident in the 1964 *Island of the Blue Dolphins.* Given the century-long Hollywood suppression of Tongva two-spirit genders in film, videos by Manriquez and Torres are all the more remarkable. L. Frank's integrated identifications as both two-spirit and Tongvetam/Ajachmem/Rarámuri correct a century of Hollywood gendercidal and genocidal tropes. Despite the suppression of Indigenous cultures and genders, L. Frank affirms their two-spirit indigeneity, especially as a two-spirit Tongva. Resisting queer repression in Native California, both Torres and L. Frank reclaim a two-spirit presence in their Tongva land that should be remembered in Indigenous Hollywood and two-spirit film history.

6

UP

Queering Wakandan, Afro-Indigenous, and Bla(c)k Futurisms

Tracing an upward movement from earth to sky, this chapter features various LGBTQI2+ Bla(c)k and Indigenous people of color (BIPOC) futurisms that ultimately contrast with trans and cisgender settler-colonial cinematic visions of sci-fi escapes to outer space trans*racial utopias.[1] First, singer Zaachariaha Fielding's A<u>n</u>angu vertical spatiality and futurity demonstrate a future and outer space marked by queer Indigenous and queer settler cooperation. Their art recalls the origin narratives and songline connections to the Pleiades constellation. This Indigenous futurism linked to the stars contrasts with the Hollywood settler Euro-American-directed science fiction films *2001: A Space Odyssey*, *Avatar*, *Avatar 2: The Way of Water*, and *Cloud Atlas*, which replicate assimilationist and transracial tropes in space, even as *Avatar* attempts to critique settler violence and *Cloud Atlas* tries to uphold abolitionist and transgender messaging. Black futurism and sci-fi also make impact. The transgender māhū and Black visions of Janet Mock reorient Afro-Indigenous connections from the orí (head) of the Black body to the Yorùbá orun (sky) in the FX series *Pose* that supplies a Yorùbá/Afro-Taíno transgender futurity.[2] While the *Pose* series briefly realizes a subtly sky-linked Black LGBTQI2+ representation only hinted at in *The Wiz*, *Black Panther: Wakanda Forever* offers Hollywood visions with limited queer Indigenous African science fiction futurity, though limited in sovereign queer erotics and complicated by the Maya's coded subhuman mutations to live deep below the ocean surface. In the contrasting "Chaac + Yum" video, the rain deity Chaac and corn deity Yum are embodied in contemporary genderqueer lovers in San Francisco, reuniting the Maya earth–sky verticality that is absented to the deep-sea Maya in *Black Panther: Wakanda Forever*. The environmental context of the Mayan rain deity Chaac gains new meaning in this time of global climate change, with queer Indigenous insights from around the globe.

Blak Futuristic Space in Music and Art Performance

Electric Fields' electronic music performances are one Indigenous model for earth–sky connections. When the queer duo of Electric Fields represented

Australia's entry in the Eurovision Song Contest 2024, Zaachariaha Fielding sang "One Milkali (One Blood)," on futuristic unity and planetary consciousness with its Pitjantjatjara, Yankunytjatjara, and English lyrics. In the Eurovision semifinal video, the dark-skinned Fielding appears wearing a beautifully sculptured and leg-revealing dress made of an iridescent cream fabric. In a powerful voice that soars into a supported falsetto, Fielding sings the lyrics, "I stand in the eye of the spiral . . . and I descend to the center of the earth," making an ancient earth–sky connection.[3] Accompanied by an up-tempo didgeridoo, Fielding's own art fills the digitized floor with its dynamic circle, spiral, and dot patterns (fig. 15) that reference the Aṉangu aesthetics and representation of cosmic and earthly migration patterns that begin with earliest oral traditions that span over sixty-five thousand years in Australia. This lyrical movement from sky to earth also references the songlines that preserve these original migrations, including that of Seven Sisters stars' descent, migration paths across Zaachariaha Fielding's Aṉangu territories, and their return to the sky. Fielding himself worked with Mimili youth to sing the Seven Sister Dreaming story and record it in media as an act of Aṉangu futurity.[4] Permutations of these sky–earth migrations reappear in Fielding's performances, art graphics, and lyrics (fig. 15).

Through lyrics and visual art, Electric Fields situate an outer space grounded in Aṉangu vision, land, and language. The "One Milkali" song chorus, "Escape with us to the planets / to the Fleetwood Macs and the Janets / Milkali la / while entertaining the gods," invites interplanetary change based upon both Euro-American (Fleetwood Mac) and Black American (Janet Jackson) music artists' visions. The song's chorus word "Milkali" references a painting, *Milkali Kutju*, by Zaachariaha's father, Robert Fielding. The painting consists of black and white dots over shades of red. Robert Fielding explains,

Figure 15 Close-up of Zaachariaha Fielding singing in "Electric Fields - One Milkali (One Blood) - Semi Final 1" at Eurovision (2024).

"In Anangu culture . . . Milkali kutju means one blood. The painting is about Indigenous and non-Indigenous working alongside one another, learning and sharing two different cultures ngapartji–ngapartji (50–50)."[5] This to say that, despite skin color differences, all blood is similarly red, and is a foundation for Indigenous and white settler cooperation, just as red is the foundation of the white and black dots of Fielding's painting. This fifty-fifty futuristic vision in the artwork and song is appropriate given that Electric Fields is composed of both Blak vocalist and painter Zaachariaha Fielding and white queer keyboardist Michael Ross, who together wrote "One Milkali (One Blood)." The "One Milkali (One Blood)" video's vision of earth and space travel allows for both queer white settler and First Nation Australian futurity. Electric Fields' anti-assimilationist idea of Indigenous futurism and sharing space with Euro-Australian settlers visually and sonically accomplishes what most pop secular trans*racial Western science fiction films do not.

Settler Sci-Fi in Outer Space

Fielding's vision of a future in space in which unassimilated Indigenous peoples and settler Europeans coexist is rarely found in settler Hollywood sci-fi films, especially before the 2010s. In fact, a Diné director somewhat reversed the Western assimilationist trope in a 2012 film about Diné migration to Mars. In Nanobah Becker's (Navajo Nation) "The 6th World," it is a Dr. Smith (Luis Aldana), a Latinx astronaut, who is destined to have children with the Diné women on the spaceship, perhaps with the Diné woman protagonist, Tazbah Redhouse (Jeneda Benally, Navajo Nation).[6] But because of the matrilineal nature of Diné society, his patrilineal line would not carry forward long in the Diné kinship system, as future generations would identify more with their Diné matrilineal clans. Both astronauts reach Mars thanks to a Diné blessing from the creatrix Changing Woman along the way and some organic Diné corn to replace the GMO corn that had rotted due to DNA instability. Estrada notes, "As the shot zooms away from the field, the visual encompasses the red planet, and the words Są'ah Naghai Bik'eh Hozhǫ́ . . . appear across the planet. It signals that Navajo, rather than English, may be the language of Mars . . . in the future . . . [with] Navajo matrilineal line[s]."[7] Becker explains that she based this very image of Mars surrounded by stars upon Kubrick's iconic *2001* shots of a mock earth from outer space.

Settler Jewish American director Stanley Kubrick's *2001: A Space Odyssey* features a famous match cut after an early male African hominid is intellectually evolved by the intercession of alien monoliths. The hominid is then able to use a bone as a weapon to kill a rival male attempting to take his watering hole and cave. In exalted victory, he hurls up his newly invented bone tool, spinning it upward into the air until it transforms after the match cut into a spinning Euro-American male space station. No human African innovations are shown in this evolution. This upward-oriented "evolution" of technology also links male aggression with hominid intellectual "evolution."[8] The clearly upward vertical movement also contrasts the more "primitive" African earthly tool-making with superior Euro-American space technology, a vertical evolution that subtly codes the scientific racist belief that Africans are less intellectually evolved than Europeans, as *2001*'s Afrocentric early hominid development contrasts starkly with its Eurocentric future in outer space. There are no people of color in the 2001 space setting of this 1968 segregated Hollywood film, a faulty and racist depiction of the future of American astronauts that did not prove true in the astronautics of the 1990s, much less in 2001, despite Kubrick's rather prescient depictions of the rise of artificial intelligence and the ongoing political tensions between the United States and Russia. To complete the Eurocentric cis-heteropatriarchy, *2001*'s U.S. women are merely attentive stewardesses and secretaries, clearly not the intellectual equals of the white male U.S. astronaut protagonists. Modern Black, women, and women of color astronauts like African American Mae Carol Jemison have disproven this sexist and racist vision of the 1960s that male Euro-Americans' supposed superior logic and physique enables them exclusively to venture vertically into space.

Given the sexist and racist segregation of Kubrick's *2001: A Space Odyssey* casting, one might mistakenly think that settler Euro-American/Canadian James Cameron's *Avatar* and *Avatar: The Way of Water* fix that situation by casting the BIPOC Zoe Saldaña in the lead alien role and Wes Studi (Cherokee Nation of Oklahoma) as the Na'vi chief. *Avatar: The Way of Water* also employed Māori actors Cliff Curtis of Ngāti Hauiti and Te Arawa descent and Duane Evans Jr. of Ngāti Whātua and Ngāpuhi descent to voice members of the sea-adapted Metkayina clan of Na'vi, an indication that the Na'vi represent Indigenous peoples on the alien planet. For *Avatar*'s disabled Euro-American protagonist Jake (Sam Worthington) to successfully lead an Indigenous Na'vi revolt against earthlings' attempts to kill off the Na'vi for their mineral riches is yet another example of the white savior trope in outer space, in which "white males master alien climes and assume the mantle of messianic liberator," a well-established sci-fi trope also seen in *John Carter* (2012) and *Dune* (2021).[9] For his efforts, Jake gets to keep his eight-foot blue alien body into which his consciousness has been fused and marry the Na'vi princess Neytiri, played by Afro-Caribbean actress Zoe Saldaña, cementing the cis-heterosexist nature of the film as well. In critique of the appropriation of Diné landmarks in western sci-fi, Watchman notes that *Avatar* is like William Burroughs's settler-colonial *John Carter* (1912) and the eponymous

2012 film adaptation of that book, contributing "to the tired cliché of a white savior who rescues an 'Indian princess,' common in Hollywood Westerns."[10]

John Russell calls Jake's assumption of the racial other "didactic blackface," an act meant to demonstrate an overcoming of racism by having Euro-Americans become one with the racially Othered alien Na'vi, who resemble Native American, African, and Polynesian peoples. Russell criticizes the blueface postracial social justice messaging: "it nonetheless utilized the privileged I/eye-witness testimony of white authority as a means to authenticate the black experience by making it one's own. It presumed that the recording of that experience by actual blacks themselves was somehow inadequate to the task."[11] Russell's prohibitive article title, "Don't ~~It~~ Make My Black Face Blue," confirms the "No More Blueface!" viral Twitter messaging of trans Diné woman Yuè Begay regarding the *Avatar: The Way of Water* sequel. Begay called for a boycott of the *Avatar* sequel, citing the film's "(white) man's savior complex."[12] *Avatar* and *Avatar: The Way of Water* each grossed over $2 billion, occupying the first- and third-highest grossing spots in movie history,[13] and these white savior narratives gain popular belief through their repetition of viewing. The problem with outer space in *Avatar* isn't the general idea of its anticolonial and environmental science fiction messaging; it is the lack of Indigenous writing, directing, and consultation that resulted in the problematic transracial noble savage blueface.

The irony of white imaginings of a seamless Afro-Indigenous alien race in space is that white settlers have historically driven partitions between African and American Indigenous peoples, separating those who were mixed with Africans from those who were mixed with Europeans, especially in the context of enslavement and tribal enrollment practices. Several authors from outside federal- and state-recognized Indigenous communities have been critical of anti-Black racism of the Indigenous Southeast. Writing for his Creole and Atakapa-Ishak communities, Andrew Jolivétte states, "As with other mixed-blood Indigenous groups anti-Blackness has been central to settler-colonial projects that attempt to erase and disenfranchise Creoles as an Afro-Indigenous people."[14] In her two-spirit "Re(Counting) Wo(Man)" video, Mikasuki Seminole mixed-blood Jennifer Lisa Vest recounts that this racial division wasn't always so, as many peoples and races came together to become Seminole. She names Native Americans such as "Hitchiti, Cherokee/Yuchi, Yamassee/Tunica, Oconee," as well as the different African peoples "Ibo, Dahomey, Ga/Fon, Hausa, Yoruba / . . . Ewe and Dagon" that joined to create and recreate Indigenous communities in Florida and throughout the Southeast in resistance to white settler colonialism that displaced, enslaved, and attacked all of these peoples.[15] As Southeast Native Americans intermarried with settler Euro-Americans who enslaved Africans, the practice of enslavement became normalized, as did the tension between mixed European Indigenous and mixed Black Indigenous people, who were separated by racist settler norms, laws, and enrollment processes. Some Afro-Indigenous Seminoles later found themselves excluded from Native American enrollments and faced enslavement or re-enslavement at different times in their histories. Here, one recalls the legacy of mixed Afro-Seminoles like John Horse, who fought U.S. settler-colonial intrusions into Mikasuki Seminole territory, later leading Black Seminoles into Mexico to escape the prospect of re-enslavement in Oklahoma by Seminoles, Creeks, and Cherokees who had stronger investments with chattel slavery.[16] Muskoke language teacher Marcus Briggs-Cloud recounts the history in which African descendants who joined the Muskoke society as escapees from white enslavement or were emancipated from Muskoke enslavement, were granted citizenship in the Moskoke Nation via the 1866 U.S. Treaty with the Creek Nation and then were disenrolled in 1979. He writes that Freedmen and their descendants have "lived with [and] intermarried with" Muskoke people and at times even spoken the language and practiced ceremonies, concluding that Muskoke language analysis shows that "anti-Blackness, experienced in Maskoke communities today, prove to be incompatible with and contradictory to Muskoke traditions."[17] Jodi Byrd (Chickasaw Nation of Oklahoma) and Joseph Pierce (Cherokee Nation of Oklahoma) also note the resistance to discussing anti-Blackness within their respective nations, with Byrd concluding, "I hope there is something queer and nonnormative to say it doesn't serve Chickasaw sovereignty to not talk about our participation in slavery . . . because my Chickasaw family owned slaves. . . . I can't undo that except to make it legible and honest." Byrd and Pierce also try to parse the differences between the "disconnection or undocumentability tied to real issues of disenfranchisement" of Five Tribes Black and Afro-Indigenous Freedmen, with other claims to being Cherokee outside of federal recognition.[18] And yet these ongoing complications of race and Indigenous nationhood are erased in outer space within the white savior narratives of mixed Afro-Indigenous people, whether they are made by cisgender or transgender settlers.

When Lana Wachowski publicly declared her trans woman identity just before *Cloud Atlas* opened in 2012, followed by Lilly Wachowski's similar declaration in 2016, film critics finally began to make trans connections in the Wachowskis' previous science fiction films, including *The Matrix* trilogy. The Euro-American transmasculine film scholar Cael Keegan notes the criticism of the Wachowskis' works that strive to depict a "postracial" solution to "the problem of racial authenticity through a transcendent universalist humanism." Keegan problematizes the Wachowskis' tendency to conflate transgender identity with transracial identity, noting, "To the extent that it treats race as if it were like gender, *Cloud Atlas* thus over-relies on a deconstructive equivalence that endeavors to align incongruous cinematic traditions" of cross-gender performance and the cross-race performances of blackface, yellowface, and redface.[19] Perplexing to viewers who did not read the British author David Mitchell's 2004 *Cloud Atlas* novel upon which the film is loosely based, the same actors sometimes change gender and race via parallel editing as they reincarnate to face the different historical oppressions: South Pacific slavery in 1848, homophobia in 1936 Scotland, nuclear environmental threats in 1973 San Francisco, institutionalized ageism in 2012 Edinburgh, clone oppression in 2144 Neo-Seoul, and intertribal wars in an environmentally unstable postapocalyptic and post-2321 Hawai'i.[20]

This chapter's materials both precede and follow Keegan in that transgender analytical direction, but with Indigenous critiques of vertical spaces in *Cloud Atlas*. The settler nature of *Cloud Atlas*'s narrative of ascent from earth to space evidences that the Wachowskis' uncritical transgender white settler colonialism cannot be resolved in their transracial and postracial gaze up toward a futuristic outer space. With Tom Tykwer, the Wachowskis directed *Cloud Atlas* (2012), hoping to challenge the whiteness of space with a multiracial cast of characters who ultimately leave an ecologically poisoned earth for the safety of outer space after centuries of human struggle in the futurist Hawai'i. Only on another planet is human peace finally achieved as the racially mixed grandchildren of the Black Meronym (Halle Berry) and the white Zachry (Tom Hanks) protagonists gather around a nighttime fire to hear stories of the old earth twinkling among the distant stars. Both Meronym and Zachry prepared to leave earth through signaling for help at the Mauna a Wākea observatory, with the tech-savvy Black Meronym being the "modern" person who must save the white Zachry, whose superstitious "tribal" culture leaves him ignorant of the advanced technology that will save him. In a key scene, Meronym scales the high craggy Mauna a Wākea peak to activate the satellite that signals for outer space help. Bathed in white tropical light, a sweeping aerial shot ascends the summit of the Mauna a Wākea proxy digitized and filmed in the Mediterranean as she leads Zachry to enter the observatory door. The succeeding aerial shot shows the defunct Mauna a Wākea telescopes surrounded by clouds on the mountain peak. This shot is supported by the vigorous stringed and brass instrumentation of the *Cloud Atlas* sextet diegetic soundtrack as rising arpeggios represent the ascent up the mountain and to the stars.[21] The ascension of the aerial shot is also meant to signify the soaring feminist and antiracist aspirations enabled by secular technology. It also foreshadows Meronym's physical ascension to the safety of another planet. As Meronym explains to Zachry inside the telescope as they walk through rooms of corpses left since an apocalypse killed them all,

"Before The Fall, Oldens built dwellings beyond the sky, among the stars, and this place joined here with there."[22] Mauna a Wākea is the connection to ascent into space. After several parallel scenes in other time frames, Meronym activates the signal. When she does so, a third aerial shot depicts a white satellite opening like a huge lotus flower and sending out a blue burst of information that will bring spaceships to save her, Zachry, her fellow band of Prescients, and some white "tribal" Hawaiians. That the Mauna a Wākea satellite looks like the lotus crown chakra of enlightenment is perhaps meant to symbolize both a technological enlightenment and a social enlightenment of intersectional race, class, and gender equality. *Cloud Atlas* problematically celebrates the controversial telescope atop the Big Island mountain Mauna a Wākea as the salvation of humanity. Here *Cloud Atlas* clearly favors Western technology and dismisses Kānaka Maoli beliefs regarding the sacredness of their Hawai'i Island summit.

Kānaka Maoli, Black, and Afro-Indigenous Futurisms

Kealoha Pisciotta of Mauna Kea Anaina Hou explained the sacredness of the peak of Mauna a Wākea in the documentary *Mauna Kea: Temple Under Siege* (2001). Likewise, Kumu Hina's three-minute short in which she teaches her mele "Kū ha'aheo e ku'u Hawai'i" (2015) clearly expresses her aloha 'āina, which resists the thirty-meter-telescope construction on Mauna a Wākea, "the highest peak and piko in all Oceania."[23] In an interview with the author, Kumu Hina explained that while "piko" originally refers to the umbilical cord, it can also encompass the head, umbilical cord, and genitals as centers of the body with temporal connections.[24] While the piko of the "po'o, or head" connects to the "'aumākua, the ancestors," the actual umbilical cord connects Kānaka Maoli to their mothers and present relatives. The third piko of the genitalia represents the connection to the future generations.[25] This descending order of ancestors/head, present/navel, and future/genitals reverses the Western conviction that the past is represented by earth below and the future by outer space above. The piko of Mauna a Wākea represents the crown and its connection to the kūpuna. The filmmakers at Kamakako'i recorded one of the many sessions in which Kumu Hina presents her mele in defense of the Mauna against the construction of the thirty-meter-telescope, an example of her aloha 'āina. Hina recalls hearing her mele being sung on Mauna a Wākea by aloha 'āina activists. She responds, "My mele was being sung. . . . How could I remain at home and not look for the nearest opportunity to go up to that mountain and show my face? They were using my composition as a rally cry to unify the people."[26] In the Kamakako'i video, Kumu Hina sports a hae Hawai'i dress while teaching Kānaka Maoli and other supporters of all ages to sing her mele "Kū ha'aheo e ku'u Hawai'i" as they sit around her on Mauna a Wākea. Her māhū voice is strong, and the crowd begins to repeat her lyrics as the short video progresses. She leads both men's and women's choruses:

> Kaiko'o ka moana kā i lana nei Hawai'i / The sea of Hawai'i surges in turmoil
> Nāueue a hālulu ka honua a Haumea / The earth of Haumea rumbles and shakes
> Nākulukulu e ka lani ki'eki'e kau mai i luna / The highest of heavens shudder up above
> Auē ke aloha 'ole a ka malihini / Alas! Woeful indeed are the heartless foreigners
> (Hooho—chorus)
> Kū ha'aheo e ku'u Hawai'i / Stand tall my Hawai'i
> . . .
> Hoe a mau hoe a mau no ka pono sivila / Paddle on in our pursuits of civil justice
> A ho'iho'i hou 'ia mai ke kū'oko'a. / Until our dignity and independence is restored.[27]

When "Hamea rumbles" and the "highest heavens shudder," it is in part in protest of the settler-colonial misuse of the sacred piko at Mauna a Wākea. Earth and Sky communicate in signs that their Kānaka Maoli children can read. The māhū Kumu Hina teaches a mele to fight for ea, for Mauna a Wākea, and to be free of the thirty-meter telescope and U.S. occupation, a clear contrast to the trans settler visions of the Wachowskis.

Black science fiction Hollywood films have offered high-production Afro-futuristic visions of vertical ascent into space with mostly unrealized queer potential. In the sci-fi/fantasy all-Black cast retelling of the *Wizard of Oz* classic film *The Wiz* (1978), directed by the non-Black Sidney Lumet, the old maid protagonist Gale (Diana Ross) escapes from being set up by her aunt to meet a man at a holiday dinner. Instead of meeting the man, Gale is whisked away in a Harlem snowstorm tornado to the fantastic Oz, where she must journey with friends to defeat the evil witch Evillene (Mabel King), unmask the fraudulent Wiz (Richard Pryor), and find her way home with the help of Glinda the Good (Lena Horne). As Gale makes her ascent in a snow tornado into space from her Black Harlem community in New York City, she is momentarily held in the cosmic palm of Glinda the Good, who is dressed in a voluminous blue dress adorned with silver stars that matches the night sky with a host of baby stars surrounding her. While Glinda could represent some aspect of the Egyptian sky goddess Nut or the West African moon goddess Mawu, she could also represent a Black Christian guardian angel in heaven.[28] Gale's escape from compulsory heterosexuality into the parallel space of Oz was picked up in resistant readings by queer audiences of the time. Black lesbian author La Donna Forsgren shares, "I found Dorothy's refusal to conform to heteronormativity refreshing and delighted in her ability to construct alternative visions of black womanhood with queer possibilities."[29] When Gale has completed her tasks in Oz, she once again ascends, this time to the lofty abode of the Wiz, who runs the sci-fi city of Oz. When Gale meets Glinda the Good, she appears to enter Glinda's starry space, ascending above the city below. As a powerful wisdom holder overseeing all from space, Glinda instructs Gale to return home by clicking her magical silver slippers three times and to think of home. Before Gale does so, she sings of the "love and affection" that "home" represents to her.[30] The original Broadway musical song "Home" was written by the Black composer Charlie Smalls and rearranged for the Motown Productions film by the Black music legend Quincy Jones, who went on to produce *The Wiz* co-star Michael Jackson's *Thriller*. Forsgren explains how, for herself and some queer audiences, *The Wiz*'s "Home" song came to represent the yearning of queer Black communities who have often been excised from their queerphobic families and churches and whose desire to have a home meant remaking family from their chosen queer community who fill in for cis-heterosexist blood relatives.[31]

There is an openly queer and trans rendition of this climactic "Home" song in the FX *Pose* series, one of many queerings of *The Wiz*. Instead of having to imagine a queer Black escape up to space and away from compulsory heterosexuality, *Pose* brings the reality of LGBTQI2+ Blackness back to Harlem and New York City. In an act of revisionist trans Afro-Latinx/Indigenous futurism, Janet Mock both cowrote and directed *Pose* season 1, episode 6, "Love Is the Message." In a key scene, the ballroom mother Blanca Evangelista (Michaela Antonia Jaé Rodriguez) of the Black and Afro-Latinx House of Evangelista sings *The Wiz* soul ballad "Home" in a late 1980s AIDS hospital ward. Blanca has HIV, and she is singing to the ballroom emcee Pray Tell's (Billy Porter) boyfriend Costas (Johnny Sibilly), who is dying of AIDS. In this context, the song becomes about making home from one's own love and relationships, even when transgender, queer, and combating AIDS in the 1980s–1990s setting of the series. Recalling that Afrofuturism is about seeing a future and justice for Black folks rather than simply creating sci-fi with black cast members, Blanca's "Home" predicted her own loving successes as the House of Evangelista mother and her ability to survive the AIDS pandemic, even when others including Costas and Pray Tell do not. Based in part upon the 1991 *Paris Is Burning*, *Pose* openly spoke about the HIV/AIDS struggles within 1980s–1990s ballroom houses in New York City that *Paris Is Burning* did not take up, even though three of its main icons, Angie Xtravaganza, Willie Ninja, and Dorian Corey, would subsequently die from AIDS-related causes.[32] Forsgren also documents that the male film role of *The Wiz*, played by Black bisexual actor Richard Pryor, was subsequently played in drag-king style by Black lesbian icon Queen Latifah in the 2015 *The Wiz Live* televised event.[33] In addition, the iconic Oz dance scenes from *The Wiz Live* are reimagined to explicitly play upon queer and trans drag ballroom culture featured in *Pose*. While a queer Black woman's vision of Dorothy's escape from heteronormativity required a queer reception of the science fiction/fantasy world of Oz, *Pose* transforms *The Wiz*'s Harlem and New York City setting to that of a contemporary reality with open Black and Afro-Latinx/Indigenous transgender and queer representation. *Pose*'s trans and queer Afrofuturism foresees greater self-representation in a time in which there are precious few examples of such directing, production, and cast inclusivity.

In *Pose*, the Afro-Taíno Indya Moore played Angel Evangelista, a trans woman member of a Black and Afro-Latinx/Indigenous ballroom house who finds love and a career as a model by overcoming barriers of poverty, racism, transphobia, and sex work. Upon wishing for a victory at a ballroom dance competition finale, Angel referenced the Yorùbá orí-orun head-heaven connection when she said, "I've been praying all week. Our orishas are working overtime." While the term "orisha" can generally refer to a major Yorùbá deity, author Baba Ifa Karade explains that the orí, or spiritual head, is also composed of two parts, with the inner head being the "orí apari" and the outer "orí apare" being the sign of the individual's orisha.[34] Afrofuturist Jon Ivan Gill emphasizes the dual earth and heaven communication in Yorùbá culture. He writes of the "Yoruba-esque metaphysic in which the ancestors (oku-orun) participate in earthly affairs."[35] While "oku" can refer to a deceased person, "orun" refers to their place of residence, heaven. With a similar critique of the Christian and Western distancing between heaven and earth, Odogame explains, "In the Yoruba worldview, the cosmos is divided into orun and aye. Orun refers to heaven/sky as the abode of the spiritual entities while aye implies the world/earth of human habitation," though both are "intricately intertwined."[36] Thus, intertwined orun and aye vertical spaces facilitate the ongoing relationships of Yorùbá ancestors and descendants, and these relations are part of the Yorùbá metaphysical body that include the orí (head). Moreover, Angel's contemporary actions of praying to orishas that descend from orun into the orí can be considered a kind of Afrofuturism, given Kodwo Eshun's British Fante sense that while science fiction is an "engineering feedback between its preferred future and its becoming present," Afrofuturism "is concerned with the possibilities for intervention within the dimension of the predictive, the projected, the proleptic, the envisioned, the virtual, the anticipatory and the future conditional."[37]

Queer Black Panther, Mayan, and Water Futurisms

While the FX series *Pose* featured a trans and queer Afro-Caribbean and Afro-Indigenous cast, crew, directors, and writers, mainstream Hollywood science fiction cinema is much more queerphobic and transphobic. First authored in Marvel *Black Panther* comics by Black feminists Roxane Gay and poet Yona Harvey, the openly queer Dora Milaje Aneka (Michaela Coel) and Ayo (Florence Kasumba) shared subtle affections in Afro-American Ryan Coogler's *Black Panther: Wakanda Forever* (2022).[38] The fearless *Black Panther* Dora Milaje Wakanda elite woman royal guard included a queer leadership and affections easily missed by most. While this *Black Panther: Wakanda Forever* Marvel queer affection is brief, it marks an important pop culture moment in which Black and other queer audiences are no longer having to merely imagine queer narratives for science fiction and Afrofuturist characters.[39]

Aneka and Ayo's kiss (fig. 16) occurs during the final *Black Panther: Wakanda Forever* scene celebrating the truce between warring African Wakanda and underwater Mayan Talokan peoples, the main conflict in the film. In the scene, Ayo sits in her Dora Milaje red, gold, and black warrior's gear at a party. The Dora Milaje protect the Wakandan royalty, whose language is based upon the Indigenous Xhosa language of southern Africa. Though these women warriors represent a pan-African Wakandan society, the Dora Milaje weaponry not shown in the peaceful scene includes a high-tech version of an Indigenous Zulu warrior spear from southern Africa. Ayo's Dora Milaje beading may also be inspired by the Indigenous Turkana people

Figure 16 Aneka (Michaela Coel) kisses her lover and fellow Dora Milaje warrior Ayo (Florence Kasumba) in *Black Panther: Wakanda Forever* (2022), directed by Ryan Coogler.

of Kenya and eastern Africa.[40] In the background plays a relaxing song from Nigerian Yorùbá singer Fireboy DML, who sings

> Well, I pray that the universe
> gives you way more than you deserve
> And when the tears fall like shooting stars
> Remember who you are
> Just look up to the sky, you'll see

In the first two song lines, Ayo's romantic partner Aneka approaches her in a sleek modern orange sports dress and kisses Ayo on top of the head. Ayo looks up at Aneka and gently responds in English, "Thank you, my love."[41] While audiences likely missed this love reference, it is indeed a long-term romantic love to which she refers. The connection of the Dora Milaje warrior lovers with the lyrics that invoke "the universe" and the reminder to "look up to the sky" would also fit the Yorùbá orí-orun head-heaven connection of living one's fate and destiny. In this case, the lesbian lovers Ayo and Aneka are living their best destiny in both defending Wakanda and living to marvel in each other's presence and love.

Ghanaian British actor Michaela Coel explained that taking on the queer role was a way to combat anti-LGTBQ legislation in Ghana. She reported, "For me, it was about why I took the role and what it meant to me to portray a queer character, being from Ghana, where there's a lot of confusing LGBTQ+ laws going on."[42] Coel's own writing earned her a Peabody Award for her 2020 TV mini-series *I May Destroy You*, which also won Coel a GLAAD award for her complex queer representation of sexual assault, including that of the queer co-star Kwame played by fellow Ghanian-British actor Paapa Kwaakye Essiedu.[43] Despite the fact that the 1930s Motion Picture Production Code that banned all positive LGBTQI2+ depictions ended in 1968, global public queerphobia continues to minimize LGBTQI2+ presence in blockbuster science fiction films, which market around the world to mixed reactions. Even the small queer affections of Aneka and Ayo matter in a film with a worldwide audience, as do the Marvel superhero America Chavez's flashbacks of her two lesbian mothers in *Dr. Strange in the Multiverse of Madness* (2022), a film that excluded the Latinx America Chavez's lesbian comic book identity while at the same time testing world markets' abilities to screen a lesbian couple.

To extend the "Yorùbá-esque" analysis that Gill begins of Wakanda, the women of Wakanda appear to resemble Tsang's queer community descriptions of the Yorùbá Yemayá, the compassionate and powerful ocean mother Orisha, who at times "wields a machete" and "hitches up her skirts for battle," in addition to caring for her human children as "the sovereign mother, whose dignity transcends all human afflictions . . . [and] commands the respect of all orishas."[44] The rhetorical hallmarks of Wakanda's freedom from patriarchal European colonial norms are their technological advancement and their relative advancement in gender equality. Starring in both films, Mexican Kenyan actress Lupita Nyong'o noted the balanced gender dynamics of *Black Panther*, stating how woman are "allowed to realize their full potential alongside the men; and the men are not threatened by the power of the women. . . . The powers are complementary." This power extends into queen, military, and queer roles for women. Noting Queen Ramonda's (Angela Bassett) leadership representation in *Black Panther*, Copeland offers a deeper look into the legacy of queen mothers in Africa, stating that "the position is still prevalent today. . . . For instance, queen mothers and chiefs exist among the Akan ethnic group; they reside over the towns and villages."[45] In fact, the queen mother of the Akan Ashante empire, Yaa Asantewaa, led armed resistance for sovereignty against the British empire in 1900,[46] a feat dramatized in the 2009 independent film *Warrior Queen* that predates the Dahomey warrior woman film *The Woman King* (2022). When the deceased King T'Challa's sister Shuri (Letitia Wright) ascends to the military leadership Black Panther role in *Black Panther: Wakanda Forever*, she occupies the main protagonist lead in another statement of women's strength, physical prowess, and intelligence. Rather than become an overt lesbian presence, however, Shuri is asexual, finding no romance across the two 2018 and 2022 *Black Panther* films. Though a lead in the second film, she remains somewhat in the shadow of her brother's heterosexual romance. Like the queer Nigerian American Nnedi Okorafor's *Binti* protagonist, however, Shuri's genius science abilities decolonize the images of African women as impoverished, oppressed, and technologically lagging and offer instead an African woman exemplar in science, technology, engineering, and mathematics achievement.[47] For example, when Shuri saves the life of the white CIA agent Everett Ross (Martin Freeman) with vibranium-enriched medical equipment not available in the United States, she tells him that she achieved the impossible healing of his bullet wound "not by magic, by technology."[48] Shuri and Wakanda's scientists are able to use vibranium to construct superior weapons and levitating ships that also come in handy during battles and world reconnaissance scenes.

To compel Wakanda to keep vibranium's power secret in the second *Black Panther* film, the Maya leader Namor floods Wakanda and kills Queen Ramonda in the process. In contrast with the technological abilities of the Wakandans of *Black Panther: Wakanda Forever*, the Maya are less morally and technologically developed. Furthermore, their location underwater ambiguously marks them as having lesser ethics, lesser technology, and less gender equality. This vertical placement below sea level was bought by mutations from vibranium itself. In the film, the Maya, who worship the rain god Chaac, consume a plant mutated by a powerful vibranium asteroid, turn blue, grow gills, and escape late 1500s Spanish colonization and diseases deep under the Atlantic Ocean's surface. A leader, Namor (Tenoch Huerta), is born underwater and eventually leads his 2000s underwater Maya against the advanced pan-African Wakandans to stop them from leaking secrets to the outside world of the vibranium that fuels both nations. David Lowry (Lumbee Tribe of North Carolina) had a telling conversation with his nephew about the film. When he asked his nephew if he felt represented in the *Wakanda Forever*, the nephew responded: "No—why weren't we (American Indians/Native Americans) students at MIT or working for the CIA?" as the Wakandans work with both in the film. Lowry points out that there is a scene when Wakandans visit MIT's duPont Building that now houses a Native American student group, but finally admits, "we are reduced to the fish-like beings."[49] Unlike Wakanda, the underwater Mayan Talokan city is pictured with neither labs nor scientists. Instead, Namor creates technology for his people with vibranium as a virtual demigod whose Yucatec Maya name, Kukulkan, denotes the great feathered serpent revered in many Meso-American cultures. Unlike Wakanda, which operates with a council of elders to guide the king's action, Talokan operates as a theocracy with Namor as a mythical god-king. When Namor's number one Talokan supporter and warrior Namora (Mabel Cadena) is shot as Wakandans rescue Shuri from captivity in Talokan, Namor cannot save Namora with technology as Shuri had saved Everett Ross, a Euro-American stranger to Wakanda. Namor is a patriarchal figure with only vague romantic connections to the lead women in the film. This lack of offspring points to a form of queer Maya underdevelopment compared to the past Black Panther line of kings that communicate from an orun-like heaven to the new Black Panther leaders as they undergo ceremonial initiation.

As the newest Black Panther, Shuri personally stops Namor, who agrees to desist in his attacks even as Shuri agrees to not give over vibranium technology to the world, at least not immediately. While Namor's motive for the attack is rooted in the desire to hide from the outside colonial world responsible for so much destruction that he witnessed under Spanish invasion of the 1500s, the conflict of a Maya nation and pan-African nation does feel like an internal Global South war that nonetheless benefits the Global North strategies of divide and conquer. It is Red/Brown on Black violence, with Maya parts played by dark-skinned Mestizo Mexican leads and Mayan supporting roles. However, César Albarrán-Torres and Liam Burke note the film's "critique of colonialism in the Mesoamerican region." By making Namor a Maya survivor of Spanish genocide, director Ryan Coogler radically changed the original Timely comic book character from a coded Yellow Peril nemesis who struck back against sea bombings of icebergs by U.S. ships by going "to the land of the white people" and waging a "war of revenge," as Namor's Atlantean mother commanded from the bottom of the sea.[50] To its credit, *Wakanda Forever* had an African anticolonial theme well in place that prevented many of the usual Maya New Age and antiquated racial tropes that remain the Hollywood hegemonic norm into the second millennium. What also gave Coogler's vision a pass in Maya representation for many was his use of Yucatec Maya language in Talokan, the casting of both Maya and Mexican actors, and the larger decolonial message of his film. In a review of *Black Panther: Wakanda Forever,* the Yucatec Maya–speaking Eider Perez Dzul notes, "Seeing the great work of Mayan actor Josué Maay Chi' in the film and as a language coach for the rest of the actors . . . was an inspiration," especially given the repression of Maya language in Yucatán schools and lack of Mayan and Maya-language film representation.[51] This rare language use only somewhat compensates for the seabound and vertically challenged Maya of Talokan.

Coogler's anticolonial and futuristic vision of the Wakanda Maya differs markedly from the German director Roland Emmerich's ecological and apocalyptic action film *2012* (2009) in which the very Maya traditionalists who predicted a world "change" in accordance with the ending of their cosmic 5,200-year baktun calendar cycle on December 21, 2012, are depicted in film as dying by mass suicide for fear of that change. In contrast, the *2012* film's more privileged non-Indigenous humans including a Black American president are welcomed into arks that allow them to withstand cataclysmic earthquakes and floods that wipe out the rest of life on earth, a sci-fi take on the Noah's ark trope from the Abrahamic Genesis text. The type of Maya "New Age" appropriations of *2012* that Jakaltek Maya scholar Victor Montejo broadly critiques are also present in the *Star Trek: Voyager* series set across outer space.[52] Written and directed by non-Indigenous people, *Voyager*'s second-in-command, Commander Chakotay of the fictional Rubber Tree People, was based on "New Age" Maya references, including the use of a "Mayan-descended medicine wheel."[53] Played by Mexican American actor Robert Beltran, Chakotay's role was overseen by the Ashkenazi Jewish American Jackie Marks, who had appropriated the Cherokee identity Jamake Highwater and was hired as an Indigenous cultural consultant. Without any Indigenous cultural background, Marks allowed stereotypes to go unchecked, stereotypes that a team of Native American writers and cultural consultants would likely not have allowed. Like *2012*, *Avatar*, and *Cloud Atlas*, *Star Trek: Voyager* demonstrates that hiring Indigenous writers, directors, main actors, consultants, and supporting actors is needed to correct many of the stereotypes reproduced by Hollywood science fiction blockbusters that lack Indigenous production components. Simply hiring one Indigenous consultant or one Indigenous actor, however prominent, is not enough to achieve equitable Indigenous representation.

Roberto Fatal and Xav SF's queer erotic Maya film "Chaac + Yum" (2022) is a clear contrast to *Black Panther: Wakanda Forever*'s inability to bridge sky with earth, a necessity in the rain-dependent farming of Mayan maize. A transgender two-spirit director and child of a Maya Tzotzil father of Simojoval, Chiapas, Mexico, Snowflake Arizmendi-Calvert both wrote and starred in the independent short film. The film features the erotic connection between the masculine Maya sky and rain deity Chaac and the genderqueer Maya land and maize deity Yum in representations that flash from a San Francisco disco to ancient Maya rainforests. It is a film like *Wakanda Forever* that goes back and forth between ancient spiritual spaces and contemporary Maya times. Arizmendi-Calvert's work offers an intriguing conception of two-spirit Maya rain and corn on earth and in the sky. The beginning of her film opens with a title card and a Spanish/English bilingual statement of Maya movement and queer erotics:

> The Mayan view of time is an eternal spirit. / El Tiempo para los mayas era un espíritu eternal.
> Every point in the spiral of time is connected. / Cada pinto de la espiral del Tiempo está conectado.
> Chaac, the deity of rain, is alive at all times. / La deidad de la alluvia, Chaac, vive en todos los temps.
> He seeks Yum, the deity of corn in all times. / Él busca a Yum, la deidad del maíz, eternamente.
> And now He seeks him in our time. / Y ahora busca a Yum en nuestro tiempo.[54]

What this introduction sets up is a queer erotics of Maya rain and corn that are played out in a contemporary disco in which queer deities Chaac (Xav SF) and Yum (Snowflake Arizmendi-Calvert) meet again in the spirits of their genderqueer Maya diaspora in San Francisco.

In the midsection of the short film, there are many cuts of the two dancing and embracing together in the San Francisco club to the two making love, stylized through offerings and slower ceremonial gestures in a Maya landscape. On the dance floor Yum is seduced by genderqueer Chaac wearing blue lipstick. They dance together, then the film cuts to Yum's hands twisting and tied with twine. Then there is another cut to maize, and then to the maize in Yum's hand. Yum, who is shirtless, wears braids with ribbons, and presents as femme, touches Chaac's chest as Chaac binds up Yum's hand to a pole

Figure 17 Yum (Snowflake Arizmendi-Calvert) is caressed by Chaac (Xav SF) in the erotic Maya interlude scene in "Chaac + Yum" (2022).

with maize. The colors are hypersaturated with purple, blue, and red lights to denote a sacred ritual space, as seen in the intense red hues in figure 17. Chaac smokes Yum off with incense that is likely copal. Chaac washes Yum sensually with Chaac's own urine and then unbinds Yum and they embrace. There is a fade back into techno dance club where they embrace and dance. Chimes fade in as they were in the beginning.[55] This film takes elements of contemporary consensual bondage with the tying of Yum's hands by Chaac—combined with the act of tying maize, which represents Yum—and the urine elements of some fetishistic sex play simulate the sky father's semen, which fertilizes Mother Earth, but with genderqueer twists (fig. 17). Chaac's urine is also emblematic of the monsoon rain that Yum needs to grow as the spirit of maize. Both presentations of Chaac and Yum are also of contemporary urban two-spirit Maya, showing sovereign erotic links to the Maya spirit of rain and corn of antiquity and today. It is strange to think that the Maya of the fictional city Talokan would have connection neither to maize, their source of life, nor to the sun, so central in Maya conceptions of time. Without either, it is unclear how much they have become like the most intelligent of fish, and how they can relate to the contemporary world above water.

Arizmendi-Calvert makes connection to the rain and corn cycles deeply tied to the identity and environmental health of the Maya in the Yucatán who are suffering severe droughts. While the Yucatec Maya of the 1500s *Wakanda*

Forever pray to Chaac to stave off the 1500s plagues and encomienda system brought by Spaniards, contemporary 2020s Yucatec Maya are also praying to the rain deity Chaac for rain in light of devastating long-term drought in the Yucatán in a time of global climate change.[56] A Nahua and Maya Tzeltal of Chiapas, Yuria Celidwen prefaces her *Flourishing Kin: Indigenous Wisdom for Collective Well-Being* with a "Reverencing" of "Mother Earth" and acknowledgment that her "remnant cloud-forest" Chiapas homeland "is now under threat of disappearing by 2050 due to climate change."[57] Oji-Cree Indigiqueer author Joshua Whitehead (Peguis First Nation) confirms in the introduction to *Love After the End: An Anthology of Two-Spirit and Indigiqueer Speculative Fiction* (2020), "I, too, write this during the massive global climate strike, the onslaught of colonial consumption bringing about the end of the world, the era of Trump and Trudeau's proposed pipelines, and the newly cresting wave of Two-Spirit, queer, trans, and non-binary writing," yet also notes, "we have already survived the apocalypse—this, right here, right now, is a dystopian present," given the settler-colonial histories, epidemics, and other ecological losses that are also evident in *Wakanda Forever*'s history.[58] In contrast, the non-Indigenous Robert A. Saunders's sense of the lack of ocean environmentalism from Namor in *Wakanda Forever* does not sufficiently articulate settler colonialism to climate change. He defines the "the Anthropocene as the ultimate obscenity," as if it were something new because it only now also threatens settler Western population. He also finds Disney's decolonial themes undermined by its films' adherence to the capitalist "neoliberal consumption of natural resources" that most feeds environmental catastrophe.[59] Noting the influence of Grace Dillon's "Indigenous futurism" term and writings, Kyle P. Whyte (Citizen Potawatomi Nation) critiques these Western conceptions of the oncoming Anthropocene in which planetary life declines due to human action, also confirming the ongoing dystopia, writing, "We confront climate change having already passed through environmental and climate crises arising from the impacts of colonialism."[60]

Indigenous LGBTQI2+ artists and activists are making different futuristic relationships that have environmental water impact. For example, in the queer Māori of Ngāpuhi and Ngāti Kahu descent Jen Cloher's "I Am the River, the River Is Me" YouTube video, the Māori chorus chant is "Tiaki mai i ahau / Maku ano koe e tiaki" and references the Law of Tangaroa, which is a primary relationship of human reciprocity with the well-being of the ocean.[61] This "Tiaki mai i ahau, maku ano koe e tiaki. . . . If you look after me, then I will look after you," philosophy also appears on the "'Enua Mānea (2021)" video installation of the Kūki 'Āirani (Cook Island) artist and climate activist Morgan Hogg "reflecting upon the current state of climate change within the Pacific Islands."[62]

In addition, Miccosukee Everglades ecological activist Houston Cypress (Miccosukee Tribe of Florida Indians) confirms their rightful place in between genders and species as a two-spirit person. Wearing disco ball earrings and a patchwork shirt and holding yet another disco ball and medicinal bay leaves threatened by ecological crises, Cypress concluded their talk on restoring the Everglades with the confirmation, "There are ways to walk respectfully between worlds. That's what the protocol is about. That's what the relationship guidelines are about, working respectfully with Indigenous communities, working respectfully with the elements, and all of the universe around us. So, there . . . are family all around us that can help give up glimpses between worlds, and these are the family who thrive outside the gender binary."[63] Here Cypress is homing in on that in-between space of gender that can facilitate seeing connections between elements, communities, and species in a Miccosukee way and serve to improve ecologies and the broader relationships of life in the Everglades. Within their ". . . What Endures . . ." (2021) short film, Cypress considers the work of the Creator in shaping the Everglades wetlands as told through Miccosukee Seminole songs and stories. In the video, Cypress credits the outdoor lighting to "Breathmaker," the Miccosukee Creator. Famed Big Cypress Miccosukee elder Josie Billy explained, "A long while back the Breathmaker blew his breath toward the sky and made the Milky Way . . . where the Big Cypress Seminole goes when they die."[64] Cypress's Breathmaker lighting credit has larger cosmological meanings, showing ancestral connections up to the sky and Milky Way as part of the call to continue to protect medicines and relative species of the Everglades wetlands today and tomorrow.

Conclusion

LGBTQI2+ "Electric Fields—One Milkali (One Blood)," "(Re)Counting (Wo) Man," *Pose*, and *Black Panther: Wakanda Forever* offer Bla(c)k and Afro-Indigenous sky-connected futurism that centers honoring Indigenous ancestors, languages, gender diversity, and cultures. Bla(c)k, Mikasuki Seminole, Maya, Aṉangu, and Yorùbá people all demonstrate a decolonized and futuristic connection from earth to sky. This growing LGBTQI2+ Afro-Indigenous diversity is nascent but noticeably absent in most of Hollywood's current settler-colonial depictions, despite *Black Panther*'s global success and the clear examples set in independent LGBTQI2+ BIPOC-directed film. Independent films like "Chaac + Yum" demonstrate that more work is needed in popular culture to bring Indigenous American representations up to the standards of some Black and Afrofuturistic representations in Hollywood. While modern Maya turn to Chaac to help with drought, many queer Indigenous peoples offer resilient visions based upon longtime environmental adaptations and resistance to dystopic settler-colonial incursions. Nonetheless, the LGBTQI2+ vision produced by Afro-Indigenous and BIPOC directors and writers demonstrate the possibility of gender variant reconnections from sky to earth, moving forward with new Indigenous and Afrofuturistic visions while echoing oral traditions from time immemorial.

7 CENTER

Nepanta Raven Film Reflections

Having completed six directions of cinema orientations, I conclude my book with a coda reflection on the Ravens especially strong in the Caxcan, Teslin Tlingit, and Tongva chapters. I again rely upon Lawrence Gross's Anishinaabe rhetorical insights to gain perspectives on raven rhetorics. Gross shares, "Stories become like seeds planted in one's mind that can grow and then be revisited from time to time to harvest the new wisdom they present."[1] He also notes that a common Native American reaction to hearing stories is to associate those stories with other stories that are similar or related to the new one told. After formally reviewing "Viva Diva" below, I revisit the ideas I planted in previous chapter analyses to harvest new fruits from them, but from the personal, gendered, and cultural perspectives of the center that is within myself.[2] I also braid in my Chichimeca, HIV-positive, film scholarship, and two-spirit reflections as I repeat this book's nahui ollin (four directions) chapters of the Diné (east), Caxcan (south), Kānaka Maoli (west), Teslin Tlingit (north), as well as the Tongva (down), and the Yorùbá (up), ending with a dream poem of four directions.

East to Gáagii in Diné, Tohono O'odham, and Yoeme Deserts

The nádleehí Diné actor Lilly Warhammer (Navajo Nation) stars as the Diné Rozene in "Viva Diva" (2017), a short film written by queer Yoeme and Mexican director Daniel Flores.[3] In a road trip to Mexico to get gender-affirming surgery, Rozene travels with her Black HIV-positive transgender girlfriend Diva (Mya Taylor) through the desert. Stopping on the Navajo Nation, Rozene confronts her estranged transphobic father (Joseph Runningfox, Santo Domingo Pueblo) with a gun. After a struggle, he shoots and kills her, depriving Diva of a lifetime of partnership. Flores depicts the spirit of Rozene as a beautiful bride surrounded by Yoeme "Sea Aniya or Flower World" butterflies in the concluding farewell night scene with her bride-to-be Diva.[4] Rozene stands on high upon desert boulders dressed in a white bridal gown and against the whiteness of the moon as blue butterflies swirl around her (fig. 18). Waking up in her car, Diva follows a blue butterfly and then scrambles up a few rocks before asking Rozene above her, "Are you leaving me?"

ROZENE: I am.
DIVA: No, please don't. Here, I'll go; you stay!
ROZENE: No. I'll always be in your heart. And you'll always be what you were meant to be.
DIVA: What was I meant to be? What do you mean? Please don't go!
ROZENE: Free. You were meant to be free.

As Diva reaches Rozene and they embrace, Rozene transforms into a blue butterfly and sails across the stars to the moon. "Live on my love," are her last words as Diva hears the fatal gunshots, waking from her dream of Rozene's spirit, but on a swing and not in the car where she had begun to sleep.[5] Like Lydia Nibley's film *Two Spirits* (2009) that warns about holding onto the spirits of those tragically killed in trans*phobic violence, "Viva Diva" also has a general Diné teaching to not hold onto the departing spirits, even under violent hate crime circumstance. To grieve to the extreme is to eventually become like *The Crow* (1994) protagonist (Brandon Lee), who must return to Los Angeles from the dead in crow form to avenge the violent death of his bride-to-be with no Flower World to calm him.

I'd entered the Yoeme and Tohono O'odham Sonoran Desert for my MA/PhD program HIV-negative in 1996, and returned west to San Diego, Cali-

Figure 18 Rozene (Lilly Warhammer) death/dream scene from "Viva Diva" (2017), directed by Daniel Flores.

fornia, with my MA, PhD, and HIV-positive status in 2002, but I didn't learn of my HIV status until 2003. While teaching American studies and American Indian studies at Palomar College, I began to date a German American guy in San Diego and talked to him about my time in Tucson. He said that he also had traveled to Tucson in Arizona, "but . . . ," he said, trailing off into silence. "But what?" I answered. "You are not going to believe this," he tested. "Try me," I intuitively answered. As he recalled the experience to me, I could envision it. I saw him walking the blanched yellow desert after a rain, approaching a partly unburied clay pot in curiosity and reaching out his hand toward it. Suddenly, a large black raven appeared before he could reach it. It attacked him from above again and again until he ran off. I looked at him; of course I believed him. Even as a five-year-old living in the Palouse of eastern Washington, I quickly returned to earth an obsidian arrowhead I'd found in the wheat fields by my house once I recognized what it was, shining glittery black like a raven's eye. Somehow, I seemed to know what was right for me: Do not take from the spirits of the dead. Within weeks of hearing this story, I approached him on the same corner in Hillcrest, a queer neighborhood in San Diego. "I just tested positive for HIV," I said to him. "I love you," he answered. But a space of fear opened and widened between us. It was as if a part of me was already buried, and a raven was set to swoop down upon those who might approach me. It was as if I was Rozene, a bride in white standing on a rock about to enter the Dream World or Death World. The fear that came from the subsequent dates I told become more smothering, as if I were being buried alive. Yet I never got sick, never developed AIDS, and never died. In time, dating HIV-positive and HIV-negative guys taught that there was definitely life beyond HIV stigma. HIV/AIDS groups also filled in with many supports along the way.

"Viva Diva" touches on HIV issues, which also recalls to me my time in the Red Circle Project of AIDS Project Los Angeles. After a dozen years of living off medications and under the supervision of my National Institutes of Health doctor, I began to see a rise in my HIV viral load. When I approached Tasha Rose, a transgender Diné and fellow member of the Red Circle Project, she said that I should start taking the HIV medications as she had done and that I would be fine. However, Tasha died of AIDS shortly thereafter. She is one of many HIV-positive Diné and Apache LGBTQI2+ folks whom I have seen struggle in LA and Tucson. These deaths have been hard on me and the two-spirit community in different ways. Initially, I could not stomach the "Viva Diva" final lines about leaving this world as they reminded me of Tasha's passing. When I learned that *Drunktown's Finest* actor Carmen Moore died, I stopped working on my first book chapter that featured her film, not wanting to think about her death. Moore passed in 2018 at the age of thirty-two.[6] Part of the source of this emotional avoidance was knowing other transgender Diné women friends like Tasha Rose who have died or been in harm's way as a result of their transgender, HIV/AIDS, and Indigenous status. As time passed, I was able to heal from the shock of Moore's and Rose's passing and return to finish chapter 1. Freed from grief, I can note the strength and resolve of Ms. Warhammer's acting performance as Rozene in her last lines. I also now appreciate the Diné chapter 1 as a memory of Moore's courage and as a reminder of how the transgender Diné director Sydney Freeland continued to rise as a director in Hollywood over the last decade.

South to Cacalot in Caxcan Chichimeca Deserts

When I was in third grade, I moved in with my mom's parents on 67th Street in South Sacramento. It was not far from the historic Nisenan Kadema village on the Kum Sayo/Roundhouse River, now called the American River on settler-colonial maps.[7] Even when my mom, sisters, and I relocated to Tallac Village in the next neighborhood west, I would find myself back there after grammar school while my mom worked. My grandparents Joe and Sarah Villalobos had a California black walnut tree by their front yard sidewalk, and I liked walnuts. But those nuts were especially tough, not like the dried treated ones in the store bins I could scoop out and break into easily. The street walnuts' outsides were fleshy green, and even after those parts rotted black and fell off, the tan walnuts inside were hard to crack. I remember trying to get at them one year during grammar school. I tried throwing them against the street asphalt with all my might, hitting them with rocks, and stomping on them with my rubber sneakers, but those walnuts would just bounce and not break. Seeing no success, I gave up.

My Grandpa Joe liked to sit in the garage with the door up and smoke his pipe, I guess watching me while I played in the front yard. One day he spoke to me in an encouraging voice that I now know he only used when I was a kid. Smiling and nodding and motioning with his pipe toward the walnut tree with some crows in it he said, "Watch those crows. Watch them. They're smart." I knew those crows would peer at me from the walnut tree, but it hadn't occurred to me to return their gaze. So I went out to watch them another day where they gathered in the walnut tree. There, I saw it. Carefully, one black glossy crow swooped down to the street and picked up a tough walnut already ripened and fallen. Quickly, ze returned to a perch on a walnut branch that hung over the street and waited. At just the right moment, ze dropped zir walnut in front of a car speeding down the road and under that walnut tree. I heard the smash and crack as the heavy car tires flattened out the nut. Once the car passed a safe distance, ze swooped back down and picked out the fleshy walnut parts scattered on the road. Amazed, I stood and watched the crows do this several times with success, more success than I'd had as they'd watched me.

As my Grandpa Joe on my maternal side was a light-skinned Mexican American World War II veteran born in Clifton, Arizona, it didn't occur to me that there was anything Chichimeca about him or me, even though he admitted that he was "a little" Indian from Zacatecas.[8] In segregated California, my Grandpa Joe was fairly passing as white, racially identifying more with his Basque Mayagoitia patrilineage, though taking his father's mother's Spanish last name Villalobos. I was a contrast to him in that, like my father and paternal grandfather, I grew up racialized as "indio/dark-skinned." My genealogical research shows centuries of baptisms of "Yndio" and "Yndia" on my Estrada patrilineal side up and down the Caxcan Juchipila River. This also means that there was no original Estrada Spaniard to found that line; the Estrada surname is a fiction of the Catholic church and its castas system in which Chichimeca were the base of the racial pyramid. In fact, one of the few Nahuat last names I've found, Xalapa, actually appears in my Grandma Sarah's genealogy.[9] Racially mixed with Rarámuri, Chichimeca, Mexica, Spanish/Basque, and African ancestry, I was never white-passing in the desegregating Washington, Idaho, and California U.S. states where I was raised. However, while I was born after the 1964 Civil Rights Act and during the Black, Chicana/o, American Indian Movement eras of Washington, Idaho, and California history, my parents and grandparents lived through earlier U.S. legal segregation, eras built on localized Indigenous genocides. It wasn't until I went to my Grandpa Joe's maternal pueblo Jerez in Zacatecas that I was greeted with "Bienvenidos a tierra indígena" (Welcome to Indigenous land). When I asked my tía (aunt) in Jerez what our Indigenous lineage is, she said, "Chichimeca," what is also called more specifically Zacateco or Caxcan, related Nahuatl-speaking desert peoples who tend toward matrilineal descent, as well as Guachichil, who are now called the Huichol or Wixárika and speak a closely related Uto-Aztecan language. "Chichimeca" is a regional term for the many original peoples of the desert famed for revolting in the Chichimeca War against Spanish settler and Mestizo/Indigenous settler/ed colonial mining and colonization beginning in the mid-1500s.

As I'd watched those crows crack walnuts, I wasn't aware that both my grandfathers also had roots from the Caxcan borderlands of Zacatecas and Jalisco in which Mother Crow is a central creatrix figure in ceremonies celebrating the summer monsoon rains. In my paternal abuelo (grandfather) Santiago's Caxcan pueblo, Juchipila, Zacatecas, the Mother Crow's flower or cacaloxóchitl (crow flower) is the main offering to give Xochipilli thanks for the monsoon rains, for nature's regeneration, and for the ability to procreate and enjoy life.[10] My abuelo Santiago told stories of La Aguila Blanca (The

White Eagle Woman) and El Don Coyote (Old Man Coyote/Huehuecoyot), who were clever, strong, and transformational. These are patrilineal stories from time immemorial. There, in sight of the Caxcan Creation Mountain Tlachialoyantepec outlined by the Juchipila River, my Pueblo elders affirmed, "¡Sí somos Caxcanes!" ("Yes, we are Caxcans!") when I returned to Juchipila with my dad as a young adult. I saw many cacaloxóchitl in Juchipila, and now understand that they represent the Crow Mother's first gift of thanks at Tlachialoyantepec, as we saw in the chapter 2 offering of plumeria for Xochipilli and summer monsoon rains.

West to ʻAlalā in the Kānaka Maoli Islands

As soon as my foot touched ground on the volcanic soil at Hilo airport, I felt a wave of fear course through my body, feeling the active volcano of Pele. Making a full circle on the Māmalahoa Highway clockwise from Hilo, I was amazed by the windward side's tropical jungle, bright flowers, and clean air. I became only slightly calmer upon seeing Pele's caldera at Kīlauea before sunset. Looking around at the dense tropical jungle and the lehua trees at Kīlauea growing from the lava, I began to calm, understanding how the violence of eruptions transforms into life. I moved on from Kīlauea, having connected Pele, the lehua, and the queer moʻolelo of the ʻaikāne Hōpoe of Hiʻiaka that I recounted in chapter 3.

As night fell and I left Kīlauea, I kept an ear out for the drums of Marchers, as I'd been warned to strictly avoid those by a hospitable Kānaka Maoli man in Honolulu. To my surprise, the nighttime air only carried the crescendo of calls from the coqui frogs somehow transported from the Taíno island of Puerto Rico to the Hawaiian Big Island, a place with no native amphibians, and no predators that would keep their numbers in check. "KO-kee! KO-kee! KO-kee!" the frogs incessantly cried over the last night miles of my circle. I knew what they were from Puerto Rican friends who'd imitated then, but I was baffled to find them so far from home.

Only upon reflection and with later research have I noticed something I did not hear in Hawaiʻi that has been a constant in my life: the call of crows. In her defense of Mauna a Wākea in *Mauna Kea: A Temple Under Siege*, Kealoha Pisciotta lamented that "Hawaii is leading the mass extinction of this planet. In our world view, we cannot support de-creation. Extinction is that. We cannot. It is against the law of the universe and the creator to eliminate a species."[11] The absence of wild ʻalalā (crow) species found only in Hawaiʻi makes her case. Even nearly twenty years after the ethnographic book *Seeking the Sacred Raven: Politics and Extinction on a Hawaiian Island*, the ʻalalā has not been successfully reintroduced into the Hawaiian Island wild from the several dozen or so ʻalalās cared for in captivity, although a new program is introducing the birds onto another island, Maui. It is with some irony that I reported in chapter 5 how L. Frank said, "And I had the ravens who are my—I like the Hawaiian term of ʻaumākua—my spirit guides" in 2010 when the ʻalalā were already missing from the wild.[12]

Without the ʻalalā, there are simply fewer ʻaumākua for the Kānaka Maoli. Walters records the words of Jimmy Medieros Jr.:

> When the ʻalalā goes, we will no longer have its protection. Luckily, through my grandfather's side we inherited the pueo or owl as ʻaumakua too. Families have several ʻaumakua. But how long will the pueo be safe? . . . There is a planned housing development not far from here that would destroy an ancient nesting area of the pueo. What happens when there is no more ʻalalā, no more pueo, no more ʻaumakua? The loss of land took away our traditional diet of taro and sweet potatoes, and it's taking away the animals. This is how the destruction of land destroys culture, health, and self-identity.[13]

The settler-colonial capitalist destruction of land has always been a main means to destroy Indigenous cultures, and Hawaiʻi is no different, only complicated by the fragility of its many unique microclimates upon smaller areas of land. Walters's prologue names the ʻalalā as one of the ʻaumākua who guide Kānaka Maoli spirits who gather at the "leaping point" into the next world, concluding that "without a spirit guide such as the ʻalalā, a soul could lose its way and drift forever through the twilight of ghosts and night moths."[14] If true, it is a difficult prospect for the spirituality of the Kānaka Maoli, unless new ʻaumākua could be found, or sovereignty won from the U.S. American settler-colonial empire.

North to Yéil in the Tlingit Lands and the Crows of the Coeur d'Alene Rocky Mountains

At the Northeast Two-Spirit Society's 2013 Two-Spirit Training conference in 2013 at the Audre Lorde Center in New York City, conference leaders Harlan Pruden (Saddle Lake Cree Nation) and Sheldon Brings Plenty Raymore (Cheyenne River Sioux Nation) screened Duane Aucoin's "My Own Private Lower Post." Aucoin's Ha Kus Teyea–informed visual film rhetoric responds to the alcoholism, domestic violence, and cultural loss that followed in the wake of the Indian residential school system in Canada. I think the Northeast Two-Spirit Society organizers showed the film knowing that it would cause many of us to think about our families and the ways that colonialism created the conditions for alcoholism and domestic violence. Understanding the ways in which historical trauma can resurface across generations shifts the way that one can begin to heal. The film screening also occurred to reinforce two-spirit "traditional practices" as a way to begin healing the "historical trauma" that "led to the dissolution of the role and the displacement of Two-Spirit people from within their Nations and Native communities."[15]

Directed by Sherman Alexie (Spokane Tribe of Indians), Victor's (Cody Lightning, Samson Cree Nation) *Smoke Signals* performance as a Coeur d'Alene boy of two alcoholic parents occurred not that far from where my own memories of parental alcoholism lie, the Coeur d'Alene woods of Idaho. Victor's parents are Arnold Joseph (Gary Farmer, Cayuga Nation) and Arlene Joseph, who is played by Cree Métis Tantoo Cardinal. As the child Victor waits alone in the car in the woods, far too young to drive away, his parents drunkenly appear from the nearby bar and dance around Victor's car. The more Victor expresses his anger to them at being abandoned in a car, the more his parents laugh at him as they prance around. I once woke up afraid and alone in the dark of my dad's VW van outside a bar in the woods in Banff Park on a road trip to British Columbia, where he'd left me to drink at night. During his Chicano activism days around the Coeur d'Alene Reservation, he would somehow survive a series of drunken car crashes and blackouts. On another road trip, he once woke up in a Folsom Prison holding cell in California. Luckily, I wasn't with him during those times.

As a young child, crows would rise in masses from the wheatfields across from my home in Pullman, Washington, and block out the sun. All I knew about crows while growing up in the Palouse lands of Pullman, Washington, and Moscow, Idaho, is that my dad would *CAAA CAAA* at the crows, and they'd *CAAA CAAA* back. In fact, "cacalot" is the Caxcan Nahuatl variant word for crow/raven, and to me that word sounds like their raucous calls, something I've also only wondered about when I've heard or read the Diné word for crow "gáagii," the Tongva Aawkut in "Tovaagnar," and the Nisenan words for crow and raven, "a·k" and "ka·k," respectively.[16] Mixing Edgar Allan Poe, my love of cornflakes and strawberries, and Indigenous crow stories, my dad once frightened me in Idaho with a story of a crow who plucked out a blind old man's eye and fed it to him in his cornflakes like a bloody strawberry. In the weeks after, this story would make me check the strawberries in my cornflakes to make sure they were not bloody eyes. Although this story was different from the Caxcan eagle, rabbit, and coyote stories that my dad's great-grandfathers passed across generations, it still reflected the larger sense that Raven and other transformers can both make us pay dearly for our lack of vision and give answers to problems that we sometimes did not know even existed.

Yet, even when my dad drank daily, he dreamed and wrote of healing. I remember Don Gregorio, the Mexican Indigenous curandero (healer) and his bird-bright eyes as he'd watch me eat the blackened scrambled eggs he'd cooked for me while my dad worked as a college counselor in Moscow. The elderly Don Gregorio stayed with us as he helped to heal my dad from alcoholism, for a time filling the void left by my abuelo Santiago's passing and opening up a spiritual link to a larger world. When I was six, I saw crows silently gather on the wintering tree outside a hotel window on a trip with my dad back to California. It began the first year of what would become my dad's decades-long sobriety supported by twelve-step programs.

Like my dad, both my grandfathers were alcoholics, and our families fractured in different ways because of that. Both of my sets of grandparents remained together, but my parents divorced when I was five years old due to my dad's drinking and using. I mostly grew up with my mom and her parents. Like her mom, my mom didn't drink, and they both form part of my matrilineal feminine spirit that I value. For my grandfathers, it wasn't Indian residential or boarding schools that prompted alcoholism. It was centuries of Mexican Indian colonial-induced epidemics, enslavements, wars, racialized conflict, racial mixing, and forced migrations. The widespread alcoholism and drug addictions we see in many of our peoples today aren't Indigenous to the Americas. Our seasonal Chichimeca medicines like tequila, sacred datura, tobacco, corn beer, and peyote were once respected more widely, only used in ceremonies guided by strict protocols that ensured community health and well-being. As colonization progressed, Indigenous and Mestizo men in Mexico have been more apt to fall into alcoholism than women. The machismo of drinking is now something of a cult in many places in Mexico and the United States, but it has many roots. Chichimeca Wars, the Mexican Revolution, World War II, and the Vietnam War are the string of wars in which my father, grandfathers, and ancestors fought that impacted their drinking and mental health. What remains is a paradox. My dad and grandfathers were alcoholics and differently impacted by colonial wars and racism, and yet they also taught me something about crows, eagles, hawks, and other birds central to our Chichimeca belief systems of Zacatecas. While their drinking days made them erratic, they also cared for me when few other men did. They cared enough to share their stories with me as their parents and grandparents shared stories with them. Even after decades of effort, I am still in the process of understanding this wide sweep of changes.

The cacalot/raven/crow are sowers of memory and stories. Now, I think they were showing me how to crack through a tough walnut exterior of a Mexican/American/Indian alcoholic family to get to the Chichimeca medicine stories inside. Without my Grandpa Joe, I wouldn't have seen the crow crack the puzzle of how to open up California black walnuts with the use of human cars.

Aawkut Down in Tovaangar

Getting a job as assistant professor in Chicano/Latino studies and American Indian studies at California State University, Long Beach, was just the lift I needed to show that I could work through my HIV-positive status and continue work in Indigenous communities. When I turned forty in 2010, I turned to riding my bike thirty miles up the coast from San Pedro to Los Angeles. Biking up through the Ballona Wetlands on a bike trail uniquely raised above the wetlands on both sides, I was enjoying the feeling of sailing above the water. Passing under the gray freeway overpasses, I began to notice the crows gathered by the dozens, fishing, talking, and resting. I hadn't seen so many crows in one place in Los Angeles. And then an awe-filled feeling thickened with each turn of my pedals as I took in the realization, "This is a Tongva Village and these are spirits returned." Not having tobacco on me, I held the space for a moment and then sped away as fast as I could and only later learned of the hundreds of Tongva unburied in that Sa'angna or Guashna Village in Playa Vista and reburied in Discovery Park with Tongva oversight. In 2004 Tongva activists and Ballona Creek environmentalists had protested Steven Spielberg's Dreamworks studio proposed to be built in this area. Crying "Tamayáawut!" (Mother Earth), they eventually managed to stave off the famed Jewish American director's project.[17]

L. Frank Manriquez remembers lying in that area when pó was younger and hearing their ancestors speak. Pó briefly recounts the place "where they buried those four hundred women" in a Hammer "Artist Talk" video.[18] I turn back to L. Frank in "Tovaangar," and repeat L. Frank voicing the animated crow Aawkut, who comes singing in Tongva to Jasper and his friends. There by the concrete Los Angeles River upstream from Yaagna, Aawkut affirms:

> When times change, you will never be lost because you will
> always know what holds you and who holds you.
> And that will be your ancestors and the people around you,
> more than you've ever known, that you are not alone.[19]

I have a better understanding of Tongva villages and crows thanks to L. Frank's voicing of the crow Aawkut who wears a necklace by a river as pó speaks to the cartoon youth (fig. 19). When I see crows and ravens in the coastal Tongva village sites, I'm aware that they will almost inevitably be

Figure 19 Aawkut, voiced by L. Frank Manriquez, from *City of Ghosts* episode 4, "Tovaangar" (2021), directed by Ako Castuera.

here long after Los Angeles has disappeared as they were here long before it appeared. L. Frank is right about that. It wouldn't be the first time that rhetor Raven gets the last laugh.

Crows Up in Oz and Coogler's Afrofuturistic *Sinners*

As I grew up in the late 1970s and 1980s, *The Wiz* (1978) was one of the few high-production Black films that would regularly play on TV, even though its lack of box office profits convinced a decade of already anti-Black Hollywood producers that Black films could not be profitable. *The Wiz* features one crow scene in which Gale first meets the Scarecrow who joins her journey to Oz along the yellow brick road. Beneath an abandoned project overflowing with debris in *The Wiz,* Michael Jackson appears as Scarecrow stuffed with trash and surrounded by Black men in crow costumes. The Oz crows admonish Scarecrow against thinking and reading, and the Scarecrow's lack of a brain points toward scientific racism that posited that Black men were incapable of rational thought and therefore destined for an "enslavement of the mind."[20] Asking to get down, Scarecrow is mocked by the crows and forced to sing the Crow's Anthem "You Can't Win," which is clearly meant to keep him in a perpetual state of self-defeat. To the crows' delight, Jackson sings the song's chorus, influenced by the blues in coloring, glides, and lamentations:

> You can't win child
> You can't break even
> and you can't get out of the game[21]

Given the rural setting of the Native American corn and sunflowers and the image of being chained, it makes sense to see the scene as based in the enslavement era in which cornbread first became adopted as Black soul food. This dual Black/Native image occurs in a setting in which Blacks mixed with Native Americans, as some have said about Jackson's family.[22] However, *Rumble: The Indians Who Rocked the World* (2017) makes a good case for the Native American, African American, and Euro-American influences in creating the genres of blues and rock that are mostly now credited to the Black community and clearly a musical influence in *The Wiz*. Jackson's Scarecrow character reads to the crows the strip of quotes on papers that stuff his body, including affirmations of education and personal liberation from Bacon, Cicero, and Confucius, and these thoughts manifest as Gale arrives to free him and shoo the crows away forever.

Jackson makes a good performance in *The Wiz*. Just as Scarecrow had overcome the lack of brains in bondage, so Jackson had leaped over most every metric of commercial success. His record sales for *Thriller* in the mid-1980s have yet to be matched. For me, growing up in South Sacramento in a working-class mixed-race neighborhood in the 1980s, there was no greater star on the street than Michael Jackson. It was before Jackson's pedophilia charges, skin bleaching, and radical plastic surgery dominated tabloids' front pages. Some girls wanted to marry him. Some boys getting into breaking fights at school imitated his Moonwalk. I wanted neither but was amazed by his sparkling "Billie Jean" performance, televised in 1983 at the Motown twenty-fifth anniversary special.

That same year, the zombie-themed video "Thriller" helped to desegregate the video channel MTV. What is it about Black horror that so attracted audiences? There is a potential answer in the Afrofuturism of *Sinners* (2025), which Ryan Coogler directed after his *Black Panther* original and sequel. In what is destined to become one of the greatest film musical examples of Afrofuturism, Preacher Boy's blues rendition of "I Lied to You" incorporates Black and African music and dance from both well before and after the secure 1932 Mississippi Delta setting of the film. The narration by the hoodoo healer Annie, played Nigerian British Wunmi Mosaku, explains the appearance of an original West African griot musician along with New York City 1980s turntables and a plethora of dances across centuries and places of Black history. "There are legends of people with the gift of making music so true, it conjures spirits from the past and the future," Annie says as even the ancestral spirits of the Chinese Americans are called into the juke joint room by Preacher Boy's blues song.[23] One of the spirits called in is of the Zouli dance, which "is exclusively danced by men to honor the feminine spirit, grace, and energy of women in the community."[24] A male dancer is always masked as a female dancer, and this in itself speaks to a queering of African genders before Christianity and Islam began to normalize cis-heterosexism in colonial eras.

After watching *Sinners* with the HIV Elders groups at the Long Beach Pike, I was taken back to a moment in high school in which music transported me into a vision of African ancestors. It was at a Tower Records in South Sacramento that I happened to play a record of The Last Poets. I didn't know that they were credited as influencers in the creation of rap; I just liked their music, which spoke of justice for Black people, infused with ancestral African rhythms and instruments. As I intensely listened to the song with puffy headphones, the Tower Records floor that was a speckled black and white linoleum began to take the form of African ancestors with shields, and spears, and traditional wrapped clothing. The more I looked and listened the more detailed the vision became, until I could distinguish the fine features, teeth, and open expressions of the figures that radiated in the hundreds around me. It was the power of that music, I now know through Annie's insights, to show these ancestors to me, and whether they were from the several freed African descendants that I found in my genealogical lines, most likely reflective of my Senegambian and Nigerian DNA regions, or purely derived from the ancestors of The Last Poets, or both, I can't say. Perhaps it is the spirit of past and future of freedom for African peoples that draws the spirit of people into Black music, despite the deepest racist conditioning of the present age.

While this seventh direction that is inside recounts lived experience in relation to the film of *Queer Indigenous Cinemas*, there are many levels of interior experiences that include the dream worlds that are much larger than this physical one. My dreams are also what center this book. Taking Modern Huastecan Nahuatl classes on Chichimeca lands in Zacatecas, I once put four dreams into poetry form. They represent the impact of traveling in the Americas and ancestral migrations. One of the greatest gifts of any land is a dream. For example, when my Grandma Sarah passed in 2017, I had a dream that showed me the road below her old home in Bisbee on Chiricahua Apache lands while a voice directed: "Walk where your grandmother walked so that the rocks may get to know you," showing my healing path at that time. While the first stanza below is about finding love in a Yellow World pueblo that stemmed from trips through Chihuahua and the Southwest, the second dream takes place at the Xochicalco teocalli (pyramids) near Puebla, where I also traveled with family. The third dream is the farthest extent to which I have not traveled in this lifetime, down along the spine of the Americas to the Andes. The fourth dream was inspired by a family trip to the Black Hills. The Chichimeca lands of Zacatecas form the unnamed center of the poem below, with the dream locations only roughly located in four directions around it. I end this book with my poem of four dreams in four directions called "Taltemicquet" (Earth Dreamer).[25]

Taltemicquet

•

Nocuate huan na timomaitzquiah.
Tinehnemih pan miac zoquicali coztic.
Nican altepet campa nemih miac
macehualmeh Pueblo ten huahcapameh.
Tonatiuh, toyoyohuan huan toixxayac
ininixnezca coztic quehuac necti.
Teipan nocuate quimaitzquia iyolchi.
Moixtlahchiliah.
Pepetacah coztic quehuac tonatiuh.

••

Itzalan teocali ten Quetzalcoat,
notayi moquetza iihtic tilostot.
Zan neci imah huan iihti.
Quiixmelauhtoc amat ten quipiya ce tahtoli
ica Nahuatl ten huahcapat.
Nopayo pan amat quiihtoa,
"TLALTICPAC."

•••

Pan tahcoyohual nictemiqui
nicochi iihtico cali
ten tepet pan Peru.
Cali quipiya tapepecholi ten ohuat.
Calaqui miac tahuilzetali.
Quemman nimihyocui yolic
niccaqui ehecat hualauh huan yohui
huan quioholonia ohuacali.
Noihyo quiza pan notacayo
huan yohui ica itzonco cali.
Niquitta hue at huan tepet ica echcapan

••••

Tonatiuh temoc iica Paha Sapa
quemman ninehnemi itzalan tepet.
Nionnehnemi pan noteixmatca
motectoc ipan petat ten tet.

Earth Dreamer

1.
My twin and I hold hands
We walk by many yellow adobe houses.
Here in the pueblo live many
ancient Pueblo people.
The sun, our clothing and our faces
are yellow like honey.
Then my twin takes her lover's hand.
They look into each other's eyes.
They glow yellow like the sun.

2.
Beneath the pyramid of Feathered Serpent,
my uncle stands inside a dark cave.
Only his hands and stomach appear.
He extends a paper that has one word
in ancient Nahuatl.
There on the paper it says,
"ON EARTH."

3.
Around midnight I dream
I sleep inside a house
on a mountain in Peru.
The house has walls of reeds.
Much starlight enters.
When I breathe slowly,
I hear wind enter and leave
and shake the reed house.
My breath leaves my body
and goes through the roof.
I see ocean and mountain below.

4.
Sun dives behind Black Hills
as I walk beneath the mountain.
I walk towards my relative
laid down on a bed of rock.

NOTES

Introduction

1. Following the Hawaiian language notes by Kānaka Maoli scholar Goodyear-Ka'ōpua, I do *not* italicize Indigenous-language words in order to avoid Othering Indigenous languages and normalizing settler-colonial English. Like Goodyear-Ka'ōpua, I provide translations, often in parentheses, after most but not all Indigenous terms. See Goodyear-Ka'ōpua, "Introduction," 30.
2. In this book, I include federally recognized Indigenous Nations of the USA and Canada in parentheses after the full names of the citizens of those Nations. I may note non–federally recognized state, local, community, clan, tribe, or transborder Indigenous affiliations without the parentheses.
3. José R. Martinez Cobo's United Nations study on Indigenous Peoples provides a workable definition of indigeneity: "Indigenous communities, peoples and nations are those which, having a historical continuity with pre-invasion and pre-colonial societies that developed on their territories, consider themselves distinct from other sectors of the societies now prevailing on those territories, or parts of them," in Martinez Cobo, "Study on the Problem of Discrimination against Indigenous Populations," 1981, quoted in *Indigenous Peoples at the United Nations*, https://social.desa.un.org/issues/indigenous-peoples/indigenous-peoples-at-the-united-nations.
4. For the translation of Abiayala from the Dule/Guna/Kuna language, see Burdette, *Revealing Rebellion in Abiayala*, xi; for the translation of Moana from the Hawaiian language, see Arvin, *Possessing Polynesians*, 8; for the song to Yemayá, see Tsang, "Different Kind of Sweetness," 113.
5. These directional ideas applied to cinema went into parts of my first article publication, "The 'Macho' Body as Social Malinche," in the 2003 anthology *Velvet Barrios: Popular Culture and Chicana/o Sexualities*. I repeated this methodology of applying four directions teachings to understand film in my 2016 publication "Ojibwe Lesbian Visual AIDS: On the Red Road with Carol laFavor, *Her Giveaway* (1988) and Native LGBTQ2 Film History" in the *Journal of Lesbian Studies* and in my 2017 article "Two-Spirit Mexica Youth and Transgender Mixtec/Muxe Media: *La Mission* (2009), *Two Spirit: Injunuity* (2013), and *Libertad* (2015)" in *Journal of Religion and Film*. See Estrada, "The 'Macho' Body as Social Malinche," 41; Estrada, "Ojibwe Lesbian Visual AIDS," 395; Estrada, "Two-Spirit Mexica Youth," 3.
6. Raheja, *Reservation Reelism*, 194.
7. Rickard, "Sovereignty," 51, 54.
8. Kuhn, *Somacultural Liberation*, 2–3.
9. Alarcón, *Snake Poems*, 6.

10. Pierce, *Speculative Relations*, 6–7, 186.
11. Gross, *Anishinaabe Ways*, 43.
12. Hernández-Ávila, "Foreword: A Meditation," xvi.
13. Louis and Kahele, *Kanaka Hawai'i Cartography*, 12.
14. Watchman, *Restoring Relations Through Stories*, 6.
15. Nepanta translates as "in the middle of" in Western Nahuat variants. For the Spanish "en medio de" translation of nepanta from the Nahuat variant of Jalisco, see Cortés y Zedeño, *Arte, vocabulario y confessionario*, 69, 96. For the Tovaangar translation as Tongva land, see Castuera and Dart, "Tovaangar."
16. Stewart-Ambo and Yang, "Beyond Land Acknowledgement in Settler Institutions," 34.
17. See the queer application of Wolfe's settler-colonial theory in Morgensen, *Spaces Between Us*, 2, 16.
18. While I've encountered of the descent of Skywoman to this continent made on the back of a turtle from Robin Wall Kimmerer (Citizen Potawatomi Nation) in Kimmerer, *Braiding Sweetgrass*, 3–4, and Shelley Niro's (Mohawks of the Bay of Quinte First Nation) 1993 experimental short *It Starts with a Whisper* mentioned in Raheja, *Reservation Reelism*, 171, Beverly Little Thunder (Standing Rock Sioux Tribe) also notes the lunar calendar aspect of the turtle among her people in Little Thunder, *One Bead at a Time*, 159. I also found mention of a Rarámuri variant in Chihuahua in which the Star Person Gawí converts into a turtle upon which the earth and mountains are formed and onto which other Star People descend to live in Servin Herrera, *Anirúame*, 23.
19. Wakpa, "American Incarceration," 174.
20. Luna and Estrada, "Trans*lating the Genderqueer -x," 256–58.
21. City of Angels Two-Spirit Society, "Meeting Minutes," Los Angeles, February 2014.
22. Driskill et al., "Introduction"; Driskill et al., *Sovereign Erotics*. For a strong Native American critique of Driskill's Cherokee and African identity claims, see Byrd and Pierce, "Settler-Colonial Elimination," 97; for Justice's related comments on the literary misappropriation of Cherokee identity, see his 2025 revisions of *Our Fire Survives the Storm*.
23. Los Angeles currently ranks highest in Indigenous populations from Mexico, Central America, and South America, with only smaller Indigenous populations hailing from Hawai'i, the U.S. Southwest, Canada, and Africa. All these are in addition to or mixed with the original local Native Californians, including the Chumash, Tongva (Gabrielino), Tataviam, Acjachemen (Juaneño), Maara'yam (Serrano), and Payómkawichum (Luiseño). See American Indian* and Alaska Native Alone and Tribe, Los Angeles County, LA Almanac Population (2022), https://www.laalmanac.com/population/po15.php.
24. The Indigenous population in Mexico alone accounts for around 11.8 million monolingual Indigenous-language speakers and 23.3 million auto-identified Indigenous people, about 3.2 to 6.3 times the USA's 3.7 million (American Indian/Alaska Native

alone) to 9.6 million (American Indian/Alaska Native alone or in combination) auto-identified Indigenous people. See Instituto Nacional de Estadistica y Geografía, *Principales Resultados del Censo de Población y Vivienda 2020: Estados Unidos Mexicanos*, (Mexico: INEGI, 2022), 44, 56; National Congress of American Indians, *Research Policy Update*, 4.

25. Bodhrán, *International Queer Indigenous Voices.*
26. Office of the High Commissioner for Human Rights, *United Nations Declaration on the Rights of Indigenous Peoples*, 28.
27. Jolivétte, *Indian Blood*, xi.
28. Barker, "Introduction," 5.
29. Ocampo, *Where We Belong*, 27.
30. Taking cues from Leslie Marmon Silko's Indigenous transborder mapping in *Almanac of the Dead*, Mishuana Goeman asserts both "urban" "woman's" and "migratory" Indigenous "spatial sovereignty" when she writes of "(re)mapping" Native "relationships among land, community, and writing" in a way "that addresses the violent atrocities while defining Native futures." See Goeman, *Mark My Words*, 13.
31. Stryker, "Queer Nation."
32. Wilcox, *Queer Religiosities*, 21, 25, 29. Jodi Byrd (Chickasaw Nation of Oklahoma) rightfully warns that one cannot assume that the word "queer" used in an already nonnormative Indigenous context is necessarily similar to queer work done by normative settler-colonial peoples. See Byrd, "What's Normative Got to Do with It?," 105.
33. Joshua Whitehead, "Joshua Whitehead: Why I'm Withdrawing from My Lambda Literary Award Nomination," *The Insurgent Architects' House for Creative Writing*, March 14, 2018, https://www.tiahouse.ca/joshua-whitehead-why-im-withdrawing-from-my-lambda-literary-award-nomination/; Love, "Queer," 172.
34. Harlan Pruden, "Two-Spirit Turns 30!!" *Two-Spirit Journal* (August 4, 2020), https://twospiritjournal.com/?p=973.
35. Driskill et al., "Introduction," 10–11. Also see the Britannica Dictionary (Online), "Berdache," https://www.britannica.com/topic/berdache for the etymology.
36. Naswood, "Two-Spirit People," 246. MJ Laing (Six Nations of the Grand River) confirms that many LGBTQI2+ Indigenous youth in Toronto "refuse" the term "two-spirit," often preferring instead their own language gender and sexuality terms, other regional European-language sexual and gender identities, multiple terms, or no fixed identity. See Laing, *Urban Indigenous Youth*, 6. This introduction uses the LGBTQI2+ acronym paired with the plus sign, which acknowledges gender/sexuality identities beyond LGBTQI2. After this introduction, this book mainly echoes the specific Indigenous-language gender terms found within the media featured in each chapter, such as third-gender categories nádleehí for the Diné and māhū for the Kānaka Maoli.
37. Naswood, "Two-Spirit People," 246.
38. Wesley, "Twin-Spirited Woman," 343, 344.
39. Pyle, "Naming and Claiming," 575–76.

40. Tompkins, "Asterisk," 27.
41. Tatonetti, *Queerness of Native American Literature*, 120.
42. Raheja, *Reservation Reelism*, 10, 199.
43. Estrada, "Ojibwe Lesbian Visual AIDS," 388–407; Estrada, "Trans Indigenous Visual Sovereignty," 381–95.
44. Marubbio, *Killing the Indian Maiden*; Aleiss, *Making the White Man's Indian*; Singer and Warrior, *Wiping the Warpaint Off*; Dilworth, *Imagining Indians in the Southwest*; Rony, *Third Eye*; Hilger, *From Savage to Nobleman*; O'Connor, *The Hollywood Indian*.
45. Raheja, *Reservation Reelism*, 18–19; Marubbio and Buffalohead, *Native Americans on Film*; Hearne, *Smoke Signals*; Howe, Markowitz, and Cummings, *Seeing Red*; Schweninger, *Imagic Moments*; Hokowhitu, "Theorizing Indigenous Media," 101–23; Wortham, *Indigenous Media in Mexico*, 26.
46. Epstein and Friedman, *Celluloid Closet*, 15:37; Russo, *Celluloid Closet*.
47. Raheja, *Reservation Reelism*, 61.
48. Aleiss, *Making the White Man's Indian*, 2.
49. Horak, *Girls Will Be Boys*, 66, 86.
50. Raheja, *Reservation Reelism*, 10.
51. Raheja, *Reservation Reelism*, 47; Raheja, "Visual Prophecies," 3–40.
52. Adrian Jawort, "An Indigenous Perspective on *Disclosure: Trans Lives on Screen*," *Indian Country Today News: Opinion* (November 16, 2020), https://ictnews.org/opinion/an-indigenous-perspective-on-disclosure-trans-lives-on-screen; Kasdan and Tavernetti, "Hollywood Indian in *Little Big Man*," 77.
53. Village People's gay French Moroccan creator Jacques Morali, who contracted HIV in the mid-1980s and died of AIDS in 1991, served as the inspiration for the film's main straight protagonist Jack Morell (Steve Guttenberg). Given that *Can't Stop the Music* was also transgender icon Caitlyn Jenner's film debut, playing the paragon of white cis-heterosexual masculinity, the film's gay and transgender coding run deep, as does the coding of Rose's own queer indigeneity. See Estrada, "Indian Icon, Gay Macho," 349, 346.
54. Estrada, "Ojibwe Lesbian Visual AIDS," 394; Tatonetti, *Written by the Body*, 136.
55. Morgensen, *Spaces Between Us*, 196.
56. Estrada, "Ojibwe Lesbian Visual AIDS," 390.
57. Rich, "New Queer Cinema," 21.
58. Aaron, "New Queer Cinema," 5.
59. Estrada, "Ojibwe Lesbian Visual AIDS," 394.
60. Rich, *New Queer Cinema*, 188.
61. Hafen, "Big Eden," 179.
62. Tatonetti, "Visible Sexualities," 161.
63. Schweninger, *Imagic Moments*, 128–41; Corbin, "Geographies of Identity and Belonging," 175–201; Hearne, *Smoke Signals*, 27, 29–30, 44, 54, 57–75, 91, 95–97, 99–105; Rader, "*Business of Fancydancing*," 116–20; Van Alst, "Sherman Shoots Alexie," 73–93; Youngberg, "Interpenetrations," 58; Estrada, "Two-Spirit Film Criticism," 114.

64. Fregoso, *The Bronze Screen*, 118, 93.
65. Subero, "*Muxeninity*," 175.
66. Smith, *Queer Mexico*, 101–3.
67. Estrada, "Two-Spirit Mexica Youth," 1–50.
68. Rich, *New Queer Cinema: Director's Cut*, 148.
69. Subero, *Queer Masculinities*, 110.
70. de la Mora, *Cinemachismo*, 151.
71. Castro Ricalde, "Lesbians Made in Mexico," 216.
72. Joseph M. Pierce, "Roma Is a Beautiful Film of Indigenous Erasure," *Joseph M. Pierce* (blog), December 29, 2018, https://www.josephmpierce.com/post/roma-is-a-beautiful-film-of-indigenous-erasure.
73. Danielle Mackey, "Isolation and Belonging in 'Two-Spirit,'" *New Yorker*, December 21, 2022, https://www.newyorker.com/culture/the-new-yorker-documentary/isolation-and-belonging-in-two-spirit.
74. Giesecke-Chero, "Queer Suffering in the Andes," 90.
75. "The Inka of Malvas," directed by Apolo Bautista, IMDb, https://www.imdb.com/title/tt34437484/.
76. Singer, "Video América Indígena," 43.
77. Singer, 41.
78. Waugh, *Romance of Transgression*, 13.
79. Tatonetti, "Visible Sexualities," 175, 158.
80. Jafri, "Reframing Suicide," 589.
81. Estrada, "Obscuring Two-Spirit Deaths," 57–58.
82. Tatonetti, *Written by the Body*, 174–75.
83. Scudeler, "Queer Indigenous Studies," 83, 86.
84. Mayer, "Bridge of Two Backs," 10.
85. Knopf, *Decolonizing the Lens of Power*, 210; Weatherford, "Journey's Discovery," 344–49.
86. Dowell, *Sovereign Screens*, 101–2, 113–15.
87. Alberta also reported child abuse in his film *Deep Inside Clint Star* (1999) and died by suicide in 2002. Estrada, "Two-Spirit Film Criticism," 115; Estrada, "Obscuring Two-Spirit Deaths," 59.
88. Blythe, *Naming the Other Images*, 216; Wilson, "Pathologies of Violence," 199.
89. McMullin, "Tiki Kitsch, American Appropriation," 4.
90. NZ On Screen, "Overview: Takatāpui."
91. Leo Koziol, "Indigiqueer Spirit: The New QueerVoices Rising Up for Native Pride," *Cinemascope Journal: Letterboxd*, June 22, 2023, https://letterboxd.com/journal/indigiqueer-spirit-new-queer-voices-for-native-pride/.
92. Tengan, "*Ke Kulana He Mahu*," 233; Teves, "Critical Reading of Aloha," 7.
93. Hall, "Navigating Our Own 'Sea of Islands,'" 30–31.
94. Kehaulani Watson quoted in Woodward, "Being Both," 70–71.

95. Zaborskis and Reich, "Queer Dig," 20.
96. Derry and Womack respectively quoted in Keeling, *Queer Times, Black Futures*, 3–4.
97. Parisi, "Of Black Bodies and Celestial Bodies," 360–78.
98. Green-Simms, *Queer African Cinemas*, 6.
99. Gipson, "Step into the Spotlight," 43.
100. O'Sullivan et al., "Queer Indigenous Screen Representation," 289, 291, 294.
101. Claire Bracken, "Faboriginal Drag Race Queen Jojo Zaho on Racism and Meeting RuPaul," *Triple J*, May 27, 2021, https://www.abc.net.au/triplej/programs/triplej-breakfast/faboriginal-drag-race-queen-jojo-zaho-on-racism-and-rupaul/13363812.
102. Tatonetti, *Written by the Body*, 19.

Chapter 1

1. Lee, *Nihikéyah*, v–vi.
2. Minthorn et al., "Introduction," 27.
3. Watchman, "Reel Restoration in *Drunktown's Finest*," 53.
4. Werito, "Understanding Hózhǫ́," 27.
5. Lee, "Introduction," 6.
6. Tom, "Mountain of Stories," 0:01–0:40.
7. Goeman, "Notes Toward a Native Feminism's Spatial Practice," 182.
8. Werito, "Understanding Hózhǫ́," 25, 27.
9. Werito, 37.
10. Tom, "Mountain of Stories," 0:42–0:52, 0:55–1:29.
11. Werito, "Understanding Hózhǫ́," 37.
12. Tom, "Mountain of Stories," 1:38–2:31.
13. Werito, "Understanding Hózhǫ́," 37.
14. Tom, "Mountain of Stories," 2:36–2:52.
15. Keovorabouth, "Reaching," 7.
16. Begay, *Voices to Faces*.
17. Baker, "Two Spirit—Injunuity," 0:17–0:33.
18. Baker, 0:42–0:52.
19. Lara and Facio, "Introduction," 13.
20. For the full Mexica analysis, see Estrada, "Two-Spirit Mexica Youth," 27.
21. Segura Granados, "Lecture," 1:00:38–1:02:04.
22. Stephanie Woods, "Chimalxochitl," *Online Nahuatl Dictionary*, accessed July 22, 2023, https://nahuatl.wired-humanities.org/content/chimalxochitl.
23. Reese, "Online Video: Injunuity."
24. Baker, "Two Spirit—Injunuity," 1:12–1:30.
25. Keovorabouth, "Reaching Back," 1.
26. Garrido and Tohme, "As They Are," 3:16–4:09.
27. Baker, "Two Spirit—Injunuity," 2:47–3:10.
28. Watchman, "Reel Restoration," 31, 43.

29. Watchman, *Restoring Relations Through Stories*, 80–81.
30. For an expanded analysis of *Drunktown's Finest*, see Estrada, "Obscuring Two-Spirit Deaths."
31. Watchman, "Reel Restoration," 36.
32. Watchman, 45–46.
33. Naswood, "Two-Spirit People," 69.
34. Watchman, "Reel Restoration," 39, 48.
35. Sydney Freeland, interview with the author, Los Angeles, July 26, 2014.
36. Estrada, "*Two Spirits, Nádleeh,* and Navajo LGBTQ2 Gaze," 190, 185.
37. Burns, *Living the Spirit*, 3; Beauchemin et al., "Two-Spirit People."
38. Goeman, "Notes Toward a Native Feminism's Spatial Practice," 172.
39. Kelley, *Tradition, Performance, and Religion*, 71.
40. Jim and Naswood, *Strengthening the Circle*, 7.
41. Werito, "Understanding Hózhǫ́," 27.
42. House, "I Am," 15:15–15:47.
43. Jim and Naswood, *Strengthening the Circle*, 10.
44. House, "I Am," 15:48–16:18.
45. Carrie House, text to the author, March 2018.
46. Zolbrod, *Diné Bahané*, 45.
47. Jim and Naswood, *Strengthening the Circle*, 7.
48. House, "I Am," 16:19–16:56.
49. Gross, "Preface," xiv.
50. "Damien Grey," *Bay Area Reporter*, April 24, 2018, http://obit.glbthistory.org/olo/imagedb/2018/04/26/20180426_Grey_Damien/m20180426_0.jpg.
51. House, "I Am," 19:40–21:27.
52. House, 19:18–19:39.
53. Denetdale, "No Explanation, No Resolution," 120.
54. Denetdale, "Navajo National Boundaries," 134.

Chapter 2

1. This text accents the first vowel in the Caxcan word for flower with the spellings "xúchitl," "xóchitl," "Macuilxóchitl," and "cacaloxóchitl." See Ocampo, *Where We Belong*, 60, 64. Ocampo also shares the word "cacalotxuchil" (crowflower) with the normative Caxcan *-t* ending in the word for crow, "cacalot," without the accent on the *u*, and using the *-l* ending more common in the Tuxpan, Jalisco, Nahuał variant documented in Cuauhtli, *Ma Tiłahtucan Mexicano*, 8; Ocampo, *Where We Belong*, 91, 191.
2. "Caxcan Pueblo," National Catalog of Indigenous and Afro-Mexican Pueblos and Communities, https://catalogo.inpi.gob.mx/Caxcan/.
3. Ocampo, "Where We Belong," 141–42.
4. Sanchez Medina, "Juchipila Zacatecas y el Xuchitl," 9:20.

5. "Tepechi" or "tepichi" in Caxcan is written "tepiltzin" in Classical Nahuatl, a language that descends from Caxcan and other Chichimeca Nahuat languages. The word morphemes tell part of this meaning, as "te" means "someone," "pil" or "pilli" means "child," and "tzin" is the reverential ending that Caxcans write and say as "chi" (author's translation).
6. Ocampo, *Where We Belong*, 64, 63.
7. Ocampo, 69, 144.
8. Ocampo, 145.
9. Ocampo, 60.
10. Note the *-t* ending in "pacti" differs from the *-tl* Central Nahuatl variant "pactli," with the *-t* ending being much more common in the Caxcan Nahuat variant. See Ocampo, 77; "Appendix: Uto-Aztecan Swadesh Lists," Wikipedia, https://en.wiktionary.org/wiki/Appendix:Uto-Aztecan_Swadesh_lists.
11. Ocampo, 68.
12. Chávez and Skelchy, "Decolonization in Ethnomusicology," 122.
13. Chávez-Gonzalez, "Xúchil (en vivo/live)."
14. Luna and Estrada, "Trans*lating the Genderqueer -x," 268.
15. Cruz de la Cruz, "Chicomexochitl y el maíz entre los Nahuas," 146.
16. Florida Colors Nursery, "Plumeria Seed Pollination and Pollinators," Growing Plumeria from Seed, accessed August 12, 2023, https://plumeriaseeds.com/plumeria-pollinators/.
17. Estrada, "Two-Spirit Histories," 177.
18. Gordon Wasson and others mention that entheogenic tobacco, ololiuhqui, and sinicuichi flowers are found prominently on the original Tlalmanalco Xochipilli statue. See Renteria, "Xochipilli," 18.
19. "Xōchipilli," Wikipedia, accessed August 10, 2025, https://en.wikipedia.org/wiki/Xōchipilli.
20. Requena, "Noticia y consideraciones," 46–47.
21. Murray, *Latin American Male Homosexualities*, 82.
22. Pérez, "Toward a Mariposa Consciousness," 112.
23. Salinas, "Yolotl de Papalotl," 77.
24. Pérez, "Toward a Mariposa Consciousness," 111.
25. Liz Calvario, "How Vida's Queerceañera Pays Tribute to Telenovelas and Chayanne's 'Tiempo de Vals' (Exclusive)," *ET Más*, May 17, 2020, https://www.etonline.com/how-vidas-queerceanera-pays-tribute-to-telenovelas-and-chayannes-tiempo-de-vals-exclusive-146679.
26. Milbrath, "Seasonal Calendar in the Codex Borgia," 149.
27. Renteria, "Xochipilli," 55.
28. Estrada, "Two-Spirit Mexica Youth," 18.
29. Ocampo, *Where We Belong*, 73.
30. Byland, "Introduction and Commentary," 19.

31. “Moyahua—Fiestas Patronales 2019,” 58:15.
32. Lara, “Moyahua.”
33. “Moyahua 2009 La Vieja Descarada.”
34. Luna and Estrada, “Trans*lating the ‘X’ in Caxcan,” 265.
35. Amador, *Nombres indígenas todavía,* 25, translation by the author.
36. “Moyahua 2009 La Vieja Descarada.”
37. Cortés y Zedeño, *Arte, vocabulario, y confessionario,* 160; Luna and Estrada, “Trans*lating the ‘X’ in Caxcan,” 259.
38. Ocampo, *Where We Belong,* 63, 65.
39. García, “Creating the Wind,” 28, 26.
40. Echeverría García, “Los excesos del mono,” 147.
41. See Wasson in Renteria, “Xochipilli,” 18.
42. Ocampo, *Where We Belong,* 88, 82.
43. Durán-Rentería quoted in Rachel Brown, “Go Inside a Complex Mexican Dance,” *National Geographic,* August 7, 2018, https://www.nationalgeographic.com/travel/article/photos-tastuan-festival-dance-zacatecas-history-culture.
44. Sergio de la Mora quoted in Rich, *New Queer Cinema,* 146.
45. Miranda, *Bad Indians,* 25, 31.

Chapter 3

1. Baker, “Hawaiian Issues,” 224, 221.
2. Xian and Anbe, *Ke Kulana He Mahu,* 00:00–0:37.
3. Wong-Kalu, interview with the author, Honolulu, Hawaii, May 17, 2016.
4. For makai as toward the sea, mauka as inland, and komohana as west, see entries at Ulukau: Nā Puke Wehewehe ʻŌlelo Hawaiʻi, accessed August 11, 2025, https://wehewehe.org/gsdl2.85/cgi-bin/hdict.
5. Brown, “Indigenous Religion of Hawaiʻi,” 5–6.
6. Shannon Uʻilani Lima, quoted in Wilson, “View from the Mountain,” 40.
7. Hamer and Wilson, *Kumu Hina,* 6:35–7:25.
8. Wong-Kalu, Hamer, and Wilson, *Kapaemahu,* 0:27–1:46.
9. Wong-Kalu, Hamer, and Wilson, 2:03–3:00.
10. Wong-Kalu, interview with the author.
11. Lynette Kahekili Paglinawan quoted in Wong-Kalu, Hamer, and Wilson, *Kapaemahu.*
12 Hamer and Wong-Kalu, “Kapaemahu,” 257.
13. For definitions of pō as night and darkness, see entry for “pō” at Ulukau: Nā Puke Wehewehe ʻŌlelo Hawaiʻi, accessed August 11, 2025, https://wehewehe.org/gsdl2.85/cgi-bin/hdict.
14. Wong-Kalu, interview with the author.
15. Mei-Singh, “Carcéral Conservationism,” 703, 705.
16. Xian and Anbe, *Ke Kulana He Mahu,* 00:00–0:37.
17. Louis and Kahele, *Kanaka Hawaiʻi Cartography,* 39, 69, 73.

18. Brown, "Mourning the Land," 385.
19. Brown, 379.
20. Hamer and Wilson, *Kumu Hina*, 1:04:22–1:04:36.
21. Woodward, "Being Both," 67.
22. Hamer and Wilson, *Kumu Hina*, 19:10–19:25.
23. Hamer and Wilson, 38:40–41:09.
24. Goodyear-Kaʻōpua, "Introduction," 9, 7, 13.
25. Kanehe, "Kūʻē Mana Māhele," 332, 336.
26. Goodyear-Kaʻōpua, "Acknowledgments," xvi. Unfortunately, this Hawaiian charter school closed in 2015, the year the film *Kumu Hina* was released.
27. Teves, *Defiant Indigeneity*, 1–21; Teves, "Critical Reading of Aloha," 2.
28. "*Ke Kulana He Mahu* Talkback," 09:32–10:16.
29. Osorio, *Remembering Our Intimacies*, 79–80, 78.
30. Hamer and Wilson, *Kumu Hina*, 1:12:05–1:12:10.
31. Hamer and Wilson, 52:20–52:52.
32. Hamer and Wong-Kalu, "Kapaemahu," 255, 266.
33. Karyl Reynolds, "Na Pohaku Ola Kapaemāhū A Kapuni: Waikiki's Healing Stones," *Waikiki Visitor*, April 2, 2012, http://www.waikikivisitor.com/2012/ilove-waikiki/na-pohaku-ola-kapaemāhū-a-kapuni-waikikis-healing-stones/.
34. Tengan, "*Ke Kulana He Mahu*," 233.
35. Xian and Anbe, *Ke Kulana He Mahu*, 40:12–40:54.
36. For a definition of mana as "supernatural or divine power, mana, miraculous power; a powerful nation, authority," see entry for "mana" at Ulukau: Nā Puke Wehewehe ʻŌlelo Hawaiʻi, accessed August 11, 2025, https://wehewehe.org/gsdl2.85/cgi-bin/hdict.
37. Hinaleimoana Wong-Kalu, Dean Hamer, and John Wilson, "The Healer Stones of Kapaemahu," 2025, https://Kapaemahu.com/team/.
38. Wong-Kalu, interview with the author.
39. Xian and Anbe, *Ke Kulana He Mahu*, 48:01–48:30, 48:53–49:15.
40. Xian and Anbe, 25:04–25:55, 24:20–24:42.
41. Xian and Anbe, 26:44–27:35.
42. Teves, *Defiant Indigeneity*, 98; Teves, "Cocoa Chandelier's Confessional," 295.
43. Xian and Anbe, *Ke Kulana He Mahu*, 57:57–59:17.
44. Xian and Anbe, 51:52–52:06, 54:06–55:00.
45. Hamer and Wong-Kalu, "Story Sovereignty," 255.

Chapter 4

1. "Full C&C Update on KIRS," Official Website of the Tk̓emlúps te Secwépemc, October 1, 2024, https://tkemlups.ca/ttes-articles/page/14/.
2. Snow, *These Mountains Are Our Sacred Places*, 2, 11.
3. Makokis, "Keynote—Two-Spirit Rites of Passage," 4:22–4:48.

4. Varga, "Indigenous Doctor," 4:23–4:49, 8:53–9:12.
5. Mary Lee, "Cree Nêhiyawak Teaching," Four Directions Teachings, 2006, https://fourdirectionsteachings.com/transcripts/cree.pdf.
6. Francis Whiskeyjack, "The Medicine Wheel," Windspeaker.com Buffalo Spirit Archives, accessed July 25, 2024, https://windspeaker.com/teachings/the-medicine-wheel.
7. Carroll, *Indiscipline*, 6.
8. Truth and Reconciliation Commission of Canada, *Canada's Residential Schools*, 10–12.
9. Desjarlais, "Two Spirited," 0:18–0:30, 0:47–1:03.
10. Desjarlais, 1:55–2:33, 2:34–2:45.
11. Desjarlais, 3:14–3:46.
12. Desjarlais, 3:51–4:40.
13. Thiel, "Origins of the Jingle Dress Dance," 15–16.
14. Desjarlais, "Two Spirited," 5:16–5:31, 4:43–5:00.
15. Desjarlais, 2:45–2:54.
16. Haig-Brown, *Resistance and Renewal*, 58.
17. "Mission Statement," Official Website of the Tk̓emlúps te Secwépemc, 2025, https://tkemlups.ca.
18. "Reflections on the Third Anniversary of Le Estcwicwéy̓ (the Missing)," Official Website of the Tk̓emlúps te Secwépemc, May 27, 2024, https://tkemlups.ca/ttes-articles/.
19. "An Invitation to Learn About History Through Tk̓emlúps te Secwépemc and Catholic Church's Sacred Covenant," Official Website of the Tk̓emlúps te Secwépemc, June 21, 2024, https://tkemlups.ca/sacred-covenant/.
20. Jenifer Norwell and Akshay Kulkarni, "B.C.'s Kamloopa Powwow Introduces 2-Spirit Dance, Ends Blood Ancestry Rules After Online Backlash," CBC News, July 17, 2022, https://www.cbc.ca/news/canada/british-columbia/kamloopa-powwow-changes-1.6523452.
21. Aaron Hemens, "Survivors, Two-Spirit People Honoured at 41st Kamloopa Powwow," Indiginews, August 5, 2022, https://indiginews.com/news/survivors-two-spirit-people-honoured-at-41st-kamloopa-powwow.
22. McNeil-Seymour, "Everything I Am, I Am to You," 8:10–8:24, 9:12–9:30.
23. Potts, "Trans Summit," 9:47–12:25.
24. Potts, 5:50–6:05. Sean Imitates Dog (Oglala Lakota) directed an autobiographical film *Two Spirits, One Journey* about his move as a winkte from Pine Ridge Reservation to Los Angeles. See Estrada, "Two-Spirit Film Criticism," 108.
25. Scudeler, "Fed by Spirits," 15, 6.
26. Smith, *Honey Moccasin*, 31:41–33:50.
27. Smith, 36:24–36:48.
28. Smith, 23:47–23:56.
29. Niro and Monani, "Resistance and Hope in Mohawk Cinema," 161–62.
30. Haig-Brown, *Resistance and Renewal*, 115.
31. Estrada, "Ojibwe Lesbian Visual AIDS," 396.

32. Knopf, *Decolonizing the Lens of Power*, 233–34.
33. Smith, *Honey Moccasin*, 37:42–37:58.
34. Higginson, "Shelley Niro, Haudenosaunee Nationalism," 141.
35. Smith, *Honey Moccasin*, 40:30–41:55.
36. "AFN National Chief Speaks," 30:05–30:44.
37. "Canada Mourns as Remains of 215 Children Found at Indigenous School," *BBC*, May 29, 2021, https://www.bbc.com/news/world-us-canada-57291530.
38. Aucoin, "Tlingit Prayer Song," 0:54–1:30.
39. Aucoin, 1:33–2:55.
40. Aucoin, "2-Spirit Blessings," 9:10–9:26.
41. Aucoin, 3:32–3:47.
42. Aucoin, 5:15–6:15.
43. Aucoin, "My Own Private Lower Post," 0:46–1:31.
44. Million, *Therapeutic Nations*, 38, 186, 184.
45. Chief Robert Joseph, quoted in Vivian Belik, "Putting the Legacy of Residential Schools to Rest," *Yukon News*, November 2019, https://www.yukon-news.com/news/putting-the-legacy-of-residential-schools-to-rest/.
46. Aucoin, "My Own Private Lower Post," 7:31–8:59.
47. Aucoin, "Truth and Reconciliation," 35.
48. Aucoin, "My Own Private Lower Post," 24:02–30:30.
49. Gross, "Use of Digressions," 183.
50. Boccieri, "The Roof," 11:29–11:50.
51. Little Thunder, *One Bead at a Time*, 4, 62, 175.
52. Boccieri, "The Roof," 12:01–12:27.

Chapter 5

1. Goldberg, "Counterstory of Native American Persistence," 219.
2. Allie Hostler, "Taking It on the Chin," Native News Network, October 30, 2013, https://nativenewsnetwork.posthaven.com/taking-it-on-the-chin-culture.
3. Manriquez, "L. Frank Manriquez Oral History," 1:32–1:37. Note that this chapter uses L. Frank's Indigenous pronoun "pó." See Tom Bliss, "L. Frank," Outwords Interviews, accessed October 2024, https://theoutwordsarchive.org/interview/l-frank/.
4. Johnson, *Spaces of Conflict, Sounds of Solidarity*, 160.
5. Manriquez, "L. Frank Manriquez Oral History," 1:59–2:10, 2:17–2:20.
6. Tongva Taraxat Paxaavxa Conservancy, https://www.Tongva.land.
7. Soja, *My Los Angeles*, 1–2.
8. Manriquez, "L. Frank Manriquez Oral History," 2:51–3:10.
9. Nelson, "*Moyla Tuupanga*," 40.
10. Castuera and Dart, "Tovaangar," 2:55–5:17.
11. Castuera and Dart, 15:48–16:17.
12. Manriquez, "Artist Talk," 11:43–12:20.

13. Manriquez, "Queer California," 0:17–0:19, 0:33–0:36.
14. Manriquez, 0:17–0:38.
15. Miranda, "Extermination of the Joyas," 266.
16. Waters, "Language Matters," 99.
17. Goldberg, "Sodomy in the New World," 48.
18. Miranda, "Extermination of the Joyas," 258.
19. Anastasia Moloney, "Shunned by Their Tribe, Colombian Transgender Women Find Freedom in Coffee Town," *Reuters*, September 27, 2018, https://www.reuters.com/article/colombia-lgbt-indigenous/feature-shunned-by-their-tribe-colombian-transgender-women-find-freedom-in-coffee-town-idUSL2N1WD0L2.
20. Howe, *Chiefs, Scribes, and Ethnographers*, 164, 67.
21. Wagua, "Descubriendo nuestra identidad . . . !," 1:05–1:22.
22. Russell et al., "HIV, Syphilis, and Viral Hepatitis," 2.
23. Haglund, "Dule Molas," 64.
24. Horak, *Girls Will Be Boys*, 84–85.
25. "The Home of Ramona," Rancho Camulos Museum, accessed October 9, 2024, https://www.ranchocamulos.org/home-of-ramona.
26. While D. W. Griffith's original 1910 *Ramona* was filmed at Camulos on Tataviam land, the 1928 film was shot at Zion National Park on Ute land. D'Arc, *When Hollywood Came to Town*, 63.
27. Carewe, *Ramona*, 01:31–2:24.
28. Carewe, 4:13–6:24.
29. Carewe, 2:32–3:21, 7:35–7:37, 36:46–37:05.
30. As a scholar of two-spirit studies, Mark Rifkin helped normalize non-Indigenous self-identification and positionality as a settler. Rifkin, *When Did Indians Become Straight*, 7.
31. "The Eviction of Temecula Indians," Pechanga Band of Indians, 2024, https://www.pechanga-nsn.gov/index.php/history/temecula-eviction.
32. Carewe, *Ramona*, 1:01:22–1:05:54.
33. Hearne, *Native Recognition*, 38.
34. This amnesia finale was the ending in neither Jackson's nor Griffith's versions of *Ramona*. Carewe, *Ramona*, 1:12:28–1:21:55.
35. Hearne, *Native Recognition*, 55.
36. Torres, "End Sequence," 3:31–4:31.
37. Helen Hunt Jackson, *Ramona* (1884), available via Project Gutenberg, https://www.gutenberg.org/files/2802/2802-h/2802-h.htm.
38. "History," Gabrielino-Tongva Indian Tribe, 2025, https://gabrielinotribe.org/history/.
39. "History," Fernandeño Tataviam Band of Mission Indians, accessed April 13, 2025, www.tataviam-nsn.us.
40. "History," Pechanga Band of Luiseño Indians, accessed April 13, 2025, https://www.pechanga-nsn.gov/index.php/history.
41. Goldberg and Champagne, "Ramona Redeemed?," 45.

42. Fernández Rodríguez, "Helen Hunt Jackson's *Ramona*," 210, 207.
43. Goldberg, "Counterstory of Native American Persistence," 219.
44. Fernández Rodríguez, 154.
45. Jurmain and McCawley, *O, My Ancestor*, 18.
46. Morris et al., "Nicoleños in Los Angeles," 97, 98.
47. Manriquez, "Tongva PowerPoint," 2022.
48. Kroeber cited in Morris et al., "Nicoleños in Los Angeles," 111.
49. Cheri Carlson, "Hundreds of Human Remains, Burial Objects to Be Returned to Tribes, San Nicolas Island," *VC Star*, April 20, 2019, https://www.vcstar.com/story/news/local/2019/04/20/human-remains-found-returned-san-nicolas-island-california-tribes/2957634002/.
50. Goldberg, "Counterstory of Native American Persistence," 227.
51. Peters, "Legacy of Exiled NDNZ."
52. Mo'e'hahne, "Animating the Indigenous," 88, 89.
53. Axmaker, "Stewart Stern."
54. Mann, *The Outsider*, 35:50–36:00, 39:55–40.10.
55. Barrios, *Screened Out*, 296.
56. Morgensen, *Spaces Between Us*, 31.
57. Adrian Jawort, "An Indigenous Perspective on Disclosure."
58. Kasdan and Tavernetti, "Hollywood Indian in *Little Big Man*," 77.
59. Herbert and Hanson, *Song of the Loon*, 54:08.
60. Scudeler, "'Indians on Top,'" 21.
61. Estrada, "Ojibwe Lesbian Visual AIDS," 395.
62. Beauchemin et al., "Two-Spirit People," 12:49–13:40, 18:30–19:23.
63. Manriquez, "Common Ground," 0:21–1:37.
64. Goeman, *Mark My Words*, 26.
65. L. Frank Manriquez, interviewee, in Nibley, *Two Spirits*, 46:56–47:22.
66. Castuera and Dart, "Tovaangar," 14:30–15:12.
67. Manriquez, "Welcoming Address," 0:28–1:50.

Chapter 6

1. By writing "Bla(c)k," I am referring to both Black and Blak people, which is not the usual BIPOC meaning, as the *B* just stands for Black in the U.S. usage of the BIPOC acronym. In the 1990s, the Erub/Mer (Torres Strait) and K'ua K'ua (Cape York) woman artist Destiny Deacon coined the term "Blak" as a visual artist's reclamation of the racist labeling of all First Nation Australians as a Black race. She took the *c* out of Black as she was repeatedly labeled a "Black cunt" by white women, and so the absence of *c* represented the absence of that sexist and racist "cunt" label. See Kate L. Munro, "Why Blak not Black: Artist Destiny Deacon and the Origins of This Word," National Indigenous TV, June 29, 2020, https://www.sbs.com.au/nitv/article/why-blak-not-black-artist-destiny-deacon-and-the-origins-of-this-word/7gv3mykzv.

2. Jian Neo Chen notes Mock's impactful biography as a Black and Native Hawaiian director and writer from Honolulu in Chen, *Trans Exploits*, 86–100.
3. Electric Fields, "Electric Fields—One Milkali (One Blood)," 0:06–0:33.
4. Eliza Berlage, "Indigenous Youth Transform Dreaming Songline into Digital Learning Resource," NITV News, July 15, 2019, https://www.sbs.com.au/nitv/article/indigenous-youth-transform-dreaming-songline-into-digital-learning-resource/qdr1i71qc.
5. Dale Roberts, "Five Things We Discovered About 'One Milkali (One Blood)' from Electric Fields," Aussievision, March 7, 2024, https://www.aussievision.net/post/five-things-we-discovered-about-one-milkali-one-blood-from-electric-fields.
6. Becker, interview with the author, 2012.
7. Estrada, "Navajo Sci-Fi Film," 529.
8. Abrams, "Nietzsche's Overman as Posthuman Star Child," 248–49.
9. Russell, "Don't ~~It~~ Make My Black Face Blue," 211.
10. Watchman, *Restoring Relations*, 43.
11. Russell, "Don't ~~It~~ Make My Black Face Blue," 208.
12. Yuè Begay, "Do NOT Watch Avatar: The Way of Water," Twitter, December 18, 2022.
13. IMDbPro, "Top Lifetime Grosses," *Box Office Mojo*, October 8, 2024, https://www.boxofficemojo.com/chart/ww_top_lifetime_gross/.
14. Prud'homme-Cranford, Barthé, and Jolivétte, "Introduction," 7.
15. Vest, "(Re)Counting (Wo)Man," 6:44–7:15.
16. Mulroy, "Behind the Rolls," 134.
17. Briggs-Cloud, "Ugh! Maskoke People," 273–74.
18. Byrd and Pierce, "Settler-Colonial Elimination," 92, 98.
19. Keegan, *Lana and Lilly Wachowski*, 8, 68.
20. For my larger analysis on *Cloud Atlas*, see Estrada, "Cloud Atlas," 2–3.
21. Wachowski et al., *Cloud Atlas*, 1:41:50–1:42:00.
22. Wachowski et al., 1:45:47–1:46:04, 1:57:25–1:57:47.
23. Peralto, "Hānau ka Mauna," 233.
24. Wong-Kalu, interview with the author.
25. Wilson, "Na Wahine Piko o Moloka'i," 2.
26. Wong-Kalu, interview with the author.
27. Wong-Kalu, "Mele Kū Ha'aheo e Ku'u Hawai'i," 0:02–5:22.
28. Babatunde, "Reimaging Women in African Religion," 982.
29. Forsgren, "*The Wiz* Redux," 326.
30. Lumet, *The Wiz*, 2:07:25–2:10:41.
31. Forsgren, "*The Wiz* Redux," 326.
32. Kumari Shreya, "*Paris Is Burning*: Where Are the Cast Members Now?," *The Cinemaholic*, April 22, 2023, https://thecinemaholic.com/paris-is-burning-where-are-they-now/.
33. Forsgren, "*The Wiz* Redux," 328.
34. Karade, *Handbook of Yoruba Religious Concepts*, 32.

35. Gill, "Ancestors Change Constantly," 2.
36. Adogame, "Aiye Loja, Orun Nile," 6, 38.
37. Eshun, "Further Considerations on Afrofuturism," 260, 262.
38. Gipson, "Step into the Spotlight," 43.
39. Forsgren, "*The Wiz* Redux," 326.
40. "Okoye and the Dora Milaje," *Black Panther Costume*, https://blackpanthercostu.me/dora-milaje/.
41. Coogler, *Black Panther: Wakanda Forever*, 2:20:55–2:21:07.
42. Emily Maskell, "Black Panther's Michaela Coel Shares Her Joy to Play a Queer Character: Michaela Coel Shares Her *Black Panther: Wakanda Forever* Role Is All About Representing Ghana and Playing an Authentic Queer Character," *Attitude*, November 7, 2022, https://www.attitude.co.uk/culture/film-tv/black-panthers-michaela-coel-shares-her-joy-to-play-a-queer-character-417623/.
43. Wright, "Art After the Untreatable," 3.
44. Tsang, "Different Kind of Sweetness," 116, 113.
45. Copeland, "'Did He Freeze?'" 148, 167.
46. Igomu and Musa, "Brave and Gallant Women of African History," 627.
47. Seow, "Nnedi Okorafor's Binti," 59.
48. Coogler, *Black Panther*, 1:10:07–1:10:09.
49. Lowry, "Native Lives Matter," 11.
50. Albarrán-Torres and Burke, "Postcolonial Superheroes," 10, 3, 5.
51. Eider Perez Dzul, "Indigenous and Proud: A Maya-Speaker's Reaction to 'Black Panther: Wakanda Forever,'" Global Voices, January 5, 2023, https://globalvoices.org/2023/01/05/indigenous-and-proud-a-maya-speakers-reaction-to-black-panther-wakanda-forever/.
52. Montejo, *Mayalogue*, 220, 6; see "cosmolectics" in Pierce, *Speculative Relations*, 11.
53. Macias, "Warrior Scientist."
54. Arizmendi-Calvert, "Chaac + Yum," 0:06–0:37.
55. Arizmendi-Calvert, 4:41–9:50.
56. Mark Viales, "Performing Maya Ceremonies in the Face of Record Drought," *It's Freezing in LA!*, July 2025, https://itsfreezinginla.com/articles/maya-ceremonies-drought.
57. Celidwen, *Flourishing Kin*, xii.
58. Whitehead, "Introduction," 7–8.
59. Saunders, "Black + Brown ≠ Green," 1–2.
60. Whyte, "Indigenous Science (Fiction) Anthropocene," 227, 224.
61. Cloher, "I Am the River," 1:30–1:42.
62. Morgan Hogg, "'*Enua Mānea* (2020)," Morgan Hogg, https://www.morganhogg.com/artworks/enua-manea.
63. Cypress, "Creative Time Summit Miami," 11:48–12:20.
64. Bucuvalas, Bulger, and Kennedy, *South Florida Folklife*, 32–33.

Chapter 7

1. Gross, *Anishinaabe Ways*, 183.
2. For the larger reflection on Teslin Tlingit crows, see Estrada, "Two-Spirit Tlingit Film," 201–26.
3. Warhammer is of the Táchii'nii clan born for the Tsi'naajinii clan; her maternal clan is Tó'áhání and her paternal clan is Tódích'íi'nii.
4. Flores, "Director's Statement." This film was part of the Sundance Native Lab overseen by Two-Spirit producer Bird Runningwater (Mescalero Apache Tribe).
5. Flores, "Viva Diva," 11:50–12:23.
6. Mark Kernes, "Carmen Moore, Popular Transgender Actress, Passes," *AVN*, August 30, 2018, https://avn.com/news/ts/carmen-moore-popular-transgender-actress-passes-164601.
7. I hadn't yet really thought about what protocols the local Valley Nisenan and Plains Miwok had for gathering, even after Gold Rush settler colonialism decimated their populations and only some regained federal recognition decades after the federal Rancheria Acts in 1959. Jesus Tarango, "Now That Columbus' Statue Is Gone, Let's Replace It with a Native American Monument," Wilton Rancheria, September 21, 2020, http://wiltonranchieriansn.gov/Home/News/TabId/562/ArtMID/2929/ArticleID/1174/Now-that-Columbus'-statue-is-gone-let's-replace-it-with-a-Native-American-monument.aspx.
8. My genealogical research on my Grandpa Joe showed Basque, Spanish, Mexica, and Guachichil mixes from the early 1500s, with several lines to famous historical figures like the Mexica Moctezuma and the Guachichil mestizo Miguel Caldera. See Schmal, "Moctezuma's Descendants in Aguascalientes."
9. While I'd imagined that I'd mainly find in my genealogical research the Rarámuri and Apache and Spanish ancestry from Namiquipa that I had heard of in my family, I also found settler/ed migrations to Chihuahua from Santa Fe, New Mexico; the Zacateco area Peñon Blanco in Durango; Merida, Yucatán; and Africa. My dad's mom, Grandma Lupe, left within us Indigenous matrilineal DNA from the general Acaxee/Ódami area of Durango, but only the narrative that her mother's side was Indigenous, without naming the tribe. Her Yriarte partilineage documented in a 1759 marriage in Santa Catarina de los Tepehuanes, Durango, was Basque from Irun.
10. Ocampo, *Where We Belong*, 64.
11. Lander and Puhipau, *Mauna Kea: Temple Under Siege*, 21:13–21:40.
12. Manriquez, in *Two Spirits*, 46:56–47:22.
13. Walters, *Seeking the Sacred Raven*, 217.
14. Walters, 2.
15. Northeast Two-Spirit Society, "Two-Part Two-Spirit Training." The Audre Lorde Project. March 16, 2013, https://alp.org/two-part-two-spirit-training. Though in part disbanded, NE2SS was inspirational to me. The forthcoming 2026 *The Raven and the*

Bull by Cherokee, Seneca, Cayuga, Comanche director Raven Two Feathers features many of the elders I've known in leadership in two-spirit societies, often since the 1980s or 1990s, such as Sade Ali, Marcus Arana, Steven Barrios, Joey Criddle, Clyde Hall, Raven Heavy Runner, David Herrera, Beverly Little Thunder, Theda New Breast, Miko Thomas, and Ruth Villaseñor. All are documented many times over in videos across the decades.

16. "Tsídii—Translation—Navajo-English Dictionary," Glosbe, accessed December 10, 2020, https://glosbe.com/nv/en/tsídii; Kroeber, *The Valley Nisenan*, 284. The main example of (Yéil) Raven that Aucoin narrates from "My Own Private Lower Post" does not follow this pattern.
17. Lepowsky, "Field and Home, Self and Memory," 62.
18. Manriquez, "Artist Talk," 20:46–20:55.
19. "Tovaangar," 14:30–15:12.
20. Curry, "When the Wiz Goes Black," 70.
21. Lumet, *The Wiz*, 33:50–34:33.
22. Vincent Schilling memorializes Michael Jackson "who was reputed to have Choctaw ancestry on his father's side and possible Blackfeet ancestry on his mother's" in Schilling, "Remembering Michael Jackson and the Racial Mashup of 'Black or White,'" *Indian Country Today* (June 27, 2014), https://ictnews.org/archive/remembering-michael-jackson-and-the-racial-mashup-of-black-or-white/.
23. Warners Brothers Entertainment, "Sinners," 2:40–3:03.
24. Centeno, "Sinners Dancers Revealed!!" 2:06–2:15.
25. On my ancestral Guachichil and Zacateco lands of Zacatecas, Zacatecas, this poem was written in Modern Nahuatl first, with the help of an architect of Modern Huastecan Nahuatl studies, Delfina de la Cruz, from Chicontepec, Veracruz, and then translated into English. Working toward a Caxcan orthography, I changed the Nahuatl words to more closely match Caxcan patterns of *-t* over *tl*, *l* over *ll*, with the spelling of "zetali" (star) as an example given in Ocampo, *Where We Belong*, 99.

WORKS CITED

Aaron, Michele. "New Queer Cinema: An Introduction." In *New Queer Cinema: A Critical Reader*, edited by Michele Aaron, 3–14. Rutgers University Press, 2004.

Abrams, Jerold J. "Nietzsche's Overman as Posthuman Star Child in *2001: A Space Odyssey*." In *The Philosophy of Stanley Kubrick*, edited by Jerold J. Abrams. University Press of Kentucky, 2007.

Adogame, Afe. "Aiye Loja, *Orun* Nile: The Appropriation of Ritual Space-Time in the Cosmology of the Celestial Church of Christ." *Journal of Religion in Africa* 30, no.1 (2000): 3–29.

"AFN National Chief Speaks on Anniversary of MMIWG Inquiry's Final Report." Cable of Public Affairs Channel, June 3, 2024. YouTube, 35 min. https://www.youtube.com/live/8Vd3bWx7VH4.

Alarcón, Francisco X. *Snake Poems: An Aztec Invocation, Special Edition*. University of Arizona Press, 2019.

Albarrán-Torres, César, and Liam Burke. "Postcolonial Superheroes: Unmasking *Black Panther: Wakanda Forever* and Namor, Its Mesoamerican Antihero." *Quarterly Review of Film and Video* (August 2023): 1–27.

Aleiss, Angela. *Making the White Man's Indian: Native Americans and Hollywood Movies*. Praeger, 2005.

Amador, Elias. *Nombres indígenas todavía en uso en el Estado de Zacatecas*. Tipografia del Hospicio de Niños en Guadalupe, 1897.

Annenberg Foundation Initiative. *Inequality in 1,300 Popular Films: Examining Portrayals of Gender, Race/Ethnicity, LGBTQ & Disability from 2007 to 2019*. University of Southern California Press, 2020.

Arizmendi-Calvert, Snowflake, screenwriter. "Chaac + Yum." Directed by Roberto Fatal and Xav SF. Digital Curanderas Production, 2022. YouTube, 11 min., https://www.youtube.com/watch?v=cuHOfFdOJtM.

Arvin, Maile Renee. *Possessing Polynesians: The Science of Settler Colonial Whiteness in Hawai'i and Oceania*. Duke University, 2019.

Aucoin, Duane Gastant', dir. "2-Spirit Blessings." 2020. YouTube, 10 min. https://www.youtube.com/watch?v=dyCHtIJNB5o.

Aucoin, Duane Gastant', dir. "Kichx Anagaat Yatx'i: Children of the Rainbow." DGA Media and T'senaglobe Media Inc., 2003. YouTube. https://www.youtube.com/@DGAProductions.

Aucoin, Duane Gastant', dir. "My Own Private Lower Post." DGA Productions and T'senaglobe Media, 2008. YouTube, 32 min. https://www.youtube.com/watch?v=F8IxQGUqyv8.

Aucoin, Duane Gastant', dir. "Tlingit Prayer Song." 2021. YouTube, 3 min. https://www.youtube.com/watch?v=YSlXX5NCcgk.

Aucoin, Duane Gastant'. "Truth and Reconciliation." In "International Queer Indigenous Voices," edited by Ahimsa Timoteo Bodhrán, special issue, *Yellow Medicine Review: A Journal of Indigenous Literature, Art, and Thought* (Fall 2010): 34–35.

Axmaker, Sean, "Stewart Stern: The Storyteller." *Greencine*, May 26, 2006.

Babatunde, Abodede Omowumi. "Reimaging Women Ritual Space: Gender and Power Dynamics in African Religion." In *The Palgrave Handbook of Africa and the Changing Global Order*, edited by Samual Ojo Oloruntoba and Toyin Falola, 969–86. Palgrave Macmillan, 2022.

Baker, Adrian. "Two Spirit—Injunuity." Independent Television Service, 2013. YouTube, 4 min. https://www.youtube.com/watch?v=iDyaknNmg28.

Baker, Mary Tuti. "Hawaiian Issues." *Contemporary Pacific* 28, no. 1 (2016): 220–27.

Barker, Joanne. "Introduction." In *Critically Sovereign: Indigenous Gender, Sexuality, and Feminist Studies*, edited by Joanne Barker, 1–44. Duke University Press, 2017.

Barrios, Richard. *Screened Out: Playing Gay in Hollywood from Edison to Stonewall.* Routledge, 2003.

Beauchemin, Michel, Lori Levy, and Gretchen Vogel, dir. "Two-Spirit People." Gender on a Stick Productions, 1991; Frameline, 2011. YouTube, 23 min. https://www.youtube.com/watch?v=8JcmAoderl4.

Begay, Yuè. *Voices to Faces: Two-Spirit History PowerPoint.* June 2020. Author's collection.

Bell-Metereau, Rebecca. *Transgender Cinema: Quick Takes: Movies and Popular Culture.* Rutgers University Press, 2019.

Blu Wakpa, Tria. "American Incarceration: Dances That Critique Confinement and Contribute to Prison Abolitionist Possibilities." In *Resistance and Abolition in the Borderlands: Confronting Trump's Reign of Terror,* edited by Arturo J. Aldama and Jessica Ordaz, 172–93. University of Arizona Press, 2024.

Blythe, Martin J. *Naming the Other Images of the Māori in New Zealand Film and Television.* Scarecrow Press, 1994.

Boccieri, Alexander, dir. "The Roof." Disney Enterprises, 2023. 20 min.

Bodhrán, Ahimsa Timoteo, ed. "International Queer Indigenous Voices." Special issue, *Yellow Medicine Review: A Journal of Indigenous Literature, Art, and Thought* (Fall 2010).

Briggs-Cloud, Marcus. "Ugh! Maskoke People and Our Pervasive Anti-Black Racism . . . Let the Language Teach Us." In *Otherwise Worlds,* edited by Jenell Navarro, Tiffany Lethabo King, and Andrea Smith, 273–90. Duke University Press, 2021.

Brown, Marie Alohalani. "Indigenous Religion of Hawai'i." *Oxford Research Encyclopedias Religion,* edited by John Barton, 1–20. Oxford Research Encyclopedias, 2023. https://doi.org/10.1093/acrefore/9780199340378.013.1139.

Brown, Marie Alohalani. "Mourning the Land Kanikau in Noho Hewa: The Wrongful Occupation of Hawai'i." *American Indian Quarterly* 38, no. 3 (Summer 2014): 375–409.

Bucuvalas, Tina, Peggy A. Bulger, and Stetson Kennedy. *South Florida Folklife.* University Press of Mississippi, 1994.

Burdette, Hannah. *Revealing Rebellion in Abiayala: The Insurgent Poetics of Contemporary Indigenous Literatures.* University of Arizona Press, 2019.

Burns, Randy. *Living the Spirit: A Gay American Indian Anthology.* Edited by Will Roscoe. St. Martin's, 1988.

Byland, Bruce E. "Introduction and Commentary." In *Codex borgianus,* edited by Gisele Díaz and Alan Rodgers, 11–44. Dover, 1993.

Byrd, Jodi A. "What's Normative Got to Do with It? Toward Indigenous Queer Relationality." *Social Text 145* 38, no. 4 (December 2020): 105–23.

Byrd, Jodi A., and Joseph M. Pierce. "Settler-Colonial Elimination and the *Dobbs* Decision: Relationality, Indigenous Kin-Making, and Queer Responsibilities." *GLQ: A Journal of Lesbian and Gay Studies* 30, no. 1 (January 2024): 81–102.

Carewe, Edwin, dir. *Ramona.* Inspiration Pictures, Inc., 1928; Diane Allen and Timeline Films, 2020. 1 hr., 23 min.

Carroll, Alicia. *Indiscipline: Reading Collaboratively Written Native American Autobiography.* University of North Carolina Press, 2024.

Castro Ricalde, María de la Cruz. "Lesbians Made in Mexico: Sexual Diversity and Transnational Fluxes." In *Despite All Adversities: Spanish-American Queer Cinema,* edited by Andrés Lema-Hincapié and Debra A. Castillo, 203–18. State University of New York Press, 2015.

Castuera, Ako, and Kevin Dart, dir. "Tovaangar." *City of Ghosts,* episode 4. Netflix, 2021. 18 min. https://www.netflix.com/search?q=city%20of%20ghosts&jbv=80994664.

Celidwen, Yuria, *Flourishing Kin: Indigenous Wisdom for Collective Well Being.* Sounds True, 2024.

Centeno, Mary. "Sinners Dancers Revealed!! Juke Joint Scene Explained—Dance Styles, Symbolism & Forgotten History." 2025. YouTube, 17 min. https://www.youtube.com/watch?v=QAX3b8E4wZI.

Cháves-Gonzalez, Luis. "Xúchil (en vivo/live)." https://luischavez-gonzalez.bandcamp.com. 2024.

Chávez, Luis, and Russel P. Skelchy. "Decolonization in Ethnomusicology and Music Studies in Higher Education." *Action, Criticism, and Theory for Music Education* 18, no. 18 (September 2019): 115–43.

Chen, Jian Neo. *Trans Exploits: Trans of Color Culture and Technologies of Movement.* Duke University Press, 2019.

Clark, James B., dir. *Island of the Blue Dolphins*. Robert B. Radnitz Productions, 1964. 1 hr., 35 min.

Cloher, Jen. "I Am the River, the River Is Me." YouTube. 2023. https://www.youtube.com/watch?v=RyZiAmAvytA.

Coogler, Ryan, dir. *Black Panther*. Marvel Studios, 2018. 2 hrs., 15 min.

Copeland, Tiffany Thames. "'Did He Freeze?': Afrofuturism, Africana Womanism, and Black Panther's Portrayal of the Women of Wakanda." *African Identities* 22, no. 1 (February 2024): 147–65.

Corbin, Amy. "Geographies of Identity and Belonging in Sherman Alexie's *The Business of Fancydancing*." In *Native Americans on Film: Conversations, Teaching, and Theory*, edited by M. Elise Marubbio and Eric L. Buffalohead, 175–201. University of Kentucky, 2013.

Cortés y Zedeño, Gerónimo Thomas de Aquino. *Arte, vocabulario y confessionario en el idioma Mexicano, como se usa en el Obispado de Guadalaxara*. Colegio Real de San Ignacio Press, 1765.

Cruz de la Cruz, Victoriano. "Chicomexochitl y el maíz entre los Nahuas de Chicontepec: La continuidad del ritual." *Politeja-Pismo Wydziału Studiów Międzynarodowych i Politycznych Uniwersytetu Jagiellońskiego* 12, no. 38 (2015): 129–47.

Cuauhtli, Chris. *Ma Tiłahtucan Mexicano: Let's Speak Mexicano*. Self-published, 2023.

Curry, Tommy L. "When the Wiz Goes Black, Does It Ever Go Back?" In *The Wizard of Oz and Philosophy: Wicked Wisdom of the West*, edited by Randall E. Auxier and Phillip S. Seng, 63–78. Chicago: Open Court, 2008.

Cypress, Houston. "Creative Time Summit Miami | Section 2: Houston Cypress." Lecture, *Facing Climate Realities, Reimagining a Green Future Creative Time Summit*. 2019. YouTube, 12 min. https://www.youtube.com/watch?v=83Uv4yYP_g8.

D'Arc, James V. *When Hollywood Came to Town: A History of Moviemaking in Utah*. Gibbs Smith, 2010.

Dawes, Daniel E. "Unveiling the Mask of Interracial Injustice: How the Seminole Nation Implicitly Endorses Dred Scott and Plessy." *Howard Law Journal* 50:319–44.

de la Mora, Sergio. *Cinemachismo: Masculinities and Sexualities in Mexican Film*. University of Texas Press, 2006.

Denetdale, Jennifer Nez. "'No Explanation, No Resolution, and No Answers': Border Town Violence and Navajo Resistance to Settler Colonialism." *Wíčazo Ša Review* 31, no. 1 (2016): 111–31.

Denetdale, Jennifer Nez. "Securing Navajo National Boundaries: War, Patriotism, Tradition, and the Diné Marriage Act of 2005." *Wíčazo Ša Review* 24, no. 2 (2009): 131–48.

Desjarlais, Sharon A., dir. "First Stories—Two Spirited." National Film Board of Canada, 2007. 6 min. https://www.nfb.ca/film/first_stories_two_spirited/.

Dilworth, Leah. *Imagining Indians in the Southwest: Persistent Visions of a Primitive Past*. Smithsonian Institution Press, 1996.

Driskill, Qwo-Li, Chris Finley, Brian Joseph Gilley, and Scott Lauria Morgensen. "Introduction." In *Queer Indigenous Studies: Critical Interventions in Theory, Politics, and Literature*, edited by Qwo-Li Driskill, Daniel Heath Justice, Deborah Miranda, and Lisa Tatonetti, 1–28. University of Arizona Press, 2011.

Driskill, Qwo-Li, Daniel Heath Justice, Deborah Miranda, and Lisa Tatonetti, eds. *Sovereign Erotics: A Collection of Two-Spirit Literature*. University of Arizona Press, 2011.

Dowell, Kristin L. *Sovereign Screens: Aboriginal Media on the Canadian West Coast*. University of Nebraska, 2013.

Echeverría García, Jaime. "Los excesos del mono: Salvajismo, transgresión y deshumanización en el Pensamiento Nahua del Siglo XVI." *Journal de la Société des Américanistes* 101, no. 1–2 (2015): 137–72.

Electric Fields. "Electric Fields—One Milkali (One Blood)—Semi Final 1." Eurovision, June 5, 2024. YouTube, 3 min. https://www.youtube.com/watch?v=mWdFRiiqHX0.

Epstein, Robert P., and Jeffrey Friedman, dirs. *The Celluloid Closet*. Telling Pictures Production Company, 1996. Alexander Street. 1 hr., 42 min. https://video-alexanderstreet-com.csulb.idm.oclc.org/watch/the-celluloid-closet.

Eshun, Kodwo. "Further Considerations on Afrofuturism." In *Science Fiction Criticism: An Anthology of Essential Writings*, edited by Rob Latham, 458–69. Bloomsbury, 2017.

Estrada, Gabriel S. "*Cloud Atlas*' Queer Tiki Kitsch: Polynesia, Settler Colonialism, and Sci-Fi Film." *Journal of Religion and Film* 18, no. 2/5 (October 2014): 1–32.

Estrada, Gabriel S. "Indian Icon, Gay Macho: Felipe Rose of Village People." In *Performing the U.S. Latina and Latino Borderlands*, edited by Arturo J. Aldama, Peter J. Garcia, and Chela Sandoval, 344–61. Indiana University Press, 2012.

Estrada, Gabriel S. "The 'Macho' Body as Social Malinche." In *Velvet Barrios: Popular Culture & Chicana/o Sexualities*, edited by Alicia Gaspar de Alba and Tomas Ybarra-Frausto, 41–60. Palgrave, 2003.

Estrada, Gabriel S. "Navajo Sci-Fi Film: Matriarchal Visual Sovereignty in Nanobah Becker's *The 6th World*." *Journal of the American Academy of Religion* 82, no. 2 (June 2014): 521–30.

Estrada, Gabriel S. "Obscuring Two-Spirit Deaths in the Films *Conversion* and *Fire Song*." In *Religion and Sight*, edited by Louise Child and Graham Harvey, 46–66. Equinox Publishers, 2020.

Estrada, Gabriel S. "Ojibwe Lesbian Visual AIDS: On the Red Road with Carol laFavor, *Her Giveaway* (1988) and Native LGBTQ2 Film History." In "Native American Men-Women, Lesbians, Two-Spirits: Contemporary and Historical Perspectives," edited by Sabine Lang, special issue, *Journal of Lesbian Studies* 20, no. 3–4 (June 2016): 388–407.

Estrada, Gabriel S. "Trans Indigenous Visual Sovereignty: From *Little Big Man* (1970) to *Drunktown's Finest* (2013)." In *Bloomsbury Handbook of Religion, Gender, and Sexuality*, edited by Dawn Llewellyn, Sian Hawthorne, and Sonya Sharma, 381–95. Bloomsbury, 2024.

Estrada, Gabriel S. "Two-Spirit Film Criticism: Fancydancing with Imitates Dog, Desjarlais and Alexie." In "Native American/Indigenous Film," edited by Elise Marubbio, special issue, *Post Script: Essays in Film and the Humanities* 29, no. 3 (Summer 2010): 106–18.

Estrada, Gabriel S. "Two-Spirit Histories in Southwestern and Mesoamerican Literatures." In *Gender and Sexuality in Indigenous North America, 1400–1850*, edited by Sandra Slater and Fay A. Yarbrough, 165–84. South Carolina Press, 2011.

Estrada, Gabriel S. "Two-Spirit Mexica Youth and Transgender Mixtec/Muxe Media: *La Mission* (2009), *Two Spirit: Injunuity* (2013), and *Libertad* (2015)." *Journal of Religion and Film* 21, no. 1 (April 2017): 1–50.

Estrada, Gabriel S. "The Two-Spirit Tlingit Film Rhetoric of Aucoin's 'My Own Private Lower Post.'" In *Native American Rhetoric*, edited by Lawrence W. Gross Gross, 201–26. University of New Mexico Press, 2021.

Estrada, Gabriel S. "*Two Spirits, Nádleeh,* and Navajo LGBTQ2 Gaze." In "Indigenous Performances: Upsetting the Terrains of Settler Colonialism," edited by Mishuana Goeman, special issue, *American Indian Culture and Research Journal* 35, no. 4 (2011): 167–90.

Fernández Rodríguez, Carolina. "Helen Hunt Jackson's *Ramona*: The Romance That Became a Tourist Guide and Silenced the Mestiza." *Revista canaria de estudios Ingleses*, no. 81 (2020): 193–215.

Flores, Daniel. "Director's Statement." *33rd Arizona International Film Festival.* Accessed November 3, 2024. http://filmfestivalarizona.com/film-detail.php?id=675.

Flores, Daniel, dir. "Viva Diva." Sundance Institute, 2017. Vimeo, 11:50–12:23, https://vimeo.com/video/234837622.

Forsgren, La Donna L. "*The Wiz* Redux: Or, Why Queer Black Feminist Spectatorship and a Politically Engaged Popular Entertainment Continue to Matter." *Theatre Survey* 60, no. 3 (September 2019): 325–54.

Freeland, Sydney, dir. *Drunktown's Finest.* Tulsa: Indion Entertainment, 2014. 1 hr., 32 min.

Fregoso, Rosa Linda. *The Bronze Screen: Chicana and Chicano Film Culture.* University of Minnesota Press, 1993.

García, Élodie Dupey. "Creating the Wind: Color, Materiality, and the Senses in the Images of a Mesoamerican Deity." *Latin American and Latinx Visual Culture* 2, no. 4 (December 2020): 14–31.

Garrido, Mike, and Tarek Tohme, dirs. "As They Are: Two-Spirit People in the Modern World." University of Southern California Department of Anthropology, 2012. YouTube, 18 min. https://www.youtube.com/watch?v=AYGxZL870ZE.

Giesecke-Chero, Micaela. "Queer Suffering in the Andes through the Lens of the Film Retablo." In *Decolonising Andean Identities: Andinxs, Activism and Social Change*, edited by Rebecca Irons and Phoebe Martin, 87–107. University College London, 2024.

Gill, Jon Ivan. "Ancestors Change Constantly: Subversive Religious Colonial Deconstruction in the Religion of Black Panther." *Journal of Religion and Film* 22, no. 1 (April 2018): 1–4.

Gipson, Grace. "Step into the Spotlight—Introducing the Marvel Comics 'Adored Ones,' The Dora Milaje." In *Black Panther: Wakandan Civitas and Panthering Futurity*, edited by Jorge Serrano, 35–60. Vernon Press, 2023.
Goeman, Mishuana. *Mark My Words: Native Women Mapping Our Nations*. University of Arizona Press, 2013.
Goeman, Mishuana R. "Notes Toward a Native Feminism's Spatial Practice." *Wíčazo Ša Review* 24, no. 2 (Fall 2009): 169–87.
Goldberg, Carole. "A Counterstory of Native American Persistence." In *Island of the Blue Dolphins*, edited by Sara L. Schwebel, 219–28. University of California Press, 2016.
Goldberg, Carole, and Duane Champagne. "Ramona Redeemed? The Rise of Tribal Political Power in California." *Wíčazo Ša Review* 17, no. 1 (2002): 43–63.
Goldberg, Jonathan. "Sodomy in the New World: Anthropologies New and Old." *Social Text* no. 29 (1991): 46–56.
Goodyear-Ka'ōpua, Noelani. "Acknowledgments." In *A Nation Rising: Hawaiian Movements for Life, Land, and Sovereignty*, edited by Noelani Goodyear-Ka'ōpua, Ikaika Hussey, and Erin Kahunawaika'ala, xvi. Duke University Press, 2014.
Goodyear-Ka'ōpua, Noelani. "Introduction." In *A Nation Rising: Hawaiian Movements for Life, Land, and Sovereignty*, edited by Noelani Goodyear-Ka'ōpua, Ikaika Hussey, and Erin Kahunawaika'ala, 1–33. Duke University Press, 2014.
Green-Simms, Lindsey B. *Queer African Cinemas*. Duke University Press, 2022.
Gross, Lawrence W. *Anishinaabe Ways of Knowing and Being*. Ashgate, 2014.
Gross, Lawrence W. "Preface." In *Native American Rhetoric*, edited by Lawrence W. Gross, xxiii–xv. University of New Mexico Press, 2021.
Gross, Lawrence W. "The Use of Digressions in Anishinaabe Rhetoric as a Moral Act: Connecting Speech to the Religious Idea That All Things Are Related." In *Native American Rhetoric*, edited by Lawrence W. Gross, 47–61. University of New Mexico Press, 2021.
Hafen, P. Jane. "Big Eden." In *Seeing Red—Hollywood's Pixeled Skins: American Indians and Film*, edited by LeAnn Howe, Harvey Markowitz, and Denise K. Cummings, 179–81. Michigan State University Press, 2013.
Haglund, Sue P. "Dule Molas: The Counterpoint-Counterplot Practice of the Traversable Cloth in (Non)Digital Realms." In *Indigenous Interfaces: Spaces, Technology, and Social Networks in Mexico and Central America*, edited by Jennifer Gómez Menjívar, Gloria Elizabeth Chacón, and Arturo Arias, 56–78. University of Arizona Press, 2019.
Haig-Brown, Celia. *Resistance and Renewal: Surviving the Indian Residential School*. Arsenal Pulp, 2006.
Hall, Lisa K. "Navigating Our Own 'Sea of Islands' Remapping a Theoretical Space for Hawaiian Women and Indigenous Feminism." *Wíčazo Ša Review* 24, no. 2 (Fall 2009): 15–38.
Hamer, Dean, and Hinaleimoana Wong-Kalu. "Kapaemahu: Toward Story Sovereignty of a Hawaiian Tradition of Healing and Gender Diversity." *The Contemporary Pacific* 34, no. 2 (2022): 255–91.
Hamer, Dean, and Joe Wilson, dir. *Kumu Hina*. QWaves Productions, 2013. Alexander Street. 1 hr., 17 min.
Hearne, Joanna. *Native Recognition: Indigenous Cinema and the Western*. SUNY University Press, 2013.
Hearne, Joanna. *Smoke Signals: Native Cinema Rising*. University of Nebraska Press, 2012.
Herbert, Andrew, and Scott Hanson, dir. *Song of the Loon*. Sawyer Productions Limited, 1970. 1 hr., 19 min.
Hernández-Ávila, Inés. "Foreword: A Meditation." In *Fleshing the Spirit: Spirituality and Activism in Chicana, Latina, and Indigenous Women's Lives*, edited by Elisa Facio and Irene Lara, xiii–xix. University of Arizona Press, 2014.
Higginson, Catherine. "Shelley Niro, Haudenosaunee Nationalism, and the Continued Contestation of the Brant Monument." *Essays on Canadian Writing: Cultural Memory and Social Identity* 80 (Fall 2003): 141–86.
Hilger, Michael. *From Savage to Nobleman: Images of Native Americans in Film*. Scarecrow Press, 1995.

Hokowhitu, Brendan. "Theorizing Indigenous Media." In *The Fourth Eye: Māori Media in Aotearoa/New Zealand*, edited by Brendan Hokowhitu and Vijay Devedas, 101–23. Minnesota University Press, 2013.

Horak, Laura. *Girls Will Be Boys: Cross-Dressed Women, Lesbians, and American Cinema, 1908–1934*. Rutgers University Press, 2016.

House, Carrie, dir. "I Am." Balancing Act Productions, 1997. Vimeo, 24 min. https://vimeo.com/86858139.

Howe, James. *Chiefs, Scribes, and Ethnographers: Guna Culture from Inside and Out*. University of Texas Press, 2009.

Howe, LeAnne, Harvey Markowitz, and Denise K. Cummings, eds. *Seeing Red—Hollywood's Pixeled Skins: American Indians and Film*. Michigan State University Press, 2013.

Igomu, Samuel O., and Yaki D. Musa. "The Brave and Gallant Women of African History: A Feminist Analysis of Yaa Asantewaa in Hezekiah Lewis' Short Film, *Warrior Queen*." In *Retelling History, Restaging African Women in Drama and Film*, edited by Irene Salami-Agunloye, 623–40. Kraft, 2022.

Jafri, Beenash. "Reframing Suicide: Queer Diasporic and Indigenous Imaginaries." *GLQ: A Journal of Lesbian and Gay Studies* 27, no. 4 (October 2021): 577–602.

Jim, Mattee, and Elton Naswood. *Strengthening the Circle: Curriculum and Support Workshops for Native Americans/Alaska Natives*. AIDS Project Los Angeles, 2015.

Johnson, Gaye Theresa. *Spaces of Conflict, Sounds of Solidarity: Music, Race, and Spatial Entitlement in Los Angeles*. University of California Press, 2013.

Jolivétte, Andrew J. *Indian Blood: HIV and Colonial Trauma in San Francisco's Two-Spirit Community*. University of Washington Press, 2016.

Jurmain, Claudia, and William McCawley. *O, My Ancestor: Recognition and Renewal for the Gabrielino–Tongva People of the Los Angeles Area*. Heyday, 2009.

Justice, Daniel Heath. *Our Fire Survives the Storm: A Cherokee Literary History, Citizenship and Sovereignty Edition*. University of Minnesota Press, 2025.

Kanehe, Le'a Malia. "Kūʻē Mana Māhele: The Hawaiian Movement to Resist Biocolonialism." In *A Nation Rising: Hawaiian Movements for Life, Land, and Sovereignty*, edited by Noelani Goodyear-Ka'ōpua, Ikaika Hussey, and Erin Kahunawaika'ala, 331–53. Duke University Press, 2014.

Karade, Baba Ifa. *The Handbook of Yoruba Religious Concepts*. Red Wheel/Weisler, 2020.

Kasdan, Margo, and Susan Tavernetti. "The Hollywood Indian in *Little Big Man*: A Revisionist View." *Film & History: An Interdisciplinary Journal of Film and Television Studies* 23, no. 1–4 (1993): 70–80.

Keegan, Cael M. *Lana and Lilly Wachowski*. University of Illinois Press, 2018.

Keeling, Kara. *Queer Times, Black Futures*. New York University Press, 2019.

"*Ke Kulana He Mahu* Talkback." Moderated by Ka'imina'auao Cambern, Kanoa Cleveland-Lagareta, and Keawe Parke. Ka La Hoihoi Ea, 2022. YouTube. 55 minutes. https://www.youtube.com/watch?v=8LTR6EGdu98.

Kelley, Dennis. *Tradition, Performance, and Religion in Native America: Ancestral Ways, Modern Selves*. Routledge, 2014.

Keovorabouth, Souksavanh Tom. "Reaching Back to Traditional Teachings: Diné Knowledge and Gender Politics." *Genealogy* 5, no. 95 (October 2021): 1–7.

Kimmerer, Robin Wall. *Braiding Sweetgrass: Indigenous Wisdom, Scientific Knowledge and the Teachings of Plants*. Milkweed Editions, 2013.

King, Tiffany Lethabo. *The Black Shoals: Offshore Formations of Black and Native Studies*. Duke University Press, 2019.

Knopf, Kerstin. *Decolonizing the Lens of Power: Indigenous Films in North America*. Brill, 2008.

Kroeber, Alfred L. *The Valley Nisenan*. University of California Press, 1929.

Kuhn, Roger. *Somacultural Liberation: An Indigenous, Two-Spirit Somatic Guide to Integrating Cultural Experiences Toward Freedom*. North Atlantic, 2024.

Laing, Marie. *Urban Indigenous Youth Reframing Two-Spirit*. New York: Routledge, 2021.

Lander, Joan, and Puhipau, dirs. *Mauna Kea: Temple Under Siege* (*Nā'ālehu: Nā Maka o ka 'Āina*). 2006. Alexander Street, 50 min. https://video-alexanderstreet-com.csulb.idm.oclc.org/watch/mauna-kea-temple-under-siege/transcript/building.

Lara, Eleticia Quintero. "Moyahua: La Fiesta de los Tastoanes en Moyahua de Estrada, Zacatecas." *Pulso del Sur*. Accessed 2019. http://www.pulsodelsur.com/nota/4799.

Lara, Irene, and Elisa Facio. "Introduction: Fleshing the Spirit, Spiriting the Flesh." In *Fleshing the Spirit: Spirituality and Activism in Chicana, Latina, and Indigenous Women's Lives*, edited by Irene Lara and Elisa Facio, 3–17. University of Arizona Press, 2014.

Lee, Lloyd L. "Introduction." In *Diné Perspectives: Revitalizing and Reclaiming Navajo Thought*, edited by Lloyd L. Lee, 3–13. University of Arizona Press, 2014.

Lee, Lloyd L. ed., *Nihikéyah: Navajo Homeland*. University of Arizona Press, 2023.

Lepowsky, Maria. "Field and Home, Self and Memory in Papua New Guinea and California." In *The Restless Anthropologist: New Fieldsites, New Visions*, ed. Alma Gottlieb, 49–80. University of Chicago Press, 2012.

Little Thunder, Beverly. *One Bead at a Time*. Edited by Sharron Proulx-Turner. Inanna Publications and Education, 2016.

Louis, Renee Pualani, and Moana Kahele. *Kanaka Hawai'i Cartography: Hula, Navigation, and Oratory*. Oregon State University Press, 2017.

Love, Heather. "Queer." *Transgender Studies Quarterly* 1, no. 1–2 (May 2014): 172–76.

Lowry, David S. "Native Lives Matter: Re-Prioritizing Anthropology (and Everything Else) in an Age of Technological Genocide." *General Anthropology* 30, no. 2 (2023): 11–15.

Lumet, Sidney, dir. *The Wiz*. Internet Archive, 2 hrs., 14 min. Motown Productions, 1978. https://archive.org/details/the-wiz.

Luna, Jennie, and Gabriel S. Estrada. "Trans*lating the Genderqueer -x through Caxcan, Nahua, and Xicanx Indígena Knowledge." In *Decolonizing Latinx Masculinities*, edited by Arturo Aldama and Frederick Aldama, 251–74. University of Arizona Press, 2020.

Macias, Anthony. "Warrior Scientist: *Star Trek: Voyager*'s Chakotay and American Indian Television Representation." *Americana: E-Journal of American Studies in Hungary* 18, no. 1 (2022). https://www.analecta.hu/index.php/americanaejournal/article/view/45475/44132.

Makokis, James. "Keynote—Two-Spirit Rites of Passage." Speech presented at Summit 2019: Queering Healthcare Access and Accessibility, October 31, 2019. YouTube, 48 min. https://www.youtube.com/watch?v=4Hj-a5AE-VM.

Mann, Delbert, dir. *The Outsider*. YouTube, 1 hr., 48 min. Universal Studios, 1961. https://www.youtube.com/watch?v=_9yiJbbOEu4.

Manriquez, L. Frank. "Artist Talk: L. Frank." Lecture at Hammer Museum, Los Angeles. Educational video. March 22, 2022. YouTube, 2 hrs., 3 min. https://channel.hammer.ucla.edu/video/1729/artist-talk-l-frank.

Manriquez, L. Frank, interviewee. "Common Ground: L. Frank Manriquez." Directed by Zakary Naranjo-Morse. Challenge/Solution Series, 2008. Vimeo, 12 min. https://vimeo.com/3449105.

Manriquez, L. Frank, interviewee. "L. Frank Manriquez Oral History." Directed by Paul Christiaan Klieger as part of the *California Indians: The First People* exhibition. California Museum, February 15, 2008. YouTube, 4 min. https://www.youtube.com/watch?v=fyIEeFtrOD0&list=PL2BED48C34E491B0E&index=2.

Manriquez, L. Frank. "Tongva PowerPoint." Lecture at California State University Long Beach, 2018.

Manriquez, L. Frank, interviewee. "Queer California: Untold Stories—L. Frank." Oakland Museum of California, 2020. YouTube, 1 min. https://www.youtube.com/watch?v=MZ2VgTTDPug.

Manriquez, L. Frank. "Welcoming Address: L. Frank Manriquez: Indigenous Pride LA 2020." October 11, 2020. 2 min.

Marubbio, Elise. *Killing the Indian Maiden: Images of Native American Women in Film*. University Press of Kentucky, 2006.

Marubbio, Elise, and Eric Buffalohead. *Native Americans on Film: Conversations, Teaching, and Theory*. University Press of Kentucky, 2013.

Mayer, Sophie. "This Bridge of Two Backs: Making the Two-Spirit Erotics of Community." *Studies in American Indian Literature* 20, no. 1 (2008): 1–26.

McMullin, Daniel. "Tiki Kitsch, American Appropriation, and the Disappearance of the Pacific Islander Body." *LUX: A Journal of Transdisciplinary Writing and Research from Claremont Graduate University* 2, no. 1 (2013): 1–6. Accessed August 7, 2024. http://scholarship.claremont.edu/lux/vol2/iss1/21.

McNeil-Seymour, Jeffrey. "Everything I Am, I Am to You." *TED x TRU.* Lecture filmed March 2018. YouTube, 23 min. https://www.youtube.com/watch?v=_59gXiy4NL8.

Mei-Singh, Laurel. "Carcéral Conservationism: Contested Landscapes and Technologies of Dispossession at Ka'ena Point, Hawaii." *American Quarterly* 68, no. 3 (September 2016): 695–721.

Milbrath, Susan. "Seasonal Calendar in the Codex Borgia." In *Cosmology, Calendars, and Horizon-Based Astronomy in Ancient Mesoamerica,* edited by Anne S. Dowd and Susan Milbrath, 139–62. University Press of Colorado, 2015.

Million, Dian. *Therapeutic Nations: Healing in an Age of Indigenous Human Rights.* University of Arizona Press, 2013.

Minthorn, Robin Zape-tah-hol-ah, Christine A. Nelson, and Heather J. Shotton. "Introduction." In *Indigenous Motherhood in the Academy,* edited by Robin Zape-tah-hol-ah Minthorn, Christine A. Nelson, and Heather J. Shotton, 12–29. Rutgers University Press, 2022.

Miranda, Deborah A. *Bad Indians: A Tribal Memoir.* Heyday, 2013.

Miranda, Deborah A. "Extermination of the Joyas: Gendercide in Spanish California." *Gay and Lesbian Quarterly* 16, no. 1–2 (2010): 253–84.

Mo'e'hahne, Ho'esta. "Animating the Indigenous, Colonial Affects, and 'Going Native' in the City: Kent Mackenzie's *The Exiles.*" *Western American Literature* 52, no. 1 (Spring 2017): 75–94.

Montejo, Victor. *Mayalogue: An Interactionist Theory of Indigenous Cultures.* SUNY Press, 2021.

Morgensen, Scott Lauria. *Spaces Between Us: Queer Settler Colonialism and Indigenous Decolonization.* University of Minnesota Press, 2011.

Morris, Susan L., John R. Johnson, Steven J. Schwartz, René L. Vellanoweth, Glenn J. Farris, and Sara L. Schwebel. "The Nicoleños in Los Angeles: Documenting the Fate of the Lone Woman's Community." *Journal of California and Great Basin Anthropology* 36, no. 1 (2016): 91–118.

"Moyahua—Fiestas Patronales 2019." Mozame, July 31, 2022. YouTube, 1 hr., 34 min. https://www.youtube.com/watch?v=XQeGx1FL72E.

"Moyahua 2009 La Vieja Descarada." YouTube, September 27, 2009. https://www.youtube.com/watch?v=bFW11a50rh4.

Mulroy, Kevin. "Behind the Rolls: Pompey Fixico Bruner." In *IndiVisible: African-Native American Lives in the Americas,* edited by Gabrielle Tayac, 133–37. Museum of the American Indian/Smithsonian Institution, 2009.

Murray, Stephen. *Latin American Male Homosexualities.* University of New Mexico Press, 1995.

Naswood, Elton. "Two-Spirit People." In *A Guide for Contribution to Keywords for Gender and Sexuality Studies,* edited by Mishuana Goeman, et al., 1–4. New York University Press, 2021.

National Congress of American Indians. *Research Policy Update: A First Look at the 2020 Census American Indian/Alaska Native Redistricting Data.* NCAI Policy Research Center, 2021. https://web.archive.org/web/20220126061718/https://www.ncai.org/policy-research-center/research-data/prc-publications/Overview_of_2020_AIAN_Redistricting_Data_FINAL_8_13_2021.pdf.

Nelson, Melissa K. "*Moyla Tuupanga*: The Moon Is in the Sky: An interview with L. Frank Manriquez." *ReVision Journal* 25, no. 2 (Fall 2002): 39–48.

Nibley, Lydia, dir. *Two Spirits.* Say Yes Quickly Productions, 2009. 51 min.

Niro, Shelley, and Salma Monani. "Resistance and Hope in Mohawk Cinema: Iroquois Cosmologies and Histories." In *Ecocriticism and Indigenous Studies: Conversations from Earth to Cosmos,* edited by Salma Monani and Joni Adamson, 172–87. Routledge, 2017.

NZ On Screen, "Overview: Takatāpui." *NZ On Screen/ Iwi Whitiāhua.* Wellington: Front of the Box Productions, 2005. https://www.nzonscreen.com/title/takatapui-2004.

Ocampo, Daisy. *Where We Belong: Chemehuevi and Caxcan Preservation of Sacred Mountains.* University of Arizona Press, 2023.

O'Connor, John E. *The Hollywood Indian: Stereotypes of Native Americans in Films.* New Jersey State Museum, 1980.

Office of the High Commissioner for Human Rights. *United Nations Declaration on the Rights of Indigenous Peoples: Adopted by the General Assembly on 13 September 2007.* United Nations, 2018. https://www.ohchr.org/sites/default/files/Documents/Publications/Declaration_indigenous_en.pdf.

Òkéwándé, O. T. and A. K. Adébáyọ̀, "Investigating African Belief in the Concept of Reincarnation: The Case of Ifá and Ayò ọlọ́p ọ́n: Symbolism Among the Yoruba of Southwestern Ni-

geria." *Bulletin of Saint Petersburg University: Oriental and African Studies* 13, no. 2 (2021): 267–81.
Osorio, Jamaica Heolimeleikalani. *Remembering Our Intimacies: Moʻolelo, Aloha ʻAina, and Ea*. University of Minnesota Press, 2021.
O'Sullivan, Sandy, Han Reardon-Smith, Alana Blakers, and Teyah Miller. "Queer Indigenous Screen Representation: Beyond a Gift from the Past or a Problem to Be Solved." *AlterNative: An International Journal of Indigenous Peoples* 20, no. 2 (June 2024): 289–97.
Parisi, Ariela. "Of Black Bodies and Celestial Bodies: Queer Afrofuturism and New Spatialities in Diego Paulino's *Negrum3*." *Kamchatka: Revista de análisis cultural* (February 2023): 360–78.
Peralto, Leon Noʻeau. "Hānau ka Mauna, the Piko of Our Ea." In *A Nation Rising: Hawaiian Movements for Life, Land, and Sovereignty*, edited by Noelani Goodyear-Kaʻōpua, Ikaika Hussey, and Erin Kahunawaikaʻala, 233–43. Duke University Press, 2014.
Perdue, Theda. "Native Americans, African Americans, and Jim Crow." In *IndiVisible: African-Native American Lives in the Americas*, edited by Gabrielle Tayac, 21–34. National Museum of the American Indian/Smithsonian Institution, 2009.
Pérez, Daniel Enrique. "Toward a Mariposa Consciousness: Reimagining Queer Chicano and Latino Identities." *Aztlán: A Journal of Chicano Studies* 39, no. 2 (Fall 2014): 95–127.
Peters, Pamela, dir. "Legacy of Exiled NDNZ." Red Wind Entertainment, 2014. Vimeo. 14 min. https://vimeo.com/323394336.
Pierce, Joseph M. *Speculative Relations: Indigenous Worlding and Repair.* Duke University Press, 2025.
Potts, Kairyn. "Trans Summit—Through the Lens of First Peoples: Two-Spirit and Indigenous Identity with Kai Potts." Intuit's 3rd Annual Trans Summit 2023, filmed April 9, 2023. YouTube, 29 min. https://www.youtube.com/watch?v=FbcIC41vik0.
Prud'homme-Cranford, Rain, Darryl Barthé, and Andrew J. Jolivétte. "Introduction: Ayou Komensé: Louisiana Creole Land, Community, and Recognition." In *Louisiana Creole Peoplehood: Afro-Indigeneity and Community*, edited by Rain Prud'homme-Cranford, Darryl Barthé, and Andrew J. Jolivétte, 3–18. University of Washington Press, 2022.
Pyle, Kai. "Naming and Claiming: Recovering Ojibwe and Plains Cree Two-Spirit Language." *Transgender Studies Quarterly* 5, no. 4 (November 2018): 574–88.
Rader, Dean. "*The Business of Fancydancing*." In *Seeing Red—Hollywood's Pixeled Skins: American Indians and Film*, edited by LeAnne Howe, Harvey Markowitz, and Denise E. Cummings, 116–20. Michigan State University Press, 2013.
Raheja, Michelle H. *Reservation Reelism: Redfacing, Visual Sovereignty, and Representations of Native Americans in Film*. University of Nebraska, 2010.
Raheja, Michelle H. "Visual Prophecies: Imprint and It Starts with a Whisper." In *Visualities: Perspectives on Contemporary American Indian Film and Art*, edited by Denise K. Cummings, 3–40. Michigan State University Press, 2011.
Reese, Deborah. "Online Video: Injunuity—Two Spirit." *American Indians in Children's Literature*. 2013. https://americanindiansinchildrensliterature.blogspot.com/search?q=injunuity.
Renteria, Jose Alejandro. "Xochipilli: Unveiling the Spiritual Concepts of a Nahua Deity." Dissertation, San Diego State University, 2018.
Requena, Antonio. "Noticia y consideraciones sobre las anormalidades de los Aborigenes Americana: Sodomía." *Acta Venezolana* 1, no. 1 (July-September 1945): 44–73.
Rich, B. Ruby. "New Queer Cinema." In *New Queer Cinema: A Critical Reader*, edited by Michele Aaron, 15–22. Rutgers University Press, 2004.
Rich, B. Ruby. *New Queer Cinema: Director's Cut*. Duke University Press, 2013.
Rickard, Jolene. "Sovereignty: A Line in the Sand." In "Strong Hearts: Native American Visions and Voices," edited by Peggy Roalf, special issue, *Aperture*, no. 139 (Summer 1995): 50–59.
Rifkin, Mark. *When Did Indians Become Straight? Kinship, the History of Sexuality, and Native Sovereignty*. New York: Oxford University Press, 2011.
Rony, Fatimah Tobing. *The Third Eye: Race, Cinema, and Ethnographic Spectacle*. Duke University Press, 1996.
Russell, John G. "Don't ~~It~~ Make My Black Face Blue: Race, Avatars, Albescence, and the Transnational Imaginary." *Journal of Popular Culture* 46, no. 1 (2013): 197–217.

Russell, Nancy K., Kevin Nazar, Sandra del Pino, Monica Alonso Gonzalez, Ximena P. Díaz Bermúdez, and Giovanni Ravasi. "HIV, Syphilis, and Viral Hepatitis among Latin American and Indigenous Peoples and Afro-descendants: A Systematic Review." *Revista Panama salud publica* 43, no. 10 (Jan 2019), 2, https://www.scielosp.org/article/rpsp/2019.v43/e17/.

Russo, Vito. *The Celluloid Closet: Homosexuality in Movies*. New York: Harper and Row, 1981.

Salinas, Luis Alberto. "Yolotl de Papalotl: Finding Spiritual Healing in Art." Master's Dissertation. California State University Northridge, 2020.

Sanchez Medina, Alondra, dir. *Juchipila Zacatecas y el Xuchitl*. AlondraSánchezMk, 2019. YouTube, 11 min. https://www.youtube.com/watch?v=e4r5ZMyEkio.

Saunders, Robert A. "Black + Brown ≠ Green: The Absent Presence of the Anthropocene in Wakanda Forever." *Political Geography* 111 (2024): 1–12.

Schmal, John P. "Moctezuma's Descendants in Aguascalientes: Genealogy by John Schmal." *Indigenous Mexico*. 2022. https://www.indigenousmexico.org/articles/moctezumas-descendants-in-aguascalientes.

Schweninger, Lee. *Imagic Moments: Indigenous North American Film*. University of Georgia Press, 2013.

Scudeler, June. "Fed by Spirits: Mamâhtâwisiwin in René Highway's New Song . . . New Dance." *Native American and Indigenous Studies* 3, no. 1 (2016): 1–23.

Scudeler, June. "Queer Indigenous Studies, or Thirza Cuthand's Indigequeer Film." In *The Cambridge Companion to Queer Studies*, edited by Siobhan Somerville, 79–91. Cambridge University Press, 2020.

Scudeler, June. "'Indians on Top': Kent Monkman's Sovereign Erotics." *American Indian Culture and Research Journal* 39, no. 4 (2015): 19–32.

Segura Granados, Andres. "Lecture: The Path of Quetzalcoatl." *D-Q University*, filmed 1977. YouTube, 2 hr., 10 min. YouTube. https://www.youtube.com/watch?v=GwXMc2VP9y8.

Seow, Janet Rosemarie. "Nnedi Okorafor's Binti: African Science Fiction and the Reimagined Black Girl." *Journal of Childhood Studies* 47, no 1 (March 2022): 56–69.

Servin Herrera, Enrique Alberto. *Anirúame: Historias de los Tarahumaras de los tiempos antiguos*. Oaxaca: Prensa Secretaria de las Culturas y Artes de Oaxaca, 2015.

Singer, Beverly R. "Video América Indígena/Video Native America." In "Film and Video," edited by Luana Ross and Daniel Hart, special issue, *Wíčazo Ša Review* 16, no. 2 (Autumn 2001): 35–53.

Singer, Beverly R., and Robert Warrior. *Wiping the Warpaint off the Lens: Native American Film and Video*. University of Minnesota Press, 2001.

Smith, Mona, dir. *Honey Moccasin*. Turtle Night Productions, 1998. Vimeo, 47 min. https://vimeo.com/92286410.

Smith, Paul Julian. *Queer Mexico: Cinema and Television Since 2000*. Detroit: Wayne State University Press, 2017.

Snow, John. *These Mountains Are Our Sacred Places: The Story of the Stoney Indians*. Samuel Stevens, 1977.

Soja, Edward. *My Los Angeles: From Urban Structuring to Regional Urbanization*. University of California Press, 2014.

Stewart-Ambo, Theresa, and K. Wayne Yang. "Beyond Land Acknowledgement in Settler Institutions." *Social Text* 39, no. 1 (March 2021): 21–46.

Stryker, Susan. "Queer Nation." *GLBTQ Archives*. Wik Wikholm, 2015. http://www.glbtqarchive.com/ssh/queer_nation_S.pdf.

Subero, Gustavo. "*Muxeninity* and the Institutionalization of a Third Gender Identity in Alejandra Islas's *Muxes: Auténticas, intrépidas, buscadoras de peligro*." *Hispanic Research Journal* 14, no. 2 (2013): 175–93.

Subero, Gustavo. *Queer Masculinities in Contemporary Latin American Cinema: Male Bodies and Narrative Representation*. Tauris World Cinema, 2014.

Tatonetti, Lisa. *The Queerness of Native American Literature*. University of Minnesota Press, 2014.

Tatonetti, Lisa. "Visible Sexualities or Invisible Nations: Forced to Choose in *Big Eden*, *Johnny Greyeyes*, and *The Business of Fancydancing*." *GLQ: A Journal of Lesbian and Gay Studies* 16, no. 1–2 (2010): 157–81.

Tatonetti, Lisa. *Written by the Body: Gender Expansiveness and Indigenous Non-Cis Masculinities*. University of Minnesota Press, 2021.

Tengan, Ty. "*Ke Kulana He Mahu*: Remembering a Sense of Place (Review)." *Contemporary Pacific* 15, no. 1 (Spring 2003): 231–33.

Teves, Stephanie Nohelani. "Cocoa Chandelier's Confessional: Kānaka Maoli Performance and Aloha in *Drag*." In *Critical Ethnic Studies: A Reader, Critical Ethnic Studies Collective*, edited by Nada Elia, et al., 281–300. Duke University Press, 2016.

Teves, Stephanie Nohelani. "A Critical Reading of Aloha and Visual Sovereignty in *Ke Kulana He Mahu*." *International Journal of Critical Indigenous Studies* 7, no. 1 (2014): 1–17.

Teves, Stephanie Nohelani. *Defiant Indigeneity: The Politics of Hawaiian Performance*. University of North Carolina Press, 2018.

Thiel, Mark. "Origins of the Jingle Dress Dance." *Whispering Wind* 36, no. 5 (2007): 14–18.

Thompson, Se'mana. "'Liberation': Cover of Queer Indigenous Girl, Volume 4 & 'Roots,' Cover of Black Indigenous Boy, Volume 2." In *Otherwise Worlds: Against Settler Colonialism and Anti-Blackness*, edited by Tiffany Lethabo King, Jenell Navarro, and Andrea Smith, 330–31. Duke University Press, 2020.

Tom, Nazbah, dir. "Mountain of Stories." Center for Digital Storytelling, 2012. YouTube, 4 min. https://www.youtube.com/watch?v=j_QNVfNXEgY.

Tompkins, Avery. "Asterisk." *Transgender Studies Quarterly* 1, no. 1–2 (May 2014): 26–27.

Torres, Craig, interviewee. "End Sequence." Mapping Indigenous LA, 2015. YouTube. 10 min. https://www.youtube.com/watch?v=2csqToLj-04.

Truth and Reconciliation Commission of Canada. *Canada's Residential Schools: The History, Part 2, 1939 to 2000: The Final Report of the Truth and Reconciliation Commission of Canada, Volume 1*. McGill-Queen's University Press, 2016.

Tsang, Martin. "A Different Kind of Sweetness: Yemayá in Afro-Cuban Religion." In *Yemoja: Gender, Sexuality, and Creativity in the Latina/o and Afro-Atlantic Diasporas*, edited by Solimar Otero and Toyin Falola, 113–30. State University of New York Press, 2013.

Van Alst, Theo. "Sherman Shoots Alexie: Working with and without Reservation(s) in *The Business of Fancydancing*." In *Visualities: Perspectives on Contemporary American Indian Film and Art*, edited by Denise K. Cummings, 73–93. Michigan State University Press, 2011.

Varga, Ryan, dir. "The Indigenous Doctor Helping Trans Youth." Context News. Thomson Reuters Foundation, 2020. YouTube, 12 min., https://www.youtube.com/watch?v=4Hj-a5AE-VM.

Vest, Jennifer Lisa. "Names." In "International Queer Indigenous Voices," edited by Ahimsa Timoteo Bodhrán, special issue, *Yellow Medicine Review: A Journal of Indigenous Literature, Art, and Thought* (Fall 2010): 28–33.

Vest, Jennifer Lisa, dir. "(Re)Counting (Wo)Man." Yokchee Tatee Film, 2020. YouTube, 51 min. https://www.youtube.com/watch?v=vlAiJD_drTU.

Wachowski, Lana, Tom Tykwer, and Lilly Wachowski, dir. *Cloud Atlas*. Warner Brothers, 2012.

Wagua, Duiren, dir. "Descubriendo nuestra identidad . . . !" Grupo Génesis Panamá Positivo, 2014. YouTube, 20 min. https://www.youtube.com/watch?v=5pEAq2ElXEQ.

Walters, Mark Jerome. *Seeking the Sacred Raven: Politics and Extinction on a Hawaiian Island*. Shearwater/Island Press, 2006.

Warners Brothers Entertainment. "Sinners | I Lied to You Song | Movie Clip | Warner Bros. Entertainment." 2025. YouTube, 5 min. https://www.youtube.com/watch?v=S7jo5Cr6WUA&list=RDS7jo5Cr6WUA.

Watchman, Renae. "Reel Restoration in *Drunktown's Finest*." *Journal of the Native American and Indigenous Studies Association* 7, no. 2 (October 2020): 29–54.

Watchman, Renae. *Restoring Relations Through Stories: From Dinétah to Denendeh*. University of Arizona Press, 2024.

Waters, Anne. "Language Matters: Nondiscrete Nonbinary Dualism." In *American Indian Thought: Philosophical Essays*, edited by Anne Waters, 97–115. Blackwell, 2004.

Waugh, Thomas. *The Romance of Transgression in Canada: Queering Sexualities, Nations, Cinemas*. McGill-Queen's University Press, 2006.

Weatherford, Elizabeth. "The Journey's Discovery: An Interview with Shelley Niro." In *Native Americans on Film: Conversations, Teaching, and Theory*, edited by M. Elise Marubbio and Eric L. Buffalohead, 337–58. Lexington: University Press of Kentucky, 2013.

Werito, Vincent. "Understanding Hózhǫ́ to Achieve Critical Consciousness: A Contemporary Diné Interpretation of the Philosophical Principles of Hózhǫ́" In *Diné Perspectives: Revitalizing and Reclaiming Navajo Thought*, edited by Lloyd L. Lee, 25–38. University of Arizona Press, 2014.

Wesley, Saylesh. "Twin-Spirited Woman: Sts'iyóye smestíyexw slhá:li." *Transgender Studies Quarterly* 1, no. 3 (August 2014): 338–51.

Whitehead, Joshua. "Introduction." In *Love After the End: An Anthology of Two-Spirit and Indigiqueer Speculative Fiction*, edited by Joshua Whitehead, 1–9. Arsenal Pulp Press, 2020.

Whyte, Kyle P. "Indigenous Science (Fiction) for the Anthropocene: Ancestral Dystopias and Fantasies of Climate Change Crises." *Environment and Planning E: Nature and Space* 1, no. 1–2 (2018): 224–42.

Wilcox, Melissa M. *Queer Religiosities: An Introduction to Queer and Transgender Studies in Religion*. Rowman and Littlefield, 2021.

Wilson, Janet. "Pathologies of Violence: Religion and Postcolonial Identity in New Zealand." In *Representing Religion in World Cinema: Filmmaking, Mythmaking, and Culture Making*, edited by S. Brent Plate. Palgrave Macmillan, 2003.

Wilson, K. L. Nālani. "View from the Mountain: Molokaʻi Nui a Hina." *Junctures* 5 (December 2005): 31–46.

Wilson, Kathryn Louise Kamakahukionalani. "Na Wahine Piko o Moloka'i: Pacific Women's Connections to Place." Master's thesis, Center of Pacific Island Studies, University of Hawaiʻi, Manoa, 2004.

Wong-Kalu, Hinaleimoana. "Mele Kū Ha'aheo e Ku'u Hawaiʻi ma ka Mauna o Wākea." Vimeo, 2015. https://vimeo.com/236180910.

Wong-Kalu, Hinaleimoana, Dean Hamer, and John Wilson, dir. "Kapaemahu." Kānaka Pakipika, 2020. YouTube, 8 min. https://www.youtube.com/watch?v=lnlpcumMsiw.

Woodward, Suzanne. "Being Both: Gender and Indigeneity in Two Pacific Documentary Films." *Pacific Journalism Review* 20, no. 1 (2015): 62–76.

Wortham, Erica C. *Indigenous Media in Mexico: Culture, Community, and the State*. Duke University Press, 2013.

Wright, Melissa A. "Art After the Untreatable: Psychoanalysis, Sexual Violence, and the Ethics of Looking in Michaela Coel's 'I May Destroy You.'" *Philosophies* 9, no. 3 (April 2024), 1–14.

Xian, Kathryn, and Brent Anbe, dir. *Ke Kulana He Mahu*. Zang Pictures, 2001. 1 hr., 7 min.

Youngberg, Quentin. "Interpenetrations: Re-encoding the Queer Indian in Sherman Alexie's *The Business of Fancydancing*." *Studies of American Indian Literature* 27, no. 1 (Spring 2008): 55–75.

Zaborskis, Mary, and Elizabeth Reich. "A Queer Dig: Kānaka Maoli Gendered and Temporal (Archaeo)logics in Kumu Hina." *Feminist Formations* 34, no. 2 (Summer 2022): 19–42.

Zolbrod, Paul. *The Diné Bahané: The Navajo Creation Story*. University of New Mexico Press, 1984.

INDEX

ABOUT THE AUTHOR

GABRIEL S. ESTRADA is a professor of religious studies at California State University, Long Beach, where ze teaches queer spirituality, Indigenous graduate classes, and Nahuatl texts. A Caxcan/Xicanx genderqueer author, ze published over twenty works on Indigenous LGBTQI+/Two-Spirit film and literature.